How and Why Do Courts Cite?

AF766382

Joy Steigler-Herms

How and Why Do Courts Cite?

Intertextual References in the Decisions of the Federal Constitutional Court of Germany and the Supreme Court of Canada

palgrave
macmillan

Joy Steigler-Herms
SFB 1385 „Recht und Literatur“
Universität Münster
Münster, Deutschland

ISBN 978-3-662-71933-6 ISBN 978-3-662-71934-3 (eBook)
https://doi.org/10.1007/978-3-662-71934-3

Translation from the German language edition: “Wie und warum zitieren Gerichte? ” by Joy Steigler-Herms, © Der/die Herausgeber bzw. der/die Autor(en), exklusiv lizenziert an Springer-Verlag GmbH, DE, ein Teil von Springer Nature 2024. Published by Springer Berlin Heidelberg. All Rights Reserved.

This book is a translation of the original German edition “Wie und warum zitieren Gerichte? ” by Joy Steigler-Herms, published by Springer-Verlag GmbH, DE in 2024. The translation was done with the help of an artificial intelligence machine translation tool. A subsequent human revision was done primarily in terms of content, so that the book will read stylistically differently from a conventional translation. Springer Nature works continuously to further the development of tools for the production of books and on the related technologies to support the authors.

© The Editor(s) (if applicable) and The Author(s), under exclusive license to Springer-Verlag GmbH, DE, part of Springer Nature 2025

This work is subject to copyright. All rights are solely and exclusively licensed by the Publisher, whether the whole or part of the material is concerned, specifically the rights of translation, reprinting, reuse of illustrations, recitation, broadcasting, reproduction on microfilms or in any other physical way, and transmission or information storage and retrieval, electronic adaptation, computer software, or by similar or dissimilar methodology now known or hereafter developed.
The use of general descriptive names, registered names, trademarks, service marks, etc. in this publication does not imply, even in the absence of a specific statement, that such names are exempt from the relevant protective laws and regulations and therefore free for general use.
The publisher, the authors and the editors are safe to assume that the advice and information in this book are believed to be true and accurate at the date of publication. Neither the publisher nor the authors or the editors give a warranty, expressed or implied, with respect to the material contained herein or for any errors or omissions that may have been made. The publisher remains neutral with regard to jurisdictional claims in published maps and institutional affiliations.

This Palgrave Macmillan imprint is published by the registered company Springer-Verlag GmbH, DE, part of Springer Nature.
The registered company address is: Heidelberger Platz 3, 14197 Berlin, Germany

If disposing of this product, please recycle the paper.

Contents

List of Figures

List of Tables

Chapter 1
Introduction

No judicial decision can be written without reference to other texts.[1] Quotations and citations are omnipresent in judicial decisions. Every decision must at least take into account the relevant statutory texts or, depending on the legal system, also precedents. The obligation to adhere to the applicable law—whether in the form of binding precedent or the postulate of statutory binding—requires judges to consider texts and thus ultimately to engage in intertextual work. Consulting and citing legal sources fulfills indispensable functions, such as creating and signaling coherence in jurisprudence. Through the act of referencing, courts demonstrate that their decisions are based on established legal doctrine, and they integrate themselves into the discourse-specific textual network. Integration into the existing doctrine through reference to relevant texts, in turn, legitimizes the decision and, not least, creates legal certainty through the predictability of law.

However, judicial decisions also contain references to texts that cannot be ascribed such a function. Among the sources cited by courts are not only statutory texts, but also, for example, references to foreign law, academic sources, or even literary texts. Such sources have no binding effect and thus raise the question

[1] Terminological note: The present text is based on an AI-generated translation from German which results in several terminological issues that cannot be fully resolved within this translation. In the German original, the term 'Zitat' serves as an umbrella concept encompassing various forms of intertextual forms and source reference, including direct quotations as well as non-verbatim citations. In English, by contrast, a stricter terminological distinction is customary: 'citation' generally refers to source attribution practices, whereas 'quotation' denotes the verbatim reproduction of text. A more extensive engagement with this English terminological distinction cannot be undertaken within the constraints of this translated version. For this reason, the terminology follows the logic of the German original: the term 'citation' is used throughout as an umbrella term that also includes quotations, while 'quotation' is employed only where the phenomenon discussed is explicitly limited to quotation forms and excludes other types of citations.

© The Author(s), under exclusive license to Springer-Verlag GmbH, DE, part of Springer Nature 2025

J. Steigler-Herms, *How and Why Do Courts Cite?*,
https://doi.org/10.1007/978-3-662-71934-3_1

of the function of their consideration. For instance, when the Supreme Court of Canada quotes Franz Kafka (Example 1), it consults a text that, in principle, cannot be attributed any authority over legal questions:

(1) Franz Kafka was not being entirely whimsical when he wrote, "If you have the right eye for these things, you can see that accused men are often attractive" (The Trial (1976), at p. 203). (R. v. Keegstra 1990 3 SCR 697—13.12.1990)

This example illustrates that citations in judicial decisions must fulfill further functions beyond creating and demonstrating legal coherence and integration into existing legal doctrine. How and for what purpose references to non-binding texts are used cannot be satisfactorily answered by current research approaches—even though many works highlight the great significance of citations in judicial decisions (e.g., Holzleithner/Mayer-Schönberger 2000, Nußberger 2006, Jestaedt 2010). Legal studies have found, among other things, that citations generally serve the exchange between courts and a "cross-fertilization among legal systems" (Slaughter 1991: 99). However, closer examination of concrete case examples and, in particular, empirical approaches to analyzing the functions of quotations remain a desideratum in research.

From a theoretical perspective, there is consensus that citations, in addition to the already mentioned function of coherence, can also be used, for example, authoritatively, ornamentally, or for economic purposes. The citation is regarded as a precious object that can adorn both the text and the citer in the sense of an "intellectual conceit" (Morawski 1970: 695). In this function, it can, for instance, strengthen the authority of an argument and thus help make a judicial decision unassailable and valid. Furthermore, the citation also fulfills an economic function, since citing, depending on the type of citation used, saves the citer work either at the level of formulation or at the level of substantive argumentation (Jakobs 1999: 126). Whether, in a concrete case, the economic, authoritative, ornamental, coherence-signaling function, or several functions are present in parallel, can hardly be determined with the results of previous studies. This research gap is not surprising, as reconstructing the functions of quotations brings with it numerous problems. One problem is that the functions of quotations are tied to the intention of the citer; however, the intentions are not encoded in the citation itself. The potential presence of several different functions and the lack of reconstructability have been considered so serious in previous citation analysis that the meaningfulness of analyzing citation functions has been questioned: The "implicit bundling of very different citation motives could shake the foundations of citation analysis and call its overall sense into question" (Hamann 2014: 510, in a discussion of doubts originally expressed, among others, by Ayres/Vars 2010).

In view of the problem outlined, one aim of this work is to provide impetus for empirically based analysis of citation functions. It is fundamentally based on the descriptive recording of citation features: While the question of why cannot be demonstrably inferred from the citation, it is empirically and descriptively accessible how citing is done. The manner of citing is the main focus of philological perspectives on the citation. It can be understood as the intentional design of a text-to-text relationship and thus allows—so a fundamental thesis of the present work—at least indirect conclusions about possible intended functions.

Citations can be made in a variety of ways. A pre-text (in this context understood as the source text) can be integrated verbatim into a quoting text or paraphrased; the quoter can accept the validity of the quoted content or reject it. All citation properties modeled by the citer in the act of citing can be used as indications of potentially intended functions. The extent to which citation properties can be used for reconstructing function will be demonstrated by a brief, introductory analysis of the following decision passages:

(2) The conceptual relationship between legal certainty and justice has always been understood differently (cf. W. Herschel, Legal Certainty and Legal Clarity, in JZ 1967 p. 727 (732); C. A. Emge, Security and Justice—Their Common Metajuristic Root, in Treatises of the Prussian Academy of Sciences, 1940 No. 9; O. A. Germann, Legal Certainty, in idem, Methodological Fundamental Questions, 1946 p. 54 ff.; M. Rümelin, Legal Certainty, 1924).[2] (BVerfGE 35, 41-65 08.05.1973, para. 53)

(3) As Martha Minow elegantly noted, the ability to be open-minded is enhanced by such knowledge and understanding:
None of us can know anything except by building upon, challenging, responding to what we already have known, what we see from where we stand. But we can insist on seeing what we are used to seeing, or else we can try to see something new and fresh. The latter is the open mind we hope for from those who judge, but not the mind as a sieve without prior reference points and commitments. We want judges and juries to be objective about the facts and the questions of guilt and innocence but committed to building upon what they already know about the world, human beings, and each person's own implication in the lives of others. Pretending not to know risks leaving unexamined the very assumptions that deserve reconsideration. (Yukon Francophone School Board, Education Area #23 v. Yukon, para. 34)

Two examples of the criteria examined in the present work for describing citation practices are, first, the *choice of citation types* and, second, *positioning elements* in the embedding of citations, which allow conclusions to be drawn about the evaluation of the quoted text by the citer. The choice of citation types can be revealing with regard to potential functions, as different citation types have different properties. If, for example, the pretext is adopted verbatim as a direct quotation, the quoter saves work at the level of formulation. On the producer side, this means that economically motivated quoting is conceivable for Example 3. In the case of paraphrases, theciter saves work at the substantive level; however, the work of formulation is not spared by the paraphrasing intertextual reference. On

[2] Note on examples and secondary literature: The AI-generated translation also applies to originally German quotations from the predominantly German secondary literature, as well as to the illustrative excerpts from decisions of the Federal Constitutional Court, in order to make their content accessible to a broader readership. Only a small number of examples have been retained in German, namely those that rely on specifically German linguistic features or for which the original wording is indispensable for understanding.

the recipient side, too, the functions of direct or material and indirect or immaterial quoting differ fundamentally: While the material quotation (Example 3) is present in the text and thus immediately accessible to the recipient, the recipient cannot extract any concrete substantive information from the reference in Example 2. The Federal Constitutional Court does summarize that there are different views on the terminological relation of legal certainty to justice—but which view is specifically represented by the cited sources Herschel, Emge, Germann, and Rümelin remains hidden from the recipient. For the recipient, such references are therefore not very economical, as they would have to pursue the reference independently through their own research.

Furthermore, it is relevant how a citing text *positions* itself in relation to the cited text. If one wishes to reconstruct the purpose for which a citation is used, analyzing only the cited content and the cited wording is of little value, since external content is not merely adopted but, in the act of citing, is met with both agreement and rejection. Those who cite position themselves in nuanced ways with respect to the content of the citation. They draw on external content either to endorse its validity or, conversely, to question or revise it. Affirmative adoption is—if we remain with the example of the economic function of citations—a necessary precondition for using a citation as a supporting argument. If a citer describes a cited content as positive, further engagement with the substantive aspects is, in principle, not strictly necessary—they can let the validity of the cited content speak for itself and project it onto their own text. However, if a citer distances themselves from the validity of a cited content, the basic functional conditions change. If, in Example 3, instead of highlighting the elegant formulation, the quotation were introduced with a critical distancing from Minow's words, this would entail additional argumentative effort; the rejection of a quotation cannot stand without further justification.

The selection of the exemplary decision passages may already have shown that the analysis of citations in judicial decisions in the present work is to be carried out using two courts as examples—the Federal Constitutional Court of Germany and the Supreme Court of Canada. Both courts are constitutional courts. In their decision-making, constitutional courts are, in principle, required to apply the same methods of legal reasoning as any other court. However, they are sometimes confronted with greater challenges than courts in other areas of law, since, in particular, "fundamental rights are to a large extent highly abstract, so that it is only with difficulty, if at all, that practicable principles can be derived or developed from their text" (Czermak 2021: 22 on the decision-making practice of the Federal Constitutional Court). A significant difference between the Federal Constitutional Court and the Supreme Court of Canada lies in their affiliation to legal families; the Federal Constitutional Court is a prominent representative of the continental European legal family (also Civil Law), while the Supreme Court of Canada represents the Anglo-American legal family (also Common Law). The two legal families differ in several respects, so it can be assumed that their different decision-making practices are also reflected in different citation practices. While the Federal Constitutional Court, as a continental European court, is bound exclusively to the constitution, the Supreme Court of Canada, as an Anglo-American court, must also take precedents into account. Furthermore, the decision style of Civil Law courts is considered depersonalized and scholarly. In contrast, in the decisions of Common Law courts, the judges are noticeably present as decision-makers, among other things through the use of the personal pronoun 'I'. The extent to which these fundamental differences in the decision-making practices of the two courts are also reflected in their citation practices is to be examined in the present work.

Based on the preceding considerations, three guiding questions arise for the following investigation.

1. How do the Federal Constitutional Court of Germany and the Supreme Court of Canada cite?
2. Why do the Federal Constitutional Court of Germany and the Supreme Court of Canada cite?
3. To what extent do the citation practices of the Supreme Court of Canada and the Federal Constitutional Court of Germany differ from each other?

To answer these three guiding questions, the study is structured as follows.

Chap. 2 deals with the interdisciplinary concept of citation and focuses on both philological and legal typological approaches. A relevant defining feature of the concept of quotation is its intertextual aspect. The concept of 'intertextuality' must therefore first be introduced as a framework theory for quotation. The term intertextuality goes back to Julia Kristeva (among others, 1972) and refers to the explicit or implicit referencing of texts to one another. Quotation is considered the prototypical manifestation of such text-to-text relations; philological typologies primarily analyze the form of this relation (e.g., direct or indirect adoption). Legal typologies focus on which types of sources are drawn upon in the act of citing. Thus, source-oriented typologies, as will be explored in more detail in Chap. 2, fundamentally distinguish between the citation of legally binding and non-binding sources.

Chap. 3 addresses the functions of citation and, in this context, presents in greater detail the functions of authority, ornamentality, economy, and coherence already mentioned in the introduction. Since the functions of citations cannot be inferred from the citation itself, this chapter primarily problematizes the identification of quotation functions and offers impulses for modeling an empirical evaluation. Productive analytical criteria, in addition to the already mentioned choice of citation type and the positioning by the citer, include quantitative aspects. From the frequencies of quoting and being cited, statements can be made about the weighting of a cited text and its influence on the citing text or even on an entire discourse.

On the basis of the decisive role of relations between the source of the citation and the citing text, between the poles of affirmation and deconstruction, *Chap. 4* addresses evaluative acts of positioning, or, in greater depth, what is meant by citation-related positioning elements. Especially in text types that appear objective—at least in German—such as judicial decisions, acts of positioning are carried out only very subtly. A suitable set of tools is provided by the analysis of epistemic modalization devices and evidentiality markers. A concrete example of epistemic modalization procedures are boosters (e.g., “clearly”, “definitely”), which are also discussed in greater detail in this chapter and with which the validity claim of one’s own and others’ propositions can be reinforced.

Chap. 5 demonstrates why it can be assumed that the two courts under study—the Federal Constitutional Court of Germany and the Supreme Court—differ in their citation practices. It introduces both courts and focuses in particular on their affiliation to different legal families. As will be shown, Common Law and Civil Law differ in their preference for certain sources, their approach to decision-making, and also in their decision style.

The empirical analysis of the present study can be found in *Chap. 6*. To answer the question ‘How do courts cite?’, the study conducts a multi-criteria frequency analysis of citation characteristics in a total of nearly 500 decisions of the Federal Constitutional Court of Germany and the Supreme Court of Canada, and examines, by quantifying citation characteristics, whether prototypical tendencies can be identified in the citation practices of the Federal Constitutional Court and the Supreme Court of Canada. The quantitative analysis also allows for comparative perspectives on the citation practices of the two courts and tests the identified frequencies for significant differences. The research question ‘Why do the Federal Constitutional Court of Germany and the Supreme Court of Canada cite?’ is addressed, by contrast, in the context of a qualitative analysis, in which selected case studies are used to examine which citation functions can be assigned to the recorded citation characteristics.

Chapter 2
Interdisciplinary Approaches to Citation and Quotation

In everyday usage, the German term ‘Zitat’ (English: quotation or citation) is generally understood as the verbatim repetition of a text or a speech.[1] From this everyday understanding of the term emerges a relevant definiens that is shared by both literary and legal approaches to the concept of citation: the citation constitutes a reference to something already existing; the act of citing is accompanied by the act of repeating. It is the “presence of a text within another text” (Genette 1993: 10) and, against this background, can be defined as a possible form of intertextual reference. Intertextual reference creates a connection between two texts, which can be realized in different ways. Thus, a distinction can be made between literal, or material, quotations, in which the material of a pretext is transferred unchanged into a quoting text, and indirect, i.e., immaterial quotations, in which the quoter intervenes in the formulation of the pretext during the act of reproduction, so that the quotation can no longer be considered verbatim.

While the configuration of the text-to-text relationship between the poles of directness and indirectness, and related questions of the markedness of quotations and citations, form the main focus of philological typological approaches, legal approaches, by contrast, do not distinguish between material and immaterial quotations and instead focus on categorizing the sources of citations. In legal typologies of citing, the type of source is foregrounded, and distinctions are made, among other things, between citing domestic and foreign case law.

As this brief overview shows, not all citations are the same, and the criteria for typologizing citations differ depending on the discipline (for an overview

[1] See footnote 1 for terminological notes. The following discussion is based on the German terminology surrounding the concept of ‘Zitat’. There are terminological—and, in part, conceptual—differences between the German and English frameworks that cannot be further addressed within the scope of this translation.

© The Author(s), under exclusive license to Springer-Verlag GmbH, DE, part of Springer Nature 2025

J. Steigler-Herms, *How and Why Do Courts Cite?*,
https://doi.org/10.1007/978-3-662-71934-3_2

of various definitions, see also Steigler-Herms/Wittmann 2022). It is a broad term that—especially with regard to the aim of describing citation practices in the empirical part of this work—needs to be differentiated. The present chapter attempts to do justice to the diverse manifestations of the citation and aims to provide a systematic account of philological and legal perspectives on the concept of quotation. A philological perspective on the concept of quotation is taken in Sect. 2.1, which focuses on the idea of different types of quotations and citations. For the legal perspective, Sect. 2.2 shows that the citation in law assumes a dual role: on the one hand, the citation is an important instrument of jurisprudence; on the other hand, it is itself the subject of legal rulings, with its legitimate use being determined, among other things, by copyright law.

2.1 Citation & Quotation from a Philological Perspective

The term 'Zitat' has been defined in many ways; the majority of these definitions understand the concept of citation as an act of reproduction. Thus, Helmstetter defines the quotation (2002: 896) in an encyclopedia entry as "[v]erbatim adoption and insertion from foreign texts, usually with marking and citation of the source." He further explicitly refers to the recourse to a pre-text (ibid.): "A quotation is a passage from another text, […]. It is a specific form of concretization of text-to-text relationships." Such definitions closely link the quotation to the concept of intertextuality, which will therefore be presented in more detail below.

2.1.1 Intertextuality

The concept of intertextuality has been defined in various ways in the relevant research canon. Therefore, an introductory, vaguely defined quintessence, as formulated by Holthuis (1993: 29) from a survey of the different conceptions, should precede the discussion: "Intertextuality […] as a theoretical concept initially refers to nothing more [than] the phenomenon of a relation between texts, however that may be determined."

To the "however that may be determined" relations are added fundamentally divergent notions of textuality, which complicate both the theoretical approach and the practical application of the concept. In addition, even before one can approach a comparison of the different definitions and approaches, terminological inconsistencies become apparent, since a wide range of supposed synonyms circulate for the term 'intertextuality' (such as 'intersemanticity' according to Schmid/Stempel (1983), 'interdiscursivity' according to Angenot (1983), among others). In such cases, the prefix 'inter-' can be used to derive the *tertium comparationis* of the sometimes very different conceptions; the commonality lies in the attempt to determine a relation between A and B. However, what the placeholders A and B can refer to varies greatly depending on the conception of the concept. For a broad and comprehensive view, it therefore seems appropriate, following Plett's "intertextualities" (the title of an essay from 1991), to first acknowledge the plurality of the term.

The originally literary and cultural studies concept of 'intertextuality' is based on a very broad understanding of the term, which assumes a textual and intertextual omnipresence: according to the theories of intertextuality pioneer Julia Kristeva, *all* social products are intertextual. Kristeva introduced the term 'intertextuality' in 1967 and defines it as follows:

> Nous appellerons INTERTEXTUALITÉ cette inter-action textuelle qui se produit à l'interieur d'un seul texte. Pour le sujet connaissant, l'intertextualité est une notion qui sera l'indice de la façon dont un texte lit l'histoire et s'insère en elle. (Kristeva 1969: 443)

This canonically quoted definition has earned Kristeva's conception of intertextuality the reputation of a radical paradigm shift in literary studies: whereas until the 1960s the text was still regarded as a closed whole that could be attributed to an author as its product, Kristeva breaks away from this assumption and dissolves both the notion of the authorial subject and the concept of textuality (see Pfister 1985: 7–9). According to her definition, a text unites both a passive and an active element. On the one hand, intertextuality 'produces itself' within a text; the text appears passive in relation to intertextuality, subject to it. On the other hand, the text 'reads' history; it is thus assigned an actively absorbing role. From Kristeva's cultural semiotic perspective, textuality is not bound to the materiality of writing: "This notion that history and society are something that is read like or as a text must always be borne in mind when Kristeva speaks of text or texts […]" (Pfister 1985: 7). Such a perspective on textuality may initially seem alien, especially in view of the fundamental, close connection of 'classical textuality' to the medium of language (at least from a philological perspective). However, if one detaches oneself from the concept of textuality and thinks of Kristeva's concept of intertextuality in terms of '*inter-objectivity*', it can indeed be regarded as a fundamental observation that is still widely received today: cultural studies perspectives record relations between all objects—and use the term quotation for the repetition or imitation of one object in another. Ulrich (2015) speaks in this context of "constructed quotations" and examines forms and functions of quoting in the cultural products of image, architecture, and music. The mutual fertilization of these cultural products is moreover so established in society that legal norms regulate what kind of inter-relation is to be designed in what way so as not to violate the rights of the author (see Sect. 2.3.2).

As already mentioned, Kristeva's concept of intertextuality does not only concern the understanding of texts but also the role of the author. Since the text cannot escape the influences of its social context of origin in any case, it is no longer (or at least no longer primarily) the product of its author. Through the "decentering of the subject" (Pfister 1985: 9), the authorial instance is superseded. As a result, an author does not employ intertextuality intentionally; rather, in Kristeva's broad understanding, it is a productive basic condition and not an optional, stylistic device.

This premise marks a significant difference from Bakhtin's concept of dialogism, which is generally regarded in literary studies as the basis for Kristeva's elaborations. As a result of his reflections on the relations between literature, language, and society, Bakhtin (1979) identifies the dichotomous categories of 'dialogism' and 'monologism'. Dialogism refers to the open engagement with divergent positions; monologic discourse, by contrast, closes itself off from questioning through engagement, in order to preserve tradition and authority (see also Pfister 1985: 2; Jakobs 1999: 13). Even though the concept of dialogism seems terminologically very close to the basic idea of intertextuality, there are in fact more differences than similarities between the two concepts: Bakhtin's dialogism primarily refers to a dialogue within the voices of a single text, not between the voices of different texts. His theory is therefore essentially *intra*- rather than *inter*textual (Pfister 1985: 4).

Since the break with pre-intertextual notions of textuality, the concept has undergone countless modifications. The re-conceptualizations responsible for the terminological chaos mentioned at the outset are, in fact, quite useful for the concrete operationalization of the term; Kristeva's postulate that simply every text is intertextual is hardly applicable for empirical analyses, for "[i]f one uses the concept of intertextuality in such a broad sense that every text is intertextual in all its elements, the concept loses its distinctiveness and thus its scientific usefulness, at least for the analysis of individual texts" (Broich 1985: 48).

One of the most fundamental differentiations is the distinction between intertextual system reference and intertextual single-text reference (cf. Broich/Pfister 1985; Hempfer 1983). Kristeva's definition corresponds to the system reference. System-referential inter-relations are based on the assumption that productive and receptive experiences with textuality inevitably flow into text production. Thus, a text is always also a product of the 'textual socialization' of its author. No text is a *creatio ex nihilo:*

> No act of writing is an Adamic act, in which the text producer would have to create his language from scratch at the same time as his text, and no literary author is a Kaspar Hauser who has never heard or read another literary text. (Pfister 1985: 52)

What exactly is to be understood by the specification 'system' in the compound 'system reference' is not definitively established. Depending on the focus of the study, the reference of the system concept can vary. For genre analyses, for example, it is fruitful to understand 'system' as a system of genres, since this allows valuable insights to be gained into conventionalized patterns of legal discourse (as in Busse 2002).

For the purposes of this study, however, the more specific perspective of single-text references is even more relevant than system reference. Single-text references refer structurally or in terms of content to explicitly identifiable forms of concretization of intertextuality, which "in eidetic terms, can be demonstrated as the effective presence of one text in another" (Genette 1993: 10). As a possible specific manifestation of explicit reference, the quotation can be cited, in which, in its direct literal variant, both structures and content are transferred into a new context. The same applies to content that is not directly literal and is alienated (as in the case of allusion, for example). Even in cases where word material or content is incorporated unmarked into a borrowing text, as in plagiarism (see Sect. 2.3.2.2), this constitutes a single-text reference in the sense of Genette's definition of intertextuality.

Genette also undertakes a specifying and differentiating re-accentuation of Kristeva's definition and understands intertextuality as a hyponym of his term *'transtextuality'*, which he introduces as a collective term for various text relations. As a superordinate term, it is accordingly broad and means "tout ce qui met en relation, manifeste ou secrète, avec d'autres textes" (Genette 1982: 7) [everything that puts in relation, manifest or secret, with other texts]. Genette divides transtextuality into a total of five types: The first subtype, *intertextuality* according to Genette, has already been outlined. In his definition, intertextuality refers exclusively to concrete forms of reference and not to features that a text shares with others, for example, due to genre conventions. The second type, *paratextuality,* denotes intra-relations between parts of a text, such as between the main text, its title, and its preface. *Metatextuality* refers to the explicit commentary of one text on another. Such a meta-relation is, for example, the genre-defining characteristic of reviews. Genette subsumes genre features in general under the fourth type, *architextuality.* The fifth and final category, *hypertextuality,* is itself a collective term for texts fundamentally based on others. A pretext (also 'hypotext') thus undergoes a literary-artistic transformation and is processed in a 'hypertext' in a parodic or satirical manner, for example.

The main focus of Genette's typology is on this last category. For the analysis of citation practices in court decisions, however, hypertextuality can be disregarded, since decisions are not motivated by literary-artistic purposes and the incorporation of a work for the purposes of parody or satire can thus be excluded. The other four categories—although originally referring to literary texts—can also be useful for non-literary genres such as court decisions. In the context of the subject of study, namely quotations in court decisions, the present work focuses on the first subtype of intertextuality as the demonstrability of a text. Thus, when the term intertextuality is used hereafter, it is to be understood as single-text reference. A broad understanding, according to Kristeva's original conception, is not pursued—at least for the analytical aims of this study—not least due to its lack of operationalizability.

A concept that is based on Genette's narrow definition of intertextuality is the scaling model by Pfister and Broich (1985). The criteria of the model refer primarily to the intensity of intertextual references. The first criterion addresses the distinction between *use* and *mention.* This fundamental distinction between types of embedding is also used in characterizations of types of quotations themselves and refers to the role a quotation assumes in relation to its embedding environment. Expressions that are *used* fulfill a sentential grammatical function; *mentioned* expressions, on the other hand, are integrated in order to say something *about* them and not *with* them:

> To *use* an expression linguistically is to use it as a tool; to employ it towards a linguistic end. […]. In contrast, to *mention* an individual is to say something about it; to make it the topic of conversation between speaker and listener. (Washington 1998: n.p.)

Pfister follows this distinction and describes quotations that, among other things, are structurally "seamlessly" (1985: 26) integrated into a new context as less intensely intertextual than quotations in which the original context is highlighted by emphasizing the character of the quotation (ibid.).

Emphasis and marking play a major role in the second criterion, the *communicativity* of intertextual references. Their intensity increases with the degree of awareness of the intertextual relation. The third criterion strongly recalls Genette's metatextuality: when "intertextuality is not only marked, but also thematized" (Pfister 1985: 27) and problematized, the criterion of *self-reflexivity* is present. As a content-semantic criterion, self-reflexivity stands in contrast to the fourth formal criterion of *structurality.* Here, Pfister compares "the merely occasional and incidental citation of pretexts" (Pfister 1985: 28) with comprehensive structural adoptions and syntagmatic integrations. The manner of integration of the intertextual reference also determines the fifth criterion of *selectivity.* References are always intense when they are close to the pretext and are only minimally abstracted for integration into the new textual environment. The final criterion, *dialogicity,* draws on Bakhtin's theory and terminology and denotes the semantic tension between the donor text and the new text.

Pfister himself explains the scaling criteria of intertextuality using the example of the quotation. Quotations can be described as the prototypical manifestation of explicit specific intertextuality as single-text reference. If Pfister's scaling criteria are applied to the types of quotations presented below, different intensities can be identified: a direct quotation is, in terms of structurality and selectivity, 'more intensely intertextual' than an indirect one. However, in order to locate a quotation with respect to all five criteria, it is necessary not only to analyze the type of quotation but also its embedding environment and, if necessary, to compare it with the quoted pretext. Without this knowledge, the degree of self-reflexivity and dialogicity cannot be determined.

2.1.2 Types of Quotations and Citations

Fundamentally, a distinction can be made between intertextual and non-intertextual types of quotation. Direct, mixed, and indirect quotations refer to other texts and are thus examples of intertextual quotation types. Intertextual quotations always involve a six-part relation. (1) A re-producer (P2) uses the words of (2) a pre-text producer (P1). These words can thus be found in (3) an original text[2]

[2] Instead of the term 'text', the term 'speech' can also be used; however, since the corpus of the present work consists of written language products, the former is preferred.

(T1) and (4) a reproducing text (T2). What is quoted always originates from an original context and, by being inserted into a quoting text, is embedded in a new context. This results in (5) a pre-text context (K1) and (6) a receiving context (K2). Intertextual quotation types can in turn be subdivided into material quotation types, in which the material of the pre-text is quoted verbatim, and immaterial quotation types, in which the material of the pre-text is not present verbatim. Furthermore, there are also forms of intertextual reference that are not classified as quotations, but are closely related to quotation in the act of referencing. An example of this is paraphrase. The study of intertextual forms, like the study of the concept of intertextuality itself, traditionally falls within the domain of literary studies. Literary approaches are particularly interested in the explicitness or markedness of quotations. Since literary texts, unlike, for example, academic texts, are subject to artistic freedom and thus not to any obligation of marking, the act of intertextual reference in literary texts can be openly marked or carried out cryptically (typology according to Meyer 1967).

Non-intertextual types of quotation include the pure and the modalizing quotation. Neither type refers to a pre-text, but instead uses quotation marks as pragmatic indicators, for example to signal irony. The analysis of non-intertextual quotation types falls within the domain of the philosophy of language and linguistics. Linguistics deals with both intertextual and non-intertextual types of quotation; it examines quotation as "speech within speech" and as "speech about speech" (Volosinov 1930: 115).

On the one hand, the preceding overview shows that quotation is studied by many disciplines; on the other hand, this may also be the reason why integrative typologies of quotation remain a desideratum in research. Typological attempts either focus on quotation as a term and thereby exclude closely related forms such as paraphrase (cf. Brendel/Meibauer/Steinbach 2011), or they focus on the intertextual aspect as the defining feature and thereby exclude non-intertextual types of quotation. The aim of the following discussion is therefore to develop a cross-disciplinary, philological typology.

2.1.2.1 The Direct Quotation

The direct quotation, also *oratio recta* (cf. e.g. Steinseifer 2019: 182, German: das direkte Zitat), paradigmatically is the starting point for the study of reproduction forms. Its description is usually provided in contrast to the indirect quotation as its (at least seemingly) dichotomous counterpart. The central criterion of the direct quotation is the unchanged, verbatim transfer into a new context. It is usually introduced or concluded by verbs of speech manifestation. Such verbal accompaniment, however, is optional, since the direct quotation behaves largely independently of its embedding context with regard to formal linguistic parameters:

(1a) Descartes says/writes: "Cogito ergo sum."
(1b) "Cogito ergo sum." That is our motto.

The marking of external content is obligatory. The way such marking should appear is highly regulated for written quotations. Direct quotations must (in German) be marked graphically with double quotation marks in order not to be considered plagiarism; in disputes over cases of plagiarism, missing quotation punctuation can even be relevant under copyright law. Even for the comparatively less regulated domain of oral communication, means of marking quotations have developed (for example, prosodic emphasis, see Günthner 2000: 4 f.). Example 1a also illustrates the variety of possible accompanying verbs, which in traditional grammar are subsumed under the term *verba dicendi* (e.g. to mean, to express, to say). In view of the fundamental understanding of quotations as the reproduction of speech and thought in general—and not just the reproduction of speech—the term must be regarded as inadequate. The frequent undifferentiated use of the term *verba dicendi* not only for verbs of oral utterance, but also for verbs of mental processes or verbs of writing, runs counter to the understanding of quotations as reproductions of verbalized, thought, and written language. *Verba dicendi* must therefore be understood in their broadest sense; the term also includes *verba sentiendi* and *verba scribendi* (see further Sect. 4.3.2).

Example 1b shows the independence from accompanying framing, which is also a central feature of the direct quotation: the criterion of syntactic independence serves as a potential distinguishing criterion from the mixed quotation, which is also based on verbatim reproduced elements. With this characteristic and that of verbatimness, two criteria are named, the latter of which will be discussed in more detail below.

The requirement of verbatim reproduction results in the exclusion of possible reformulations. Even substitutions with synonyms of supposedly identical real-world reference are *salva veritate* inadmissible (cf. Brendel/Meibauer/Steinbach 2011: 2). The direct quotation thus transfers both content and form into a new context; it is a *type-token* transfer. With this condition, the direct quotation is at least seemingly protected from distortion by the quoting P2, so that it is considered the ideal of truthful reproduction. It should be noted, however, that even the act of selecting a sentence to be quoted from a source text constitutes a kind of intervention by P2. By selecting a quotation and its scope, P2 introduces their subjective perspective on T1 and thus influences the interpretation of the quoted material by a recipient.

Moreover, complete verbatimness is in itself an ideal that cannot be fulfilled in all contexts of reproduction; the extension of the concept of verbatimness proves to be vague. While the written, verbatim quoting of written language is unproblematic due to its fixed nature, certain problems arise when spoken language is involved. The degree and extent of identity between the original utterance and its reproduction that must be ensured in order to speak of verbatimness—or, with even greater emphasis, of *word-for-word* correspondence—varies according to the requirements of the context of reproduction (cf. Maier 2014).[3]

2.1.2.2 The Indirect Quotation

Perhaps the most obvious difference between indirect (German: das indirekte Zitat) and direct quotations lies in the absence of graphematic markers. Instead of quotation marks, indirect quotations—also known as *oratio obliqua*—use so-called markers of indirectness to transfer an original utterance into an indirectly quoting context K2 (for the use of the term, e.g., in relation to epistemic modal verbs, see Scherr 2019: 3, as well as Chap. 4), of which some adaptations *can* be made but *do not have to be*. The majority of adaptation features used are optional linguistic procedures; obligatory procedures are limited to only a few. In order to be considered an indirect quotation, the quote must be transformed into a subordinate clause introduced or derived from a matrix verb, but the type of subordinate clause used for this transformation is irrelevant to the status of indirectness. The following examples (2b, 2c & 2d) demonstrate three possible syntactic transformations of a direct quotation (2a) into indirect quotations[4]:

(2a) The press spokesperson announces: "With the decision published today, the 3rd Chamber of the First Senate of the Federal Constitutional Court has not accepted for decision a constitutional complaint against labor court decisions regarding a dismissal due to a grossly inhumane statement."

(2b) The press spokesperson announces that the 3rd Chamber of the First Senate of the Federal Constitutional Court has not accepted for decision a constitutional complaint against labor court decisions regarding a dismissal due to a grossly inhumane statement.

[3] Difficulties in the written reproduction of oral utterances are illustrated, among other things, by different transcription conventions: while in a content-focused context it may be sufficient to reproduce only the final verbalized words, omitting hesitation signals, false starts, and appendices, the latter may be relevant for extralinguistic studies. Similar problems arise in the oral quoting of originally written language: especially in the production of spoken language, the individual speaker characteristics of P2 inevitably come into play. An influence on the reception and the actual verbatimness cannot be ruled out: (1c) Descartes already said: "I—thank uh think,—therefore—am—I." (Example after Plank 1986: 286). With this individually colored reproduction of the famous quotation, Plank illustrates possible 'disturbing factors' in a reproduction dependent on P2. It remains to be discussed whether, in the course of pauses, slips of the tongue, and dialectal variations—and as in the present example, an interlingual transposition of a sentence originally in Latin—one can still speak of complete verbatimness. Verbatimness—especially in the context of oral direct quotation—is therefore also a property that can be realized to varying degrees.

[4] Example based on a press release of the Federal Constitutional Court (BVerfG) No. 101/2020 of November 24, 2020, referring to decision 1 BvR 2727/19 of November 2, 2020.

(2c) The press spokesperson announces the 3rd Chamber of the First Senate of the Federal Constitutional Court has (German: “habe”) not accepted for decision a constitutional complaint against labor court decisions regarding a dismissal due to a grossly inhumane statement.

(2d) The 3rd Chamber of the First Senate of the Federal Constitutional Court announces not to have accepted for decision a constitutional complaint against labor court decisions regarding a dismissal due to a grossly inhumane statement.

Example (2b) connects the quoting subordinate clause using the subjunction ‘that’. This necessarily results in a change of verb position: in the original utterance—a main clause—the verb occupies the second position, while in the indirect quotation it takes the verb-final position required by the conjunction. Example (2c), by omitting the conjunction[5], instead uses the verb-second position typical of main clauses. Such verb positioning is only possible in combination with specific matrix verbs (for example, *say* and *claim*), since the lexical characteristics of the matrix verb determine the structural embedding possibilities of the reported speech. By contrast, the position of the matrix phrase itself is highly flexible.[6] In addition to the initial position used in the examples, postposed inversions (2e) as well as parenthetical insertions (2f) are also possible:

(2e) The 3rd Chamber of the First Senate of the Federal Constitutional Court has not accepted for decision a constitutional complaint against labor court decisions regarding a dismissal due to a grossly inhumane statement, announces the press spokesperson.

(2f) The 3rd Chamber of the First Senate of the Federal Constitutional Court has, announces the press spokesperson, not accepted for decision a constitutional complaint against labor court decisions regarding a dismissal due to a grossly inhumane statement.

Different orders of embedding and embedded sentence elements, in addition to formal differences, also carry different discourse functions (Brendel/Meibauer/Steinbach 2007: 10). Brendel/Meibauer/Steinbach describe “subordinate clauses with main clause-like verb-second position […]” as “less integrated than complementizer-introduced verb-final clauses.” (ibid.)

Which transformations are to be carried out in indirect quotation also depends on the respective language (for English, for example, Bucalic 2007: 61).

[5] Whether the conjunction introducing the subordinate clause can be omitted in indirect quotations depends, in addition to the matrix verb, on subject identity and sentence type. Infinitive forms (as in 1d) require the identity of the subject in both main and subordinate clause. Furthermore, ellipsis of conjunctions is, for example, impossible for interrogative sentences; interrogative pronouns and adverbs must be transferred, and yes-no questions are rendered in direct quotation with ‘whether’.

[6] This also applies to direct and mixed quotations, for which embedding with matrix verbs is optional; matrix verbs are facultative additions for these two types.

Differences in the grammatical, lexical, and syntactic repertoire of individual languages lead to the use of sometimes highly divergent markers of indirectness. Two examples in comparison between German and English resources for indirect quotation are the so-called *consecutio temporum* and the subjunctive. The *consecutio temporum,* which is also extensively discussed in school grammars, refers to the shifting of verb tenses for the purpose of reported speech. In German, by contrast, indirectness cannot be marked by tense shifts; indirectness is signaled by the subjunctive. The pragmatic dimensions of the subjunctive and the *conditional* are, at least in the context of indirectness, entirely different. Even in German, the use of the "reporting subjunctive" (Duden 2005: § 762) or the mood referred to as the subjunctive of indirectness to signal indirectness is inconsistent. The subjunctive, also recommended by school grammars, leads to a distancing between P2 and the indirectly quoted content, which in an epistemic reading (possibly unintentionally) can lead to the assumption that the cited content is being questioned (see also Sect. 4.3.1 on the role of the subjunctive as an epistemic quotative). For comparative studies, such as the present work, in which citation practices in texts of different languages are to be compared, it is an important insight that the manner of quoting is shaped not only by the quoter but also by language-specific conventions (see also Sect. 4.4 for further discussion).

2.1.2.3 The Mixed Quotation

The mixed quotation (German: das gemischte Zitat) contains elements of both direct and indirect quotation: "Mixed quotation is a label reserved for indirect speech reports in which some portion is set off in quotes to indicate literalness of rendering" (Cumming 2003: 77). By reproducing a previous original utterance, it belongs to the types of quotation that involve reproduction, i.e., intertextual types of quotation.

A first central question in characterizing mixed quotations arises from the limiting but very unspecific terms "portion" and "literalness" used in the definition: How large such a 'portion', or more precisely the extent of literally adopted elements in a mixed quotation, usually is or must be in order to count as such, is, like the term "literalness", vague.

With the criterion of the "verbatim requirement," Maier (2014: 5) offers a formal specification: Indirect quotations and their contents enclosed in quotation marks must exhibit token-identity with the original utterance (Maier 2014: 6). However, a quantitative specification of the extent is also lacking in this approach. The following (constructed) examples are therefore intended, starting from a singular token-identity, to serve as a reflection of the "verbatim requirement":

(3a) He spoke of a "human rights violation."
(3b) He spoke of "a" human rights violation.

What the two examples have in common is the quantity of literally quoted material—the portion of the integrated direct quotation in each case consists of exactly one word.[7] In contrast, at least according to an initial intuitive interpretation, there is a difference in the acceptability of what is appropriate for direct reproduction, or which terms or formulations possess the property of being 'worthy of quotation'. The reading of example (3a) is unproblematic in that the motivation for the use of the quotation by the producer is not called into question. Even if the intended function—as is generally the case with all types of quotation—is not transparent without further contextual clues, a quotation-like reproduction of an autosemantic word such as "human rights violation" appears to offer added value. This assumed added value of the message creates acceptance of the decision for a mixed quotation. Example (3b), on the other hand, quotes an indefinite article, which in isolation—especially as this is intensified by the graphic isolation through quotation marks—is devoid of content. No semantic added value can be derived from marking such a synsemantic word; the reader is inclined instead to seek a pragmatic added value and might interpret the marking not as reproductive, but as modalizing (see also modalizing quotation in Sect. 2.1.2.7). Theoretically, the variability of the reading and of the sense of appropriateness initially described as intuitive may possibly be grounded in Grice's maxim of relevance (Grice 1975), according to which recipients presuppose an added value in linguistic utterances; the reader tries to extract relevance from the act of quoting. For the minimal criterion of token-identity, the following may therefore apply: What is relevant is not only *how many tokens* are quoted, but also what added value can be gained from the act of quoting. Even though no empirical research has yet been conducted in this regard, numerous examples suggest a tendency for mixed quotation of autosemantic words as compared to synsemantic words. Furthermore, the presence of a literal portion, as with direct quotations, results in opacity, so that no substitutions can be made in order to preserve truth conditions.

A restriction regarding the quoted material lies in the "well-formedness" (Shan 2010: 422) of the mixed quotation: In comparison to direct and pure quotations, in which theoretically even meaningless sequences of letters can be quoted, the high degree of integration of the direct portion into the embedding sentence ("host sentence," de Brabanter 2019) requires grammatical correctness. The two components of the mixed quotation (literal portion and embedding sentence) are so interwoven that the reproduction must fit seamlessly into its environment: "Unlike in direct discourse and pure quotation, the syntax doesn't see the quotation marks" (Maier 2014: 9). This can, for example (as in indirect quotation), lead to a syntactic shift from SVO to SOV position.[8]

[7] In this context, "word" is to be understood as an orthographic word.

[8] All embedding possibilities of the direct portion are subject to the grammatical requirements of the embedding sentence. With this condition, indirect quotation occupies a special position in the philosophy of language: The literal portions are, according to the use-mention distinction, both mentioned and used. This dual role is also reflected in the terminological diversity: With regard to the simultaneous fulfillment of use and mention, the mixed quotation is also referred to as *double-duty quotation* (García-Carpintero 2005) or as *hybrid quotation* (De Brabanter 2019).

2.1.2.4 The Reference

Some studies conflate quotations and references (German: der Verweis): For example, Richter (2013) subtitles her dissertation on 'The Construction of Reputation' as 'References to Ferdinand de Saussure in Romance Linguistics'. However, in her study, quotations are also integrated without any indication of terminological distinctions. In Richter's terminology, quotations thus *fall under* references.

As a counterexample that follows a strict terminological distinction, Jakobs (1999) can be cited: In the subtitle *Quotation and Reference as the Result of Receptive, Reproductive, and Productive Action* of her work on *Textual Networking in the Sciences,* Jakobs explicitly distinguishes between reference and quotation. She proceeds in the same way in her analysis, in which she treats the two forms of appearance both in their kinship as forms of intertextual linkage, but also in their differing structure and functionalization.

The following discussion advocates a conceptual and terminological separation of the terms 'quotation' and 'reference', since quotations manifest the content of a pretext—whether in material or immaterial form—in another text, whereas references merely indicate the presence of a source citation in the absence of concrete pretext material. Jakobs (1999: 100) understands references—unlike quotations—as "search instructions" and as "calls to action." The reader is prompted to independently obtain additional information offered in relation to the text at hand. The character of a prompt is also expressed in accompanying imperative reference expressions such as "cf." and "see" (ibid.). While literal quotations integrate information directly and accessibly into a text, references point to information external to the text. Due to this demonstrative character, Jakobs (1999: 101) ascribes to them a deictic character (cf. Bühler's theory of deixis, Bühler 1965) and distinguishes two forms of deixis. If the reader is familiar with the text named by the reference, this is called external deixis. This is the case, for example, with canonized theories in science and norms in the case of legislation. The information is not immediately present to the reader, as with a literal quotation; however, it is located in a retrievable 'external domain'. If the reference points to a text that is not yet present in the reader's informational repertoire, this is deixis to a phantasm. This is anaphoric pointing, since the producer refers to something that, chronologically, can only be consulted after reading the referring text.

Ehlich and Rehbein (1986) attribute relevance for meaning construction by the recipient to all components of a reference source. Not only the name, but also, for example, the year, help the reader to classify the source in terms of its degree of familiarity, currency, and, if applicable, validity.

The amount of information the reader can gain in advance about the named source can be increased by the referencing producer through comprehension-modifying additions. Whether a source is to be read affirmatively or critically can be guided by the producer through evaluative additions. Such additions can serve as indications of intended quotation functions (see also Chap. 3). Jakobs (1999: 103) refers to reference additions as labels. ‘Reference labeling’ is used, among other things, in scholarly texts and in decision texts. As an example of the latter, the following passage from a decision of the Federal Constitutional Court is quoted:

(4) The term of office of a judge appointed for a fixed period is of considerable significance for the question of whether a tenured civil servant, to the extent required by Art. 92, 97 GG, can succeed not only in detaching himself from his original authority, but also in maintaining his inner independence despite the impending return within two years to the position of a civil servant bound by instructions (*critically, for example:* Ruthig, in: Kopp/Schenke, VwGO, 23rd ed. 2017, § 18 para. 4; [...]). (BVerfGE 148, 69 2nd Senate 22.03.2018, para. 125, emphasis by J.S.)

The structural and substantive integration of references in legal texts is examined by Höfler (2015) from a legal-linguistic perspective. As a “legislative-technical device” (ibid.: 325), he ascribes to references a significant role in the discourse structure of law. Höfler (2012: 33) identifies the recognizability of their reference object as decisive for the comprehensibility of references. In order for a reference object, i.e., a bibliographic citation, to be “identifiable with the least possible cognitive effort” (ibid.), explicit linguistic repetitions (i.e., quotations) can be included, among other things. References as acts of pointing in the sense of Jakobs are thus less accessible and comprehensible than quotations, which are present in the text and immediately accessible.

2.1.2.5 Paraphrase

Another form of intertextual reference is the paraphrase (German: die Paraphrase). In general, this refers to the rewording of content using synonyms in order to convey its meaning in a new context. Philological specifications do take up such a (general linguistic) understanding, but they problematize paraphrasing operations and their influence on the integrity of the content being transmitted. If one follows the definition of paraphrases as “sentences or phrases that convey the same meaning using different wording” (Bhagat/Hovy 2013: 463), the question arises as to how divergent a formulation can be, or to what degree of reformulation a conveyed content can still be transmitted unchanged in its meaning. Bhagat/Hovy (ibid.) accordingly point to the distinction between a narrow definition in logic and a comparatively more liberal terminology: the former demands complete identity of content, while the latter also designates approximate content equivalences as paraphrases.

As the following survey of paraphrasing methods will suggest, the assumption of an unchanged transmission of meaning under real language conditions is almost illusory. Even though the acceptance of content approximations complicates definitional efforts, a broadening of the concept of paraphrase to include more or less content-modifying forms is indispensable. In his considerations on the structure of synonymy, Wirth (1996: 7–11) distinguishes periphrastic and metaphrastic forms as subtypes. While paraphrases are formed primarily through substitutions at the syntagmatic level, periphrases (exemplarily for rhetorical purposes) operate at the paradigmatic level: if the sentence ‘the eagle flies’ is paraphrased as ‘the king of the skies flies’ (example after Wirth 1996: 10), the content of the signified is enriched; this is a periphrasis. As a third variant of paraphrase, Wirth introduces the metaphrase, in which content is knowingly reproduced in altered form—through additions or omissions. As an example of this type, he (ibid.: 11) cites qualitative changes such as a change of genre (e.g., the transposition of a poem into prose).

As illustrated by the examples of periphrasis and metaphrase, the congruence of content, often cited in definitions of the term, is not necessarily the aim of the paraphraser. Yet even when synonymy is intended in a paraphrase, denotation and connotation make complete equivalence of signifieds difficult.[9] Apparent synonyms can—despite referring to the same signified—evoke different connotations. Against this background, approximate equivalences in the comparison of pre-text and content are to be assumed as the rule. This condition is also taken into account by De Beaugrande/Dressler (1981: 50) in their definition of paraphrase as “approximate conceptual equivalence among outwardly material.” How far a paraphrase departs from its original text varies, among other things, depending on the paraphrasing strategy. Bhagat/Hovy (2013: 465–469) identify 25 different paraphrasing operations,[10] most of which can be summarized as substitution measures: substitutions can be carried out, among other things, using synonyms (5a), antonyms (5b), as well as metaphors and figurative language (5c).

(5a) She is extremely hungry.
(5b) She is not at all full.
(5c) She could eat a horse.

Even though all three examples are intended to denote the same state of affairs, the influence of lexical substitutions on the tone and thus ultimately on the unfolding of meaning in the sentences is unmistakable. In a similar way, a change in word class (e.g., when converting a verbal style into a nominal style) can influence the tone, the assignment to a style, and thus the overall meaning. Comparatively more subtly than lexical substitutions, elliptical paraphrases deviate from an original content (6a & 6b).

(6a) Goethe is interesting, and Kafka is also interesting.
(6b) Goethe and Kafka are interesting.

The summarizing ellipsis (6b) essentially conveys the same predication as the coordinating variant (6a). Whether both sentences actually carry the same semantic content remains open to discussion. If a sentence producer chooses such a conspicuous redundancy as in (6a), the recipient is inclined to attribute an intention to it. The loss of redundancy in (6b) could thus evoke a different reading.

---

[9] For the definition of synonymy as equivalence of signifieds, see Wirth (1996: 24).

[10] In this context, only some of the operationalizations are contrasted, exemplified, and discussed. Moreover, Bhagat/Hovy (2013) do not distinguish, as Wirth (1996) does, between paraphrases, periphrases, and metaphrases; their list thus includes operations of all three types in summary.

As a final example, following the list by Bhagat/Hovy, substitution or enrichment by world knowledge should be mentioned. Reformulations for paraphrases primarily require linguistic knowledge; secondarily, world knowledge can expand reformulation options (7a & 7b).

(7a) The Bolsheviks fought.
(7b) The Reds fought.

By identifying the reformulation measures used, Bhagat and Hovy take a major step toward an empirical grasp of paraphrase, which is especially sought after by computational linguists for the optimization of natural language processing (e.g., in Vila/Martí/Rodríguez 2014).

The preceding examples have shown that paraphrasing measures can significantly influence the transmission of meaning. However, the determinability of the relation between paraphrase and pretext is further complicated: when a reader receives a paraphrase, it is usually marked by a source reference, but the reformulations carried out are invisible without comparison with the pretext. Whether a producer has paraphrased a source objectively or (intentionally or unintentionally) subjectively cannot be inferred from the paraphrase itself and can only be partially reconstructed interpretively.

2.1.2.6 The Pure Quotation

The pure quotation is the main focus of philosophical reflections on quotation in language. Its role is so central that, in the philosophy of language, it can be regarded as the prototype of quotation as such. When canonical studies—such as those by Davidson (e.g., 1979)—speak generally of "quotation," they usually mean the pure quotation, and other types of quotation are only mentioned in passing or excluded altogether. Other studies, in turn, focus for example on analyses of the semantic status of pure quotation (Pafel 2011). What both perspectives have in common is the avoidance of concrete definitions: "It turns out that a precise characterization of pure quotation is slippery enough for authors to usually prefer examples instead of definitions" (Bazzoni 2016: 120). This problem is also addressed by Cappelen/Lepore/McKeever (2020), who approach pure quotation by identifying, characterizing, and formalizing numerous examples. They understand pure quotation in an instrumentalist sense as a "device for talking about language" (ibid., no page numbers). Similarly, it can be understood as a "device used to refer to typographical or phonetic shapes by exhibiting samples, that is, inscriptions or utterances that have those shapes" (Davidson 1979: 27). The pure quotation "turns language on itself" (Cappelen/Lepore/McKeever 2020) and thus enables the thematization of conceptual properties. These can be—not only typographical and phonetic properties, as Davidson's definition suggests, but in principle all describable properties of a pure quotation. Some examples of pure quotations and their thematization of properties are given in the following sentences (8a–8e):

(8a) The word 'Bundesverfassungsgericht' consists of 24 letters.

(8b) "Schein" and "Sein" rhyme.
(8c) *Öaklfsföhlraghioe* is a jumble of letters.
(8d) 'Ich habe Hunger' is a sentence.
(8e) *Ver-* is a prefix in German.

A comparison of the examples reveals at least four features of pure quotations: 1. The content and scope of the pure quotation are subject to no restrictions whatsoever. It is possible to quote individual words and phrases as well as entire sentences, individual morphemes, or even sequences of letters devoid of meaning and reference. 2. The lack of restriction also applies to the possibilities for thematizing the quoted material. The commonality in thematization consists in the presence of an attribution process at all; *which* attributes are thematized is irrelevant. 3. There is no binding regulation for the typographical and graphematic marking of pure quotations. For example, academic writing guides attempt to standardize the use of double quotation marks only for reported speech, according to which pure quotations should not/must not use them. In contrast, the Duden also lists double quotation marks as an option for "parts of words, words, or text passages [...] about which one wishes to make a statement." 4. According to a widespread view[11] (Brendel/Meibauer/Steinbach 2011: 17), pure quotations constitute both syntactically and semantically singular units ((8d') 'X' is a sentence). As the preceding discussion suggests, perspectives on pure quotation are largely theoretical in nature. Empirical studies on pure quotation and its real communicative functionalizations do not (yet) exist and thus represent a desideratum.

2.1.2.7 The Modalizing Quotation

Like pure quotations, modalizing quotations (German: das modalisierende Zitat; in English mostly referred to as scare quotes) do not refer to the reproduction of a pre-text. Abbott (2004) therefore alternatively proposes the term "non-citational quotation marks." However, this designation expresses that "there is no quotation-like function here at all," and this "still needs to be investigated" (Meibauer 2007: 30).

The scare quote is initially to be understood as a subjective and interpretation-dependent addition of meaning. In modalizing quotation, it is a matter of an interpretive marking of individual words or phrases, usually with the aim of signaling a meaning that deviates from the literal content or a deviation from the register of the modalizing quoting text. As the following examples show, the quotation marks in modalizing quotations signal exclusively that the quoted term requires additional interpretation; how it is to be understood and what motivates the quotation remains initially opaque without further contextual or world knowledge on the part of the recipient.

[11] Discussion and counterposition in Pafel (2011).

(9a) The apartment costs “only” €1,000,000.
(9b) That is a “bargain.”
(9c) The state of research reveals itself as a “patchwork.”

Examples 9a and 9b represent an effect often intended with modalizing quotations—a reading is evoked that, through irony, reverses the actual denotation of “only” and “bargain” into their opposites. This reversal is primarily guided by the quotation marks. Example (9c) represents another function: In the quotation of the term “patchwork,” it is not a matter of ironic reversal into the opposite, but rather the marking of a deviation in register, which arises from the stylistic tension between discussing the state of research and the use of figurative elements. The quotation marks used can thus also be described as pragmatic indicators; Meibauer (2007: 22) therefore locates modalizing quotations at the “graphematics-pragmatics interface.” A similar graphematics-pragmatics relation is described by Predelli (2003: 7) with his differentiation between *message* and *attachment.* The former refers to the content of the quoted word; the attachment to the additional meaning evoked by the quotation marks (as *attachment triggers*). Secondarily, but also influencing the interpretation (especially in example 9a), is non-linguistic world knowledge, in this case about apartment prices.

The use of modalizing quotations has so far been less analyzed descriptively than criticized as inappropriate from a prescriptive perspective. Such criticism is voiced above all by Predelli (2003), who, drawing on a dictionary, introduces his remarks on *scare quotes* with the following words: “Expressing a widespread viewpoint, the Harper Collins Concise Dictionary of English Usage warns that they are ‘not acceptable in formal writing’ and that it is far better to find words that express the writer’s intentions precisely and do so without apology” (Ehrlich/Murphy 1991: 139). Predelli (2003: 2) reduces the motivation for using modalizing quotations indiscriminately to the writer’s inability or unwillingness to find a more appropriate word:

> In a typical scenario […] the writer knows or suspects that the word […] is not properly applicable […]. Unable or unwilling to find a more appropriate expression, she uses it anyway, and apologetically recognizes her deviance from the requirement of precision by enclosing the term within quotation marks.

That such a motivation for use applies to some writers cannot be ruled out. In view of the fact that writers, by marking conspicuous terms, already demonstrate their awareness of (variant) appropriateness, the question arises as to *why* they nevertheless choose a variant that is nonconforming to the register of the respective communicative context. Predelli’s characterization of modalizing quotations as a ‘makeshift solution’ falls short and completely ignores stylistic-intentional uses: By locating quotation marks “between linguistic and rhetorical components,” Klockow (1980: 220) highlights the potential aesthetic aspect of modalizing quotations. A violation of genre- or discourse-typical conventions can—by “exploiting the connotative level” (Klockow 1980: 302)—be used deliberately and rhetorically-strategically. The proximity to rhetorical figures is also evident in the term “non-literal speech.” When academic writing guides refer to non-literal speech, they are in fact referring to nothing other than modalizing quotations. The established mention and the normative requirement of how a modalizing quotation must be marked in academic texts can also be interpreted as evidence of an accepted presence; thus, modalizing quotations—contrary to the inadmissibility in formal contexts criticized by Ehrlich/Murphy and Predelli—seem to be at least accepted in German-speaking contexts.

2.2 Citation & Quotation in Law

In the context of law, the quotation assumes two roles at once: On the one hand, it itself constitutes an *object of the law*; within the framework of copyright law and the right of personality to protection against the attribution of false statements, criminal dimensions of unlawful handling of quotations are regulated. On the other hand, the quotation itself is also an *instrument for the realization of the law.* The quantitative increase in the number of quotations observed in the 1990s (for the increase in exchanges between courts, see e.g. Glendon 1991) in decisions attests to the ongoing establishment of intertextual and inter-judicial references. In legal citation typology, these references are not classified according to structural criteria as in philological characterization (*how* is it cited?), but are primarily based on a classification according to the sources of the quotations and their (hierarchical) relation to the citing instance (*who* is being cited?).

In legal scholarship, the concept of the quotation is usually understood very broadly, as a summary of literal quotations and non-literal quotations, references, and paraphrases. The legal citation and reference typology presented in Sect. 2.2.2 accordingly treats these types together and not (as in the philological perspective) separately from one another.

2.2.1 Intertextuality in Law

Morlok describes legal work as "thoroughly intertextual" (2015: 69), consisting for the most part of the "use of (other) texts" (ibid., 70). Intertextuality is a fundamental phenomenon of law: On the one hand, in the production of legal texts (for example, court decisions), lawyers regularly refer to other texts in the form of citations and references. On the other hand, the existing law itself requires intertextual work in interpretive practice. According to the binding effect of the law under Art. 97 para. 1 of the Basic Law, judges are subject to the law (which exists in the form of texts) and must, in their case decisions and the reasoning for those decisions—in other words, in the entire production of their decisions—refer to the existing normative texts. The postulate of the binding effect of the law is thus, at its core, ultimately the obligation to intertextual work.

To illustrate the constitutive role of intertextuality in law, the four fundamental methods of interpretation[12] in legal scholarship can be named (Morlok 2015: 71; see also ibid., 179 f.): Systematic interpretation requires, for the determination of the meaning of a legal provision, a comparison of existing norms. The same applies to grammatical, historical, and teleological interpretation, among others, if only because the reconstruction of supposed legislative intentions—regardless of the specific methodology—always requires recourse to the medium of written fixation. Due to these obligatory textual relations, Busse (2000: 1 f.; see also Busse 1992) summarizes legal decision-making as follows: "[…] one could describe it as the production of decision texts from existing texts by means of the creation of case-related textual relationships (and thus text networks)." With the concept of text networks, he draws on the image of law as a "web" and "collage" (Morlok 2015: 70).

With Busse and Morlok, two philological positions have been discussed. Considerations of the intertextuality of law originate less from legal scholarship itself than from philology, which deals with textual interconnections. In legal scholarship, the concept of intertextuality receives less attention, which may be due to the neglect of reflection on the materiality of law as text (see also Neumeyer 2018: 104). One of the few examples of a legal analysis using the originally literary and cultural theoretical concept of intertextuality is Neumeyer's essay on the problem of intertextual interpretation of human rights treaties. With the aim of creating universal human rights standards, human rights treaties are particularly dependent on the consideration of intertextual references; they can thus be regarded as exemplary for legal intertextual work.

Even if the concept of intertextuality is rarely mentioned by name in legal scholarship, there are nevertheless numerous discussions in which the basic ideas of intertextuality are present. In the form of the terms "transjudicial communication" (Slaughter 1994), "constitutional dialogue" (Meuwese/Snel 2013), or "judicial dialogue" (Law/Chang 2011), questions of intertextuality are taken up in legal scholarship: With the concepts of inter-court communication and dialogue, it is examined whether and how courts relate to one another and in what tangible forms these relations manifest themselves. It seems as if the concept of intertextuality in legal scholarship simply hides behind another name.

2.2.2 *Legal Citation Typologies*

The typological criteria used in legal scholarship differ entirely from the philological approaches presented. In legal scholarship, the authorship of the referenced content is used as the primary criterion. The linguistic form in which the content

[12] For more on legal methods of interpretation, see Canaris/Larenz (1995). The fifth method, comparative law (Häberle 1989: 913), which is also highly intertextual, is not counted among the classical methods.

is integrated—whether as a literal quotation or as an indirectly paraphrased content—is of secondary importance. Thus, it is primarily a categorization of types of authorship, and the philological focus on the question 'How is it cited?' gives way in legal typology to the question 'Who is being cited?'.

A typology that refers more generally than specific citation typologies to forms of communication between courts in general is the typology of transjudicial communication according to Slaughter (1994). Even though Slaughter encompasses all communicative forms of making contact (she also discusses, among other things, oral exchanges between judges), her typology is certainly suitable for citations and references: citations and references are one of the various potential manifestations of transjudicial communication. The typology opens up three categories of classification[13], each of which is further subdivided into several subcategories. First, under "geometry" (Slaughter 1994: 103) of transjudicial forms of communication, the status of the citing and the cited court is placed in a hierarchical relationship. From this hierarchy, three possibilities for locating the citation and thus for categorizing the form of communication arise: *Horizontal* communication takes place between courts of identical status. Ultimately, both national borders and hierarchical relationships can influence the likelihood that a court will refer to the statements of another court: "National supreme courts, for instance, may be more likely to take account of each other's judgments than of the judgments of lower foreign courts." (Slaughter 1994: 103). *Vertical* communication takes place between judicial bodies at the national and supranational level. An example of this is the citation of certain ECtHR decisions by national courts that are parties to the European Convention on Human Rights. The decisions of the ECtHR are binding for these states in any case; nevertheless, citing them can be described as an exchange: "Such citations can be read as the beginning of a direct court-to-court communication." (Slaughter 1994: 111) Vertical and horizontal forms of communication can also appear together as a *vertical-horizontal hybrid form.* The communication between national courts and the ECtHR, cited as an example, is also an example of Slaughter's second typological category of *reciprocity* (1994: 112 f.). *Dialogic* communication in the form of mutual acknowledgment, exemplified by mutual citation, can be described as directly reciprocal. This variant stands in contrast to the judicial *monologue,* in which a court borrows content from another court, while the latter does not in turn respond to the content of the former. Whether a "judicial dialogue" actually exhibits features of dialogicity, or whether judicial communication is in fact more one-sided and monologic, is discussed by Law and Chang, among others (2011: 528–531), using the dialogicity features of the *Oxford Dictionary.* In view of the determination of the addressee, the designation as a dialogue proves to be highly problematic. Even if courts cite each other, they do not address each other, and there is not necessarily a common subject to which both parties respond, as is characteristic of dialogues. This also applies to Slaughter's third subtype of reciprocity: In "intermediated dialogue"

[13] The third category refers to the function of transjudicial communication.

(1994: 113 f.), courts do not respond directly to each other and are thus closer to monologic structures. In this form, the content of both is brought together by a third mediating instance. Other legal typologies that explicitly refer to judicial citations resemble the non-specific typology according to Slaughter, especially in that the relationship between the citing court and the cited court is always highlighted as the decisive criterion.

A similar approach is also followed by Nußberger's typology (2006). Nußberger classifies citations according to the national and legal-systematic relationship between the citer and the cited, and extracts from this the three categories of internal to the system, external to the system, and foreign to the system. The first category, *internal to the system,* includes all citations that refer to sources belonging to the same legal system as the citing court. These can be citations of statutes as well as references to interpretive formulas and decisions, or even to scholarly texts. Nußberger does note that among these are citations whose inclusion is mandatory, as well as citations of a legally facultative nature, but she does not explicitly use the poles *facultative vs. obligatory* as criteria for internal differentiation. An example of references that must be included is the binding to statutes in general, or more specifically, the "almost pedantic" (Nußberger 2006: 763) approach of the ECtHR to this postulate. The ECtHR introduces all case analyses with a verbatim citation of the norm whose violation is to be adjudicated. Such an approach, however, is rare (ibid.); usually, courts are content with a non-verbatim reference to the relevant paragraph(s). Common for the interpretation of a norm—but not legally binding—is the reference to scholarly positions. The handling of scholarly positions in jurisprudence is variable according to legal culture. For the judicial style of the German Federal Constitutional Court (BVerfG), the consideration of relevant scholarly literature is indeed formative (Nußberger 2006: 765, see also Sect. 5.1.1 on the continental European legal tradition). *External to the system citations* are references that have become established in the course of international and supranational networking. For the European context, these are above all the CJEU and the ECtHR. The extent to which national courts cite these two internationally composed bodies, however, depends on several factors. International law is subject to European law (cf. Nußberger 2006: 765); the latter must therefore be cited. For the citation of the ECtHR, there is no corresponding constitutional requirement (ibid.: 766).

Nußberger refers to as *foreign to the system* citations "from the decisions of other countries," "from the scholarly literature on the norms of another legal system" (2006: 767), as well as "general political and philosophical citations" (2006: 763).

With this definition, Nußberger implicitly undertakes a twofold classification of scholarly literature. References to (legal) scholarship can, on the one hand, be counted among the internal to the system citations, insofar as they deal with the same legal tradition. On the other hand, they can also be foreign to the system if they discuss matters that do not belong to the legal system of the citing court.

Furthermore, within the type of foreign to the system citations, Nußberger distinguishes between *explicit* and *implicit* citations. Explicit citations are those that are clearly marked as a supplement to one's own reasoning. For implicit citations, the origin from a foreign legal system is not made clear (Nußberger 2006: 768). In this way, Nußberger essentially follows the literary studies distinction between marked and cryptic citations.[14]

A differentiation according to systems is certainly useful for the analysis, aimed at by the typology, of the development of a common European law. In contrast, a sometimes undifferentiated terminology, which makes the classification of citations more difficult, is problematic: In the first half of the article, Nußberger refers to a system in terms of national borders and legal traditions. However, by assigning all philosophical literature—regardless of its national affiliation and its embedding in a legal tradition—to foreign to the system citations, the first two criteria of a system are not consistently maintained. Overall, Nußberger seems to be tacitly working with two different interpretations of the term 'system'.

A third legal categorization, which is compatible with the categories internal, external, and foreign, but names only two categories, is the division into *self-citation and foreign citation* according to Jestaedt (2010: 152–155). Using the example of citations by the Federal Constitutional Court (BVerfG), Jestaedt distinguishes between the court's own authorship and foreign authorship of the cited content. The Federal Constitutional Court mainly uses, and especially when arguing in genuinely constitutional matters, self-citations (Jestaedt 2010: 154; see also Sect. 5.3.1 on existing studies of the citation practice of the BVerfG).

2.2.3 The Citation as an Object of Jurisprudence

There are legal regulations governing how to cite and in which contexts false citation or quotation constitutes a legal violation. Incorrect citation is to be understood in two ways: on the one hand, as unmarked citation, and on the other, as protection against the reproduction of statements that were not made, through the right to personality. For the former, for example, the obligation to indicate intertextual references in non-artistic works arises from copyright law. Failure to indicate can be sanctioned as unlawful plagiarism. However, as will be explored below, the definitional foundations necessary to distinguish between citation and plagiarism for the identification of copyright infringement are inadequate. A similar situation exists with the identification of incorrect quotation, understood as a distorted or fictitious reproduction. Among the issues to be discussed here are, for example, when quotation is deliberately falsified and when reproductions are unintentionally distorted through processes of interpretation.

[14] Literary and cultural studies use the characterization 'cryptic' for citations that are not explicitly identified as such (e.g., in Benninghof-Lühl 1998).

2.2.3.1 The Citation in Copyright

"Reproduction, distribution, and public communication of a published work for the purpose of citation" is permissible under copyright law, "provided that the use to its extent is justified by the particular purpose" (German Copyright Law, § 51 UrhG). The regulation is open with regard to the medium of the citation and refers not only to the quotation as the reproduction of linguistic material, but also to musical quotations (ibid., para. 3) and the use of images. The thus permitted use of third-party copyrighted intellectual property limits copyright law as an exception provision (Rehbinder/Peukert 2019: § 25 Rn. 477 f.). This limitation is, as contained in the wording of the regulation, functionally justified: The "particular purpose" is exemplified in paragraph 1 for independent scholarly works as "explanation of the content."

The function, alongside the extent, is the decisive criterion for assessing the legal conformity of a citation: The citation may, for example, explain, exemplify, develop, supplement, and substantiate the expression of one's own thoughts, but not replace them (cf. Schack 2013: 89). At what extent a citation is considered legally infringing as 'too long' cannot, in view of the widely varying lengths of works providing and using citations, be universally specified numerically. Schack (2013: 89) notes that a citation can be integrated into independent works, which, however, must not be built entirely on citations. Within the framework of artistic freedom (German Basic Law, GG Art. 3, para. 5), artists enjoy extensive freedom, so that citation in extensive use can form the foundation of artistic forms such as parody or pastiche, without constituting a copyright infringement.

2.2.3.2 Citation and Plagiarism

Art forms that employ quotation, such as parody and pastiche, are exempt from the explicit requirement to mark quotations, for example through quotation marks and source references. In contrast, marking is obligatory and highly regulated in non-artistically motivated texts, such as in academic writing.

If a quotation—apart from artistic uses—is used without marking, it constitutes plagiarism, since every author has the right to recognition of their authorship (§ 13 UrhG). Plagiarists present the intellectual property of others as their own and thereby commit not only a legal but also a social transgression (Bloch 2012: 13–26). As a social matter (cf. Bloch 2012: 13–26), the plagiarism debate—regardless of whether it is conducted in legal, academic, or philological discourse—always also constitutes a debate about morally reprehensible violations of norms. The generally accepted reprehensibility of plagiarism, according to Jakobs (1999: 223), lies, among other things, in the social esteem accorded to textual products. This, in turn, is rooted in the high value placed on "qualities such as originality, novelty, and individuality." The fact that the perceived reprehensibility correlates with a violation of values considered desirable can be illustrated by the example of academic texts: Plagiarism in academia is regarded as a "threat to the moral structure of academic integrity" (Bloch 2012: 6), especially in view of its functions of knowledge transfer, knowledge representation, and knowledge expansion (cf. Jakobs 1997: 158), and is thus considered a violation of norms and immoral. Plagiarism disregards "the intellectual effort of other authors" (ibid.).

While there is broad consensus regarding the (legal and socio-moral) reprehensibility,[15] there are no universally valid definitions for the identification of plagiarism: There is no catalogue of criteria for determining plagiarism that specifies "whether the criterion of formal correspondence of three or more consecutive words is sufficient, or whether one must also take into account content-related criteria, such as the originality claim of the reproduced material" (Jakobs 2011: 100).

The question of criteria for determining plagiarism, which is frequently problematized but only partially or not at all answered in relevant studies, for example in forensic linguistics, ultimately results in practice in the fact that the assessment of plagiarism "allows for considerable subjective leeway" (Reichmann 2013: 176). In the absence of citation markers or source references, the examination of formal criteria between a suspected plagiarism and a suspected source text primarily focuses on establishing verbatim identity. Fundamental to the assumption that verbatim identity provides information about the plagiarism status of a text is the supposed individual uniqueness of the encoding of linguistic utterances ("uniqueness of individual utterances" in Coulthard 2004: 431). Given the abundance of choices offered by the linguistic inventory, it is assumed that even when verbalizing the same subject matter, two communicators—except for some topic-related lexico-grammatical overlaps (ibid.: 435)—will use different words and structures. The following if-then relation may therefore seem plausible: The longer the sequence of verbatim identity, the less likely it is that identical word choice is due to chance, and the more likely it is to be plagiarism (Johnson 1997). In summary, for the quantitative measurement of similarity between two textual products, the proportion of shared vocabulary and the length or extent of the borrowed material are used as indicators of plagiarism (Coulthard 2004). While this procedure empirically eliminates the subjectivity in plagiarism detection criticized at the outset, there are still no fixed numerical thresholds that determine from what phrase length a passage is indisputably considered plagiarism.

A seemingly opposite, but suitable complementary approach is described by Woolls (2003) with the analysis of so-called *hapax legomena*. Hapax legomena are words that occur only once in both the plagiarized and the plagiarizing text. The probability that two people would choose the same word to describe a matter, and each use it only once, is low.

---

[15] Both the tendency to plagiarize and attitudes toward its reprehensibility are considered to be culturally variable (Krekeler 2013, Bloch 2012). From the perspective of Western culture, the most frequently cited example of the cultural variability of plagiarism is China. Due to collectivism, which stands in contrast to Western individualism, texts there are regarded as "common property" and "verbatim intellectual appropriation [...] as a virtue" (Jakobs 1999: 223; cf. Bloch 2008: 219).

Stylistic analysis, which employs both quantitative and additional qualitative methods for evaluating formal identity, is also used for the detection of plagiarism and forgery (e.g., in Dern 2003). In cases of suspected plagiarism, the identification of stylistic inconsistencies can provide evidence of plagiarized sections. The features to be considered in a stylistic analysis are extensive and cover all linguistic levels, from the analysis of salient vocabulary, such as especially neologisms, to the analysis of sentence length.

Another analytical tool, situated between formal and content analysis, that can provide indications of plagiarism, is the handling of content and function words. Plagiarists tend to conceal the unmarked appropriation of external content by reformulating content words with synonyms. Function words, such as connectors, are retained in the act of plagiarism (Olsson 2009: 22–34). Even more detached from fixed criteria than formal plagiarism analysis, and therefore even more problematic, is the detection of content plagiarism. Even completely 'successful' reformulations, whose wording in the plagiarism does not allow any conclusions to be drawn about the wording of the original, are by definition still plagiarism. This is problematic insofar as, for content, in contrast to formal aspects, no universal criteria can be formulated. The lack of a requirement to mark 'general or basic knowledge' (as found in guides to academic writing) further complicates the accusation of plagiarism: It is difficult to draw a line between content that should be considered foundational knowledge and 'original' content.

2.2.3.3 Protection Against Misrepresentation Within the Framework of Personality Rights

The reproduction of false quotations is to be regarded as a violation of personality rights and can therefore be subject to legal action. A person who has been unlawfully misquoted may sue both for injunctive relief and for (financial) compensation for the non-material damage incurred as a result of the false quotation (BVerfGE 54, 208; BVerfG, NJW 1993, 2925; BGH, NJW 1998, 1391; BGH, NJW 2011, 3516). These regulations primarily give rise to two questions: to what extent does a false quotation violate personality rights, and at what point does a quotation constitute a misrepresentation?

To answer the first question, Seibert (1992: 263) refers to the Imperial Penal Code of 1981 as background, in which the right of expression is based on the Old Testament injunction "Thou shalt not bear false witness against thy neighbour" (quoted in ibid.). According to current law, the assertion and dissemination of unprovable facts are prosecuted as defamation (German Criminal Code, § 186 StGB) and, together with slander and insult, are classified among the offences of injury to honour, which are "capable of making [the affected person] contemptible or of degrading him in public opinion or of endangering his credit [...]". Such a diminution of social standing (cf. Seibert 1992: 264) also occurs when statements are attributed to a person that they did not make, or when statements they did make are not reproduced truthfully. The protection of honour (German Basic Law, GG Art. 5 para. 2) may come into conflict with the right to freedom of speech and expression in the adjudication of offences against honour (cf. Forkel 1994: 641), which is why a balancing of the two rights is always required in deciding whether a person accused of misquotation should be convicted.

A quotation is generally considered false and therefore unlawful whenever it reproduces a statement incorrectly, in a distorted, or in a falsified manner (Forkel 1994: 639). In view of the different types of quotations (cf. direct, indirect, and mixed quotation), however, the question remains open as to what degree of modification and adaptation is permissible when integrating a quotation into a new context.

As an example of a false quotation that violates personality rights and of a highly problematic decision by the Federal Constitutional Court (BVerfG), Forkel (1994) discusses the case of the protection of honour involving the writer Heinrich Böll and the journalist Matthias Walden. In a television commentary in response to the murder of the President of the Berlin Court of Appeal, Günter von Drenkmann, in 1974, Walden—purportedly quoting—relied on several statements by Böll. The latter, in turn, sued the journalist for false interpretation and thus for the untruthful reproduction of his original statements. The VI Civil Senate of the Federal Court of Justice (BGH) initially dismissed the claim, arguing that Walden had reproduced the words in accordance with the understanding and interpretation of an average reader. Two years later, the case gained constitutional relevance through the Federal Constitutional Court, and Böll's claim was upheld: there was no truthful quotation, as the defendant should at least have made it clear that it was his personal interpretation. Without the addition of a disclaimer indicating interpretation, there was a serious violation of personality rights (case summarized after Forkel 1994: 637 f.). The decision of the Federal Constitutional Court and the quotation rules established to protect personality rights were controversial, since the average reader "cannot know how the author wishes their ambiguous sentences to be understood" (Forkel 1994: 638; see also the reasoning for the rejection of the first claim by the BGH, 30.05.1978—VI ZR 117/77).

The discussion about the actual practicability of these requirements was renewed more than ten years later with a quotation by the Federal Constitutional Court in the Maastricht ruling. In this, the Court reproduced a quotation for which it named Manfred Zuleeg, formerly a judge at the European Court of Justice, as the source. In a statement published, among other places, in the Juristenzeitung, the alleged source of the quotation distanced himself from it: "The statements for which I am quoted on page […] are not mine" (quoted in Forkel 1994: 637).

The fact that the Federal Constitutional Court itself does not comply with the protection against false quotations—for the breach of which it had previously held Matthias Walden liable for financial compensation of 40,000 DM—has prompted calls to review the relevant case law (cf. Forkel 1994: 640).

2.3 Interim Conclusion I

As the preceding discussion has shown, the general linguistic understanding of quotations as verbatim reproduction is too narrow and does not do justice to the diverse forms of quotations and citations. Different criteria can be applied to typologize these various forms. Philological approaches focus on the configuration of the pretext-text relationship between the poles of materiality and immateriality. Legal approaches do not deal with the configuration of pretext presence, but rather with the categorization of sources. Further essential findings of the interdisciplinary theoretical approaches can be summarized as follows.

- The concept of intertextuality was introduced as the overarching theory of quotation and citation. For intertextual references, it is fundamental to distinguish between a broad understanding of intertextuality as system reference and a narrow understanding of intertextuality as single-text reference. The present study focuses on the latter and examines exclusively intertextuality that is explicitly marked by source references.
- Possible forms of marked intertextual references are direct, mixed, and indirect quotation, as well as paraphrase and reference. These types differ in terms of the presence of the consulted pretext: while, for example, in direct quotation the pretext is integrated both in its content and form, intertextual reference in the case of a reference is limited to the citation of source information, which may optionally be provided with a so-called reference label. Unlike the intertextual types of quotation, modalizing and pure quotations do not refer to a pretext, but use quotation marks for pragmatic purposes without referring to another linguistic product. Both types of quotation, i.e., pure and modalizing quotation, have therefore not yet been examined in connection with the concept of intertextuality. Whether, in fact, only one's own content is cited purely and in a modalizing way, or whether these two pragmatic strategies are also applied to external content, is to be examined in the present work.
- The legal regulation of the use of quotations and citations demonstrates the relevance of intertextual reference as a social practice. The law not only regulates the obligation to mark quotations in order to protect copyright, but also makes use of the practice of quotation and citation itself for its realization. Legal-theoretical reflections on the instrumental aspect of quotation and citation categorize *whom* legal texts refer to. Among other things, hierarchical relations between the quoted and the quoting court are central here. The background to these relation-oriented categorizations is the assumption that recourse to different categories of sources of citations entails different motivations for use.

As the previous chapter has shown, there are many ways to describe intertextual references. If one wishes to combine philological and legal perspectives on quotation and citation, both the configuration of text-pretext relations and the types of sources consulted must be taken into account. These two analytical criteria—type of quotation and type of source—not only serve the aim of the study to descriptively capture citation practices, but also provide indications for reconstructing the functions of quotations. The following chapter will further elaborate on the usefulness of these analytical criteria with regard to determining the functions of quotations and citations.

Chapter 3
Functions of Citations

The act of citing conveys more than mere content—citations can fulfill a wide variety of functions. Marked and thus deliberately employed intertextual references always pursue at least the "minimal intention" of drawing the attention of a group of recipients to another text (Helbig 1986: 153).[1] The concept of 'minimal intention' already implies the potential existence of further intentions, since 'drawing attention' can itself serve a wide range of purposes. The diversity of citation functions is already evident from the etymological roots of the term. The German term 'Zitat' is derived from the Latin verb 'citare', which can be literally translated as "to set in motion, to stimulate, to excite, to agitate" (Benninghof-Lühl 2009: col. 1539). In its broader usage, the term in the mid-16th century also referred to "summoning before a court" and "calling forth by virtue of social power or authority" (Grimm n.d., col. 1658, cited in Benninghof-Lühl 2009: col. 1539). This already names three possible functions: First, citations can stimulate and evoke emotion; second, they can be used to verify (or falsify) facts; and third, they confer authority on the person citing. As an enumeration by Hamann (2014: 510) illustrates, however, the functional potential is by no means exhausted by these three functions. Using the example of legal texts, Hamann identifies a "bundling of very different citation motives," which he sees as linked to "evidentiary, self-referential, referential, explicatory, digressive, commentary, and meta-footnotes," "as well as alibi, ornamental, evidentiary, erudition, secondary treatise, dispute or flattery, and reserve footnotes" (ibid.).

Although citations are "ubiquitous in [...] legal discourse, whether in academic scholarship, legal briefs or judicial opinions" (Levin 2019: 764), the study of

[1] This statement cannot be transferred to the broad concept of intertextuality as defined by Kristeva, which eludes the intentional aspect and understands intertextuality, among other things, as an inescapable fundamental condition of text production in general.

© The Author(s), under exclusive license to Springer-Verlag GmbH, DE, part of Springer Nature 2025

J. Steigler-Herms, *How and Why Do Courts Cite?*,
https://doi.org/10.1007/978-3-662-71934-3_3

citation functions in law has received very little attention (cf. ibid.). For this reason, the chapter primarily draws on considerations from rhetoric and findings on academic citation. The rich spectrum of functions presents citation analysis with the major challenge of identifying citation functions. Citation functions are not invariable, but are closely tied to the difficult-to-reconstruct intentionality of the person citing. With the resulting aim of finding empirical analytical tools for identifying citation functions, the present chapter is structured as follows.

Sect. 3.1 addresses the broad concept of function that underlies this chapter. In rhetoric, the citation functions of *authority* and *ornamentality* have been identified, which are discussed in Sect. 3.2.2. In academic texts, the functions of *coherence* and *economy* have been identified. These two functions (primarily, though not exclusively) fulfill requirements of text production and are therefore discussed together in 3.2.2. The presentation of each function also includes discussion of its role in judicial decisions.

The separate treatment of the various functions is a theoretical distinction that does not do justice to the practice of citing. As an attempt to classify citation functions (Sect. 3.4) and a summarizing discussion of the problems of functional analysis (Sect. 3.5) will suggest, citations—complicating their functional analysis—are not simply *either* authoritative *or* economical, but can combine several functions simultaneously.

3.1 Preliminary Remarks on the Concept of Function

In rhetoric, the ornamental and authoritative use of citations is considered a mean that serve the overarching goal of persuasion (cf. Bär/Vollmann/Kraus 2003; Benninghof-Lühl 2009). In this sense, it must be asked whether, for example, the ornamentality of citations itself can be described as a function, or whether it is rather an instrument for realizing a higher-level function. The examples cited at the beginning, following Hamann (2014, e.g., evidentiary vs. flattering footnotes), also show that citation functions can operate on different levels; they can enrich a text or, beyond that, the cited or citing person. By operating on different levels, the boundaries between means and ends become blurred when determining citation functions. In order to systematically consider citation functions, the present chapter first introduces the broad concept of function that underlies the following discussion.

Citation functions are not static constructs. There is no exhaustive and countable repertoire of functions inherent to the citation. Due to their dependence on intention, citation functions are, strictly speaking, *functionalizations.*

A differentiated approach to the relationship between functions and intentions can be found in Große's (1976) description of general text functions. According to Große, a text function is "the intention encoded in the text, manifesting itself in the text as a communication instrument, and—this is important—precisely as the recipient is supposed to understand it" (ibid.: 68). The text function informs a recipient whether a text is to be understood, for example, as informative or appellative. A distinction must be made between text functions and intentions. The author's intention may correspond to the text function or may deviate from it. The latter leads Große to posit a "secret intention." Authors may wish to present a text as informative (text function) and—without this being explicitly encoded in the text—simultaneously pursue persuasive aims (intention) (Große 1976, see also Brinker 1983). If this is transferred to citation functions, it means that citations can fulfill functions that relate directly to the text and are encoded, for example, by textual evidence as an ostensibly informative addition. At the same time, behind the informative-evidentiary citations, higher-level intentions such as demonstrating erudition and authority may be concealed. Große's approach provides a suitable starting point for discussing an operationalizable understanding of citation functions. However, encoding cannot serve as a criterion for differentiating between function and intention, since, for example, the citation function 'discourse coherence' (citing to situate within a textual network, see Sect. 3.3.2) is neither encoded nor can it be considered an intention, as fulfilling coherence is obligatory in many discourses. Discourse coherence is thus a citation function that, terminologically, falls under neither Große's concept of function nor his concept of intention. Große's concept of function must therefore be expanded to include text-external, non-encoded functions. Text-internal functions, text-external functions, and intentions can occur together. Such a presumed concatenation can be illustrated by the following example:

> A number of studies *demonstrate* the imbalance between the speaking time of teachers on the one hand and learners on the other *impressively* (e.g., Bellack et al. 1966; Sumfleth/Pitton 1998; Seidel 2003; Wuttke 2005; Helmke et al. 2007; Lipowsky et al. 2007; Liu/Zhu 2012). (Wuttke/Seifried 2016: 350; emphasis by J.S.)

The fact that the reference to the many studies is intended to serve as evidence for an already proven imbalance in speaking time between teachers and learners is explicitly encoded in the text—the verb 'demonstrate' can (following Große 1976) be read as a functional *text-internal* indicator. By referring to other studies, Wuttke/Seifried also establish a foundation for their own investigation, coherently link to existing research, and thus relieve themselves of the heavy 'burden of proof' for such statements in academic texts, whereby the citation also becomes *text-external* in its function. The quantity of evidence is also striking. While citing a single source in academic writing can be considered obligatory and, due to this obligatory nature, is not necessarily to be interpreted as significant in terms of intention, the reference to *seven* studies clearly goes beyond merely fulfilling text-productive conventions. It is conceivable, for example, that Wuttke/Seifried (2016) not only wish to provide evidence for their statement, but also, by demonstrating the apparent consensus in the relevant literature, seek to strengthen its validity and authority, thus using the citations *intentionally*. The authors themselves further comment on the cited results as "impressive," thereby reinforcing the validity of the cited studies already demonstrated by the verb "demonstrate" through their own evaluation (see *booster* in Chap. 4).

The brief analysis of the example is intended to illustrate one main point regarding functions and intentions: Functions encoded in the text can themselves serve higher-level purposes. The 'demonstration' in the example is thus both an end and a means to an end.

The identification of higher-level, non-encoded functions—or, in Große's terminology, "intentions"—requires reconstruction and interpretation of various textual clues. Functions that are not explicitly verbalized thus represent the main problem in the analysis of quotation functions and therefore form the focus of the present chapter, which is based on a broad understanding of the concept of function: A function is here understood broadly as an umbrella term for encoded, i.e., text-internal, as well as non-encoded, i.e., text-external functions, in other words, intentions.

3.2 Identification of Functions

Since citation functions vary, among other things, in relation to text types (cf. van den Berg 2000: 23), an integrative account of *all* possible functions is not feasible. The following identification of functions is therefore limited to the presentation of four functions that relevant research has identified as significant in the context of utilitarian text types: *ornamentality, authority, economy,* and *coherence.*

3.2.1 On the Attempt of Integrative Classifications

As mentioned at the outset, citation functions are difficult to reconstruct and categorize. Attempts at integrative classifications of citation functions are therefore rare and have not been attempted in recent research. Older approaches mostly refer to scholarly texts (for a comparison of relevant surveys, see Cronin 1984). Working out citation functions using the example of scholarly texts is advantageous in that academic citation, as well as the functional requirements for scholarly texts in general, are highly regulated. This standardization (at least theoretically) sets limits to the use of citations and seems to make it more feasible to assume a cross-textual, definable functional repertoire. For non-standardized literary texts, for example, there is no such limitation:

> In comparison to scientific, legal, political, and other pragmatic discourses, literature seems to occupy a special position in that its ability to cite virtually all text types—from the Gospel to advertising—with approval or rejection, to imitate in pastiche, to parody, or to relativize ironically, is virtually unlimited. (Zima 2000: 297)

The occurrence of artistically motivated citation, such as ironic and parodic citation, cannot be entirely ruled out even in pragmatically oriented academic discourse, but it is not taken into account in relevant collections of functions for scholarly texts. An example of such a collection is Weinstock's list (1971).

1. Paying homage
2. Background reading
3. Historical
4. Bibliographical leads
5. Narrative
6. Definition
7. Clarification
8. Illustration
9. Example
10. Experimental detail
11. Theory
12. Data
13. Methodology
14. Description
15. Current concerns
16. Development of ideas
17. Disputing
18. Criticism
19. Corroboration
20. Disclaiming
21. Substantiation
22. Similar research
23. Contradictory research
24. Further detail
25. Same paper
26. Statistics

On the one hand, Weinstock's list is illustrative of the great variety of aspects that can be understood as citation functions; on the other hand, it is a largely unsystematic compilation that, among other things, mixes questions about the content of the citation with questions about the semantic relations between the source and the citing text. Despite the lack of systematics, the compilation provides impulses for criteria that can be applied in the analysis of citation functions: A large proportion of the aspects mentioned (including, for example, *theory, data* and *methodology*) answer the question of *what* is being cited. This suggests the thesis that the choice of source contributes decisively to the characterization of citation functions. The same applies to the characterizations of text-pretext relations (such as *disputing* and *criticism*). Here, the focus is on the question of *how* a citation is used or what is done with it. The categories according to Weinstock (with the exception of category 1, "paying homage") are strongly oriented towards the texts involved.

The extent to which citations can also serve functions in relation to the citing authors, beyond the texts themselves, is not considered in Weinstock's list. Two examples of functions potentially related to the citing author are authority and ornamentality.

3.2.2 *Authority and Ornament*

According to ancient rhetoric, the two functions of authority and ornamentality serve the goal of persuasion (see also Knape 2013) and are therefore presented together in the following.

Citations can be used as ornamentation (cf. van den Berg 2000). The ornamental citation makes a "contribution to stylistic variation" and thereby also promotes a "relaxation of the ear" (ibid.: 15). The beauty and ornamentation of speech contribute to the emotional effect on the recipient (Ueding/Steinbrink 2011: 284). As Landert (2015) analyzes using the example of journalistic texts, citations can be used as "enriching with colourful expressions" (ibid.: 33). Similarly, though not for journalistic but for scholarly texts, Jakobs describes the "ornamental, stimulating, surprising, witty, or entertaining" function. The reason for this is that (especially literal) citation enables the citer to use a style that deviates from the usual register of the citing text:

> Such expressions [colourful expressions] would be inappropriate outside of quotes due to their style. In the same way as newspapers are expected to report content objectively, they are normally expected to use formal language as well. Usually, therefore, colloquial and non-standard language, colourful metaphors and verbal puns are restricted to quotes. (Landert 2000: 33, following Bell 1991: 208f.)

Ornamental effects of citations are to be understood as scalable, depending on the degree of stylistic difference. This scalability is based on varying degrees of stylistic difference and the resulting contradictions between the citing and cited text: "The more unexpected or the greater the contrast between the referencing text and the source, the greater the stimulating value is likely to be" (Jakobs 1999: 128, using the example of mottos).

Thus, a text can be ornamented through stylistic differences. Beyond this, the ornamental citation can also serve to ornament the citer themselves as a "display of knowledge acquired through wide reading" (Morawski 1970: 695). In this self-representational function, Morawski refers to the ornamental citation as an "intellectual conceit" (ibid.). Whoever is able to ornament themselves with a citation must be well-read and thus intellectual. With this self-representation as intellectual, the ornamental citation is closely linked to the authoritative use of citation.

Before discussing the *authoritative function of the citation,* some remarks on the concept of *auctoritas* should be made, as these also shed light on the act of citing itself: *Auctoritas* is initially decisive in legal evidence procedures and legal speech, since both the evidence procedure and legal speech rely on *testimonium* and proof *ex auctoritate. Auctoritas* is also relevant in domains outside of law:

> A. as topos (Aristotle), as credibility and reputation (Cicero), as venerability [...] (Quintilian) becomes a social fact in antiquity: Authority by virtue of age, wisdom, life experience, achievement (personal authority) acquires public normative and evidentiary force. Legal first decisions (precedents), positions of peoples/nations, wise men, famous citizens, significant poets, but also proverbs, customs, oracles, written works, etc., become A. Such authorities are cited as justification, and people learn from them. Alongside political authorities, there are rhetorical, literary, and linguistic authorities, as well as authorities of faith and science. (Kalivoda/Montefusco 2013: col. 1179)

From this definition, at least two aspects emerge that are also important for understanding the authority of citations. On the one hand, *auctoritas* is closely linked to social attributions such as reputation and credibility. In this sense, one must assume a reciprocal influence and 'chains of attribution'—to whom authority is ascribed, credibility and reputation are simultaneously granted. These attributes can be considered socially desirable and profitable. Kalivoda/Montefusco (2013: col. 1179) therefore define authority as an advantageous quality:

> In public and private life, A. is the ability to influence others through one's special reputation. This reputation enables the person endowed with it to enforce their will without resorting to any means of coercion. A. is thus an 'effective force,' a 'dynamic' quality.

Furthermore, authority can refer both to persons (the "wise men") and to texts (e.g., the Bible). This authoritative function of the citation is emphasized not only in antiquity but also shapes the later history of the word. In dictionaries of the 16th century, as summarized by the *Deutsche Wörterbuch* (Grimm 1862: col. 1658), the citation refers to the "reputation of an authority." This applies both within and outside the legal sphere: Within, it means "the summons to court, specifically: the document containing the summons," and "outside the legal sphere in a broader sense, the summoning by virtue of social power or authority."

The authority of a citation can thus be generated by citing an authoritative person or an authoritative text. The citation is able to project the authority of a cited author or a cited text onto the citing instance. Authoritative citing therefore presupposes the authority of the source and is thus closely linked to the question of *what* and *who* is being cited. The outline of the concept of authority reveals connections that suggest that citations are not cited primarily or exclusively for the sake of authority, but also, among other things, to intend credibility and prestige. Consequently, authority in antiquity is used precisely for these purposes; it is a means of persuasion.[2] However, in its authoritative function, the citation is not only a "weapon" but equally a shield. Content can be presented as factual through citing; it is therefore always also "a kind of immunization strategy" (Gander 2010: 19). This 'immunization' also operates on a quantitative level as a "doubling of the voice" (as in the title of Gander 2010). The more authors share the view of the citer, the more acceptance can be acquired for a statement, and the more difficult it becomes to challenge this supposedly majority claim to validity (see also

[2] According to Victorinus, an "argumentum ... cui quasi necesse habeat credi," i.e., an argument that one necessarily believes (Kalivoda/Montefusco 2013: col. 1180).

the discussion of so-called *string citations* in judgments; in this chapter). The same applies, as quantitative citation analysis shows (cf. Swales 1986), to being cited: The more often a text or author is cited, the more prestige and authority is conferred upon them.

Ornamentality and authority are both *persuasion strategies.* They can be assigned to *ethos* and *pathos,* two of the fundamental pillars of classical Aristotelian rhetoric. Ethos refers to the (ideally authentic and not exclusively strategic) self-presentation of a communicator as moral and virtuous (Mouchel/Fortenbaugh/Robling 2013: col. 157 f.).[3] Those who are considered virtuous are more likely to be attributed credibility than a speaker with a bad reputation (ibid.: col. 1519, on Aristotelian ethics). In this respect, ethos can also be understood as *ethical authority.* Reputation, credibility, and authority in general can all be strengthened by citation:

> Skillfully chosen and placed within the argumentation (argutia), [the citation] strengthens the authority (auctoritas) of the speaker or author. Citing well-known or even remote, rare works increases persuasive power, credibility, and reputation (ethos). (Benninghof-Lühl 2009: col. 1541)

Demonstrating ethos is considered such a central function of intertextual references that the citation is also interpreted in empirical studies as an expression of ethos. Sobota (1996) understands all intertextual references as indicators of ethos. In judicial decisions, they demonstrate judicial ethos in three respects: Sobota (1996: 121) distinguishes between "*arguments from authority* ('this is so because that person—a respectable person or institution—also says so')," the "*text argument* (this is so because it is written)," and "source references (that is where it is written exactly), since these indicate professional conscientiousness, a striving for continuity, and respect for tradition." Such a classification, to understand *all* citations per se as ethos demonstration, is problematic, as it neglects all other functions of citations. Sobota subsumes ornamental stylistic devices under the concept of pathos; however, she does not consider ornamental citing in this category.

In Aristotelian rhetoric, *pathos*[4] is understood as the "arousal of emotions," which can be produced by figures such as "e.g., exclamation, apostrophe, prosopopoeia, rhetorical question, alliteration, anaphora […]". This also includes types of citation, since direct speech is considered one of the particularly pathetic figures (Bär/Vollmann/Kraus 2003: col. 691; col. 698). Benninghof-Lühl (2009) similarly notes that the citation has the capacity to arouse emotions. Such arousal of affect is again linked to the ornamentation of speech (cf. Ueding/Steinbrink 2011: 284) and to the ornamentality of the citation.

[3] This interpretation is widespread, but not undisputed. In another interpretation, it is considered a precursor to pathos: "A complicated reception already in antiquity led to the reduced view that 'ethical' meant the moderate level of affect and accordingly a moderate—the so-called middle—style of speech or writing" (Mouchel/Fortenbaugh/Robling 2013: col. 1518).

[4] This term, too, has at times received different definitions; for an overview of possible dimensions of the concept and its historical development, see Bär/Vollmann/Kraus (2003).

Given its capacity to confer *ethos* upon the speaker and to evoke *pathos* in the recipients, the citation can thus be considered *persuasive* in two respects: In its authoritative use, it serves self-presentational functions and marks the speaker, among other things, as credible, educated, and virtuous (ethos). When used ornamentally, it embellishes the speech or text and can emotionally involve the recipient in this way (pathos). While the use of citations for persuasive purposes is recommended in ancient rhetoric, this very practice later meets with criticism: Montaigne, whom van den Berg calls the first theorist of citation (van den Berg 2000: 24), raises concerns about the *auctoritas* of the practice of citing in his *Essais*. Those who cites solely by invoking the authority of the source, for the purpose of projecting authority and, in the worst case, without any reflection of their own, cloak themselves in "the weapons of another" (Montaigne [1992]: I, XXV, 243). Montaigne criticizes "immodest writers [...] who insert whole passages from the ancient authors into their worthless works in order to show off [...]" (Montaigne I, 240). To invoke the words of another, he argues, only demonstrates erudition when combined with one's own activity and intellectual contribution:

> We can certainly say, Cicero says this or that, Plato had this manner, these are Aristotle's own words. But what do we say for ourselves? What do we do? What do we judge? A parrot could say as much [...] We repeat the opinions and learning of others, and that is all we do. We must make them our own. (Montaigne [1992]: I, XXIV, 222f.)

With Montaigne's remarks, it is thus possible in contexts of citation to distinguish between different kinds of authority: To use the ideas of others as a starting point for reflection attests to the *author's own authority*; citing as mere reproduction without one's own positioning, by contrast, is a reprehensible appropriation of *foreignexternal authority*. The attempt to "show off" ultimately has the opposite effect: "For, that infinitely greater brilliance [of the quoted authors] gives them such a distorted, insignificant, and ugly appearance that they lose far more by it than they gain" (ibid.: 240).

For the *genre of judicial decisions,* it is above all the *demonstration of authority* that is a frequently discussed and particularly relevant function of citation (e.g., Levin 2019). For a decision to be accepted and valid, its line of argument must also be accepted. Quantitatively, judicial decisions often employ so-called *string citations,* which string together multiple sources (see Holzleithner/Mayer-Schönberger 2000: 338 f.) and thus serve as a "doubling of the voice" (Gander 2010). Genuinely ornamental and otherwise unintended decorative citations are, according to Jestaedt (2010: 148), rare in jurisprudence. However, authority can also be conferred by referencing sources that do not possess legal authority and may therefore initially appear ornamental. DeStefano even speaks of "the common law's affection for literature" (2007: 522) and interprets such references as an appropriation of "legal authority." As a particularly illustrative example, DeStefano (2007: 523) quotes a decision of the U.S. Supreme Court in which a *dissenting opinion* is introduced with a quotation from Orwell:

> BIG BROTHER IS WATCHING YOU, THE CAPTION SAID...In the far distance a helicopter skimmed down between the roofs, hovered for an instant like a bluebottle, and

> darted away again with a curving flight. It was the Police Patrol, snooping into people's windows. (Florida v. Riley, 488 U.S. 445, 466 1989, quoted in DeStefano 2007: 523)

To explain the authoritative effect of literary quotations, he draws on the rhetorical concept of ethos:

> The citation of literature employs ethos on at least three levels: It invokes the authority of the author of the cited literature, it bestows additional authority on that author by the very fact of legal citation, and it may also enhance the judge's image in the eyes of certain readers (ibid.: 528).

Whether rhetorical supports for argumentation in general—and thus also ornamental and authoritative citations —are compatible with the rationality aspired to in law is questioned by Sobota (1986). In an analysis of decisions of the Federal Constitutional Court, she concludes that

> the court relies extensively on means of persuasion that are taboo according to modern rationalist legal theories. In the decisive passages, the judges use not arguments, but rhetorical figures that impress readers in an aesthetic-emotional way. The three means of persuasion—Logos (argumentative persuasion), Ethos (reference to morals and general views), and Pathos (persuasion through stylistic devices)—are found in a constant balance. (Sobota 1996: 115)

Ornamental and authoritative citations would thus be understood as a breach of the rationalist model of law.[5]

3.2.3 *Coherence and Economy*

The demonstration or production of coherence and economy are functions that are mutually dependent: In order to argue economically, there must first be a textual network in which an author can position themselves coherently—at the same time, a coherent positioning can in turn make further argumentation unnecessary and thus contribute to economy.

As an act of recontextualization, citing always stands for the creation of something new on the one hand and the consideration of what is old on the other. The latter locates a citing text within an existing discourse. This positioning is hereafter referred to as discourse coherence. Intertextual references for the demonstration of coherence within a discourse are described by Jakobs (1999: 114) using the example of scholarly texts as "networking and positioning" for the "safeguarding of continuity through the formation of tradition and lines of reference." This requirement of scholarly texts can be met through citation and referencing.

---

[5] Sobota further explains that the rationalist model of law, according to which rational justifiability is supposed to be the foundation of legal decision-making, is a theoretical construct far removed from practice: "Whoever equates legal correctness solely with rational justifiability fails to recognize the actual standards of practice" (1986: 115).

Following Jakobs (1999: 114–116), three subfunctions of discourse coherence can be identified.

To consult what already exists and to make this consultation transparent through references to sources functions, firstly, as the foundation of scholarly progress. Novelty, in this sense, can only be created through engagement with already existing results. It is therefore appropriate that theoretical reflections on citation often make use of the saying that the wheel does not have to be reinvented every time (see, e.g., Jakobs 1999: 115 and Jestaedt 2010: 150). To locate the citing text is, as a second subtype, also "a kind of service" (Jakobs 1999: 116), which enables the reader to receive relevant texts, i.e., those that are pertinent in the respective discourse (according to the citer's evaluation). This reception demands from the reader, depending on the type of intertextual reference, a varying degree of initiative, for while, for example, the direct quotation can be read in its material presence and integration in the quoting text without further effort, the reader must pursue references independently. As a rule, the "service" does not only include an objective and uncommented summary of previous literature, but also provides classifications—this can be considered the third subfunction of producing discourse coherence. Questions such as how a cited source relates to the citing text, to what extent similarities and differences exist between the two texts, and in what respect the cited source is relevant, can be answered for the reader by "producing knowledge of relationships and classifications" (Jakobs 1999: 117).

Taking relevant literature into account and thus establishing coherence in discourse is a fundamental and functionally determined convention in scholarship, which also creates networks. Bunia/Dembeck (2010) see intertextual networking as a characteristic of scholarship:

> Modern scholarship is always (also) a network: publications, as elementary events whose concatenation constitutes scholarship in the first place, characteristically emerge from a *network of interaction between publications.* This network is constituted and described by means of citation: the reference to already existing works serves (at least in the humanities) to support one's own arguments or to point out invalid results, pays tribute in the name of the obligation to acknowledge sources to the originator of the borrowed arguments, and last but not least, creates alliances—whether for better or for worse. (Bunia/Dembeck 2010: 161)

Networks created through citation must also be viewed critically; Bunia/Dembeck describe scholarly "alliances" as problematic when intertextual references are made not for reasons of substantive enrichment, but, for example, out of personal friendship (cf. the title "Citing Friends"; see also "citation cartels," therein: 195). This gives rise to the suspicion "that citation is where the possible corruption of scholarship by friendship takes place and is at the same time justified" (ibid.: 163).

Drawing on external content can also be pragmatically motivated and can relieve a text producer both in terms of content and formulation. Such relief through intertextual references will hereafter be referred to as the *economic function.* Taking other texts into account, or, as in scholarly writing, even being required to do so, leads on the one hand to an overall highly complex text production process (cf. Jakobs 1999: 336[6]). On the other hand, this very consideration also offers the citer the opportunity to dispense with cognitively demanding formulation work: those who cite do not have to verbalize content themselves. The degree of relief in formulation varies with the different types of citation. While direct quotations—apart from considerations regarding suitable embedding, such as introduction and conclusion—require no intervention in formulation, paraphrases are comparatively more demanding at the level of formulation. Indirect and mixed quotations also require adaptation to the textual environment. In general: the more verbal material from a pretext is adopted without adaptation or alteration, the less formulation work is required on the part of the citer (cf. Jakobs 1999: 96). "Adopting [a formulation] is advisable [...] when the author wishes to spare himself the effort of 'rethinking' and 'rephrasing' in the case of complex or complicated subject matter, or when he fears a distortion or abbreviation of the content when paraphrasing" (Jakobs 1999: 126). The literal adoption of external content also hints at another aspect, which Jakobs does not elaborate further. Citation can also shorten or even replace substantive justification work or textual actions altogether.

Both substantive and formulative economy are subject to the "suspicion" that the citer "exploits the welcome and permitted relief provided by citation [...] excessively, by letting other authors speak for him out of convenience" (Graefen 2007: 13). In order to avoid the disapproved "uncreative mere adoption and copying" in scholarship (Bänsch/Alewell 2020: 40 f.), citation guides such as the one just mentioned recommend an appropriate scope and frequency of citations.[7]

Nevertheless, economic citation can be considered necessary, for it is questionable whether, for example, the constant reformulation of a definition assumed to be known to the text's addressees offers any added value. An abbreviation through intertextual references can thus be economical both for the citer and for the recipient. In this function, substantive economy is closely related to the signaling of discourse coherence, for even if a citer does not wish to avoid the work of justification, discursive constraints as external textual conditions partly prescribe an economy in text production.

The observations on scholarly text production cannot be seamlessly transferred to *jurisprudence.* In jurisprudence, legal dogmatics emphasizes coherence rather than innovation in recourse to what already exists, namely the law.

[6] "The productive recourse to specialist literature in scholarly writing projects increases the complexity of the text production process both qualitatively and quantitatively. It contributes to the fact that writing scholarly contributions is among the most demanding forms of text production at all."

[7] Jele (2021: 124) expresses criticism of so-called patch-writing, seeing a university "economically shaped environment" that strives for "maximum success with minimal effort" as one reason for plagiarism: "Plagiarism, from this perspective, are provoked and expected products of (scholarly) requirements."

Demonstrating coherence can be regarded as a fundamental requirement of judicial decision-making. Decisions must not be made arbitrarily by judges; they must fit coherently into existing case law and be as predictable as possible. In German Civil Law, the obligation to subsume under applicable laws is manifested, among other things, in the postulate of legal binding (cf. Art. 103 II GG; § 1 StGB in its criminal law specification). In Anglo-American Common Law, the binding obligation to precedents, the *stare decisis et non quieta movere* doctrine (cf. Jestaedt 2010: 157, see also Chap. 5 for further discussion), can be regarded as a counterpart. In both, albeit very different, forms of binding, citation[8] is, in this respect, a suitable instrument. First, a citation can be used to document *what*—be it applicable law or precedents—was taken into account in the decision-making process. Second, citations also serve as a "Preserver of the Linguistic Status Quo" (Levin 2019: 769). The citation preserves argumentations and procedures and thus guarantees, among other things, inter-court uniformity in decision-making: "After all, if a court must apply the same rule previous court had applied, quotation should guarantee that the second articulation is identical to the first" (Levin 2019: 770). In this sense, it supports communication between courts ("transjudicial communication" in Slaughter 1994; see also the role of citation in the development of common European constitutional law in Nußberger 2006, cf. Chap. 2). The same applies to intra-court consistency, which can be demonstrated by means of self-citation (Jestaedt 2010: 157). Both "internally and especially externally," citation serves judicial coherence (ibid.).

The function of economy has been subject to particularly severe criticism in the context of law: the necessary economy in decision-making is also criticized as a "unfounded foundation of legal legitimacy" (Holzleithner/Mayer-Schönberg 2000). Citation does not function as justification, but rather as a "substitute for justification" (Jestaedt 2010: 15), which does not do justice to case-appropriate argumentation. Especially in Civil Law, citing similar decisions as a shortcut in argumentation also collides with the ideal of subsumption, according to which a case is to be decided solely by subsuming it under applicable norms (Holzleithner/Mayer-Schönberg 2000: 326). Criticism of this practice questions the entire influence of precedents in the continental European legal tradition. Recourse to precedents can always abbreviate (and at the same time support) a norm-oriented justification of decisions when the relation between case and norm allows for interpretive leeway (ibid.)

[8] A broad concept of citation underlies this, for even the mere mention of a bibliographic reference without literal reproduction fulfills this function and can demonstrate the consideration of binding texts.

3.3 Order of Functions

As the preceding discussion has shown, citations can serve both discourse-obligatory conditions of text production (coherence and economy) and 'optional' persuasion strategies (authority and ornamentality). This rough classification initially allows for the presentation of potentially similar levels of function from a theoretical perspective, but it is not entirely tenable—for example, coherence citations can be used for text-productive purposes, but also for purposes of self-presentation. Sect. 3.1 therefore first introduced a distinction between text-internal and text-external functions.

A systematic proposal for the operationalization and further differentiation of the latter functions can be found in Hamann (2014: 511), who suggests an analysis of citation functions (in legal studies) based on the communication psychology theory of Schulz von Thun (2010). According to von Thun, every message—implicitly or explicitly—contains four levels. He distinguishes the factual level, the relationship level (which also includes representations of others), the appeal level, and the self-revelation level; self-revelations are to be differentiated into intentional self-presentations and unintentional self-disclosures. If this multi-level model is applied to potential intentions, then an intertextual reference—as Hamann illustrates with the following example of the footnote "Likewise Heck AcP 112 (1914), 1"—can have at least six functions.

- Factual information: "The thought expressed can also be found in Heck."
- Definition of relationship: "You, reader, have a right to this evidence from me, the author."
- Appeal: "You, reader, really should engage with Heck."
- Self-presentation: "I, the author, have read and understood Heck."
- Self-disclosure: "The author apparently needs to boost his self-esteem by citing Heck."
- Representation of others: "You, reader, did not previously know where you could look this up." (Hamann's application of von Thun to citations, 2014: 511, see also 512)

Considering citation functions against this background offers the great advantage of highlighting in advance the possible simultaneous presence of *multiple functions in a single citation.* A citation can simultaneously convey, for example, factual content *and* self-presentation. In addition, Hamann's application of von Thun's theory also suggests a further sub-differentiation of the individual functions; for example, the function of authoritative citation can refer to the self or to the 'other'. What the model does not provide, however, is the possibility of examining a citation for a specific intended (or unintended) function. Of course, the footnote "Likewise Heck AcP 112 (1914), 1" can be understood as an appeal to the reader ("You, reader, really should engage with Heck."); but whether this assumption is more plausible than the assumption of self-presentation ("I, the author, have read and understood Heck") cannot be reconstructed. Even if one assumes that every statement, and thus every citation, operates on four levels, it still seems questionable to give equal weight to the factual information conveyed by a citation such as "Likewise Heck AcP 112 (1914), 1" and all other conceivable functions.

Overall, the model offers valuable insights into functions with regard to the citing author and the addressee, but not with regard to the texts involved. An integration of the cited and citing text is enabled by Helbig's fourfold distinction of levels of citation function, developed for literary texts (1996: 161–182). Helbig identifies *recipient-, reference text-, text-,* and *producer-oriented* functions. His classification is primarily based on the *cui bono* principle: citations can provide added value for the recipient, for the intertext, for the text, and for the producer. With this subdivision, he advocates moving away from a focus on the relation between pretext and citingtext and for greater attention to author and recipient (cf. ibid.: 149).

Helbig (1996: 153) describes the recipient orientation of citations as a fundamental functional prerequisite. Through the "orientation of the marking towards the recipient," it is "inherent in all functional variants in a more or less pronounced way"[9] (ibid.). In this basic function, the citation is a kind of "reader service" (ibid.: 154) and guides reception. According to Helbig, recipient orientation is the dominant function, which, however, does not exclude the simultaneous presence of other orientations. This is interesting insofar as none of the functions identified in Sect. 3.2.2 and Sect. 3.2.3 exhibits recipient orientation as a dominant element.

Citations used, for example, for purposes of self-presentation, are assigned by Helbig to the producer-oriented level. Citations at this functional level primarily do not serve the text, but rather fulfill "pro domo" (ibid.: 181) the self-presentation needs of the quoter. Under the category of producer, Helbig considers only the citing instance as (re-)producer, not the producer of the cited pretext. However, it would be quite reasonable to supplement this category with the latter: as already shown, a citation can also be used to honor an author (*"paying homage"* Weinstock 1971: 18), to build networks, and to maintain friendships (Bunia/Dembeck 2010). In this function, it is at least ostensibly intended to serve the cited party—but this does not preclude the possibility that honoring the pretext author ultimately also benefits the citer. Therefore, *both* producers should be considered; the cited author or producer of the intertext as P1, the citing (text) producer as P2. Authority can be assigned to the producer-oriented level, which can be generated both by self-presentational citing (P2) and by being cited (P1).

The texts involved in the act of reference, i.e., the cited and the citing text, are treated separately by Helbig: *Reference text-oriented functions* mean "that a reference text not only unilaterally shapes the meaning of a post-text, but that its meaning is also modified by a subsequent text" (ibid.: 169). This 'continuation' can be carried out in literary texts, for example, through the parodic use of quotations.

[9] This applies only to cases of marked intertextuality and is noteworthy insofar as Helbig himself, in his problematization of quotation functions, also addresses unmarked intertextuality. Unmarked quotations, however, are disregarded in this study.

The so-called “additional coding” as “explicitly affirmative confirmation of meaning or as radical deconstruction of its [the pretext’s] original intention” (ibid.) also belongs to the reference text-oriented level of function (for the role of affirmation and deconstruction in determining citation functions, see 3.4.2). Citing has an effect at the level of the pretext, especially with regard to the establishment of coherence; for example, if a court decision questions a previous decision, this inevitably has consequences for its status in the discourse.

Text-oriented functions are illustrated by Helbig using the example of characters in fictional texts; for instance, a first-person narrator can be characterized through intertextual references, which also serves an aesthetic function (ibid.: 175). For the purposes of this study, such a categorization is only applicable with some modifications, since (at least as a rule) there are no fictional characters in non-literary texts. Accordingly, persons in non-literary texts do not belong to the level of the text, but to the producer-oriented function. Nevertheless, the category of text-oriented functions is at least suitable with regard to characterization functions: in non-literary texts, quotations do not characterize characters, but rather the text itself. If, for example, many ornamental quotations are chosen for a text, it can be assumed that the text itself is intended to be perceived as aesthetic.

With this differentiation, Helbig offers a valuable perspective on the instances involved in the process of functionalization. Citations are functionalized with regard to whom or what they are intended to serve. As with the application of von Thun, however, the question remains unanswered as to which analytical criteria can be used to assign functions to one of the four possible orientations.

3.4 On the Analysis of Citation Functions

In the discussion of possible citation functions, several problems inherent to the identification of citation functions have already been alluded to. The attempt to empirically capture the use of citations in a meaningful way is sometimes even described as a hopeless endeavor: “Identification problems plague all our regressions. […] [T]he difficulty of identifying the true meaning of many or few citations is so endemic that to our minds it calls into question the entire enterprise” (Ayres/Vars 2000: 430). Such identification problems are responsible for the “previous reservations” towards citation analysis, for which Hamann (2014: 505) rightly notes the lack of qualitative methods. Although this deficiency and the “particularly deficient” state of research on the function of marked intertextuality were already criticized by Helbig (1986: 143), it can by no means be considered resolved in current research. The following discussion, after a summarizing problematization, therefore attempts to propose an approach to analysis.

3.4.1 Problematization

The challenges in analyzing citation functions can be summarized as two fundamental problems: the *problem of the delineation* of individual functions in a concrete citation context and the *problem of reconstructing intentionality.*

The theoretical approach to potential functions undertaken here is only of limited use for an empirical analysis of citation functions, since a separation of individual functions is not tenable in the practice of citation use. The bundling of various citation motivations has been emphasized repeatedly. A citation can *simultaneously* fulfill several functions. Even if one could identify these functional components, one would still face the problem of distinguishing means and ends, and thus the necessity of a functional hierarchy. The issue can be illustrated using the example of coherence: the function of a citation may be to establish and/or to demonstrate coherence. *Establishing* and *demonstrating* must essentially be understood as functional subcomponents of the function 'coherence'. The same function can, in turn, be motivated in different ways. This internal functional differentiation is indispensable insofar as it can be linked to other functional levels. The establishment of coherence can—using Helbig's (1986) terminology—be text-oriented or pretext-oriented. In this sense, a citer might, for example, seek to establish coherence in order to provide substantive value to the text or the pretext, or, as demonstrated in court decisions, because the requirements of the text type demand it. If, on the other hand, the subcomponent of demonstrating coherence dominates, then the self-presentational level of the producer is also affected. By demonstrating, through coherence, that they are familiar with a discourse, able to connect to it, and able to position themselves within it, the citer simultaneously demonstrates their expertise and thus strengthens the credibility of their conveyed content. Thus, even through a citation that does not appear to be used authoritatively on the surface, authority can be suggested. In a functional hierarchy, authority in such a case could be considered an overarching goal.

The same applies to ornamentality and economy, which can likewise be aimed at generating authority. Thus, it is conceivable that economy and coherence, on the one hand, facilitate text production, and on the other hand, are used to demonstrate discourse expertise—in other words, a kind of functionalization of functions. This may raise the question of whether ostensibly authoritative citations can also be subordinated to another function, such as ornamentality. At least for the text type of court decisions, this seems unlikely for the following reason: it can be assumed that the presumed functional hierarchy of citation use is oriented towards the dominant text function. For court decisions, which are particularly concerned with ensuring validity, it is to be expected that the prioritization of validity-enhancing authoritative citations takes precedence over, for example, citations intended ornamentally. This thesis does not mean that all citations in decisions are authoritative, nor does it exclude the occurrence of citations primarily intended otherwise, such as economic citations. While such theses allow for a deeper theoretical problematization, they do not directly contribute to the modeling of empirical analytical instruments.

A second problem arises from the *necessity of reconstructing intentionality.* If the use of citations is understood as intentional and citations as instruments for fulfilling certain functions, then this intention should, in principle, be reconstructible. However, when considering the citation alone, the intended function—possibly due to the communication context or the assumed text functions—can at best be surmised, but not clearly demonstrated. What intention lies behind a citation is, at least for the reader, not discernible from the citation itself, and even in citation contexts, intentions are generally not explicitly coded.

Ultimately, the very limited possibilities for reconstructing intentionality lead to a problem that can be considered particularly serious for the purposes of this study: if functions are understood as intentional uses and intentions are not accessible to analysis, then no *functional assignment* can be made. The following Sect. 3.4.2 therefore examines which analytical criteria at least allow for the consideration of possible intentions.

3.4.2 Impulses for Modelling an Empirical Analysis

As has been problematized, it is not possible to discern from the cited content itself why a citer refers to it. The aim of the following discussion is therefore—to draw on existing empirical approaches to citation analysis—to identify clues that allow conclusions to be drawn about the intended citation function. Five questions can be posed to the citation, which allow for an empirical approach to citation functions. These five questions are as follows:

1. What type of citation is used (direct quotation, indirect quotation, mixed quotation, paraphrase, reference, pure quotation, modalizing quotation)?
2. Who or what is being cited and what is the status of the cited source? (e.g., foreign case law)
3. Where is the author or source mentioned? (e.g., in parentheses or in the running text)
4. How often is citation used, or how often is each type of source cited? (e.g., in relation to the total number of citations in a text)
5. How is the citation embedded? (e.g., rejection or approval, evaluation of the citation through adjectives)1. The characteristics of the various types of intertextual references (direct, indirect, mixed, references, paraphrase, modalizing, pure; cf. Sect. 2.1.2 on the philological typology of quotations) can lead to a particular type being favored for the realization of a specific function. This was illustrated using the example of ornamentality; for decorative use, the direct quotation is particularly suitable, as its verbatim nature can create stylistic differences. However, this does not mean that other types of quotations cannot be used ornamentally, since even in the case of indirect quotation, a

(possibly slightly modified) verbatim adoption of the pretext is possible. For the intertextual types of quotation, no clear or exclusive functional assignment is possible. In contrast, the situation is clearer with the non-intertextual types of quotation, which are defined by their function. Thus, the pure quotation serves exclusively to thematize properties of the cited content, and the modalizing quotation always serves to mark, in an interpretation-guiding way, differences in register between the cited term and the citing text, or to indicate irony.

2. The question of which author and which source is cited is relevant for all of the functions presented. It is therefore necessary to discuss which properties a source must have in order to bring about a particular function. Coherence—whether in court decisions or in scholarly texts—can only be established by referring to sources that are considered relevant to the respective discourse. In the case of judicial decisions, for example, these would be precedents with binding effect. If a court cites a text that has no legal authority and does not belong to the textual network of the respective discourse, such as a literary text, it is unlikely that this citation is intended to establish or demonstrate coherence (for a systematic differentiation of source categories, legal citation typologies can be used, see Sect. 2.2.2). The citation of 'discourse-external' sources therefore likely stands for ornamental or authoritative citation, but not for coherence. For a source to be used ornamentally, it must possess the attribute of ornamentality in the sense of aesthetic value. Thus, it is questionable whether text types generally considered unadorned, such as legal texts, can be used as textual ornament in utilitarian texts. The choice of source also plays a decisive role for the borrowing of authority, since the cited author or text must first be regarded as authoritative—otherwise, no projection of authority onto the citer is possible. This assignment is only of indirect use for citation analysis, as it again raises the question of under what circumstances a text or author can be considered authoritative. The measurement of influence and authority is particularly supported by quantitative citation analysis as a branch of bibliometrics, since quantitative citation analysis assumes that the frequency of being cited provides information about the status of a text in its discourse (a prominent legal example is the citation index *Shepards Citations,* cf. Shapiro 1992). On the basis of statistical evaluations, statements are made about the influence of, among others, scholarly publications: "on the assumption that the more a journal is cited, the more important, 'visible' and prestigious it will be" (Swales 1986: 39).
3. A qualitative approach to capturing the weighting of a cited author is the description of their placement in a citing text. Following Swales (1990), a distinction can be made between so-called *integral citations,* in which the source of the citation is prominently placed in the running text, and so-called *non-integral citations,* in which the source is mentioned separately (for example, in parentheses). A similar approach is found in Richter (2015). Drawing on Griffig (2006), Richter (ibid.: 146 f.) proposes, in the search for reputation signals, criteria for a source reference that deviates from the norm and is thus also meaningful with regard to authority. If the author of a pretext is named

differently than is conventionally required, this can be taken as an indication of their prominent status in the respective discourse. Particularly revealing with regard to reputation signals are

> references to such specific authors whose reputation and degree of recognition [...] are so high that they are either referred to entirely without bibliographic localization (i.e., neither in the running text nor by mention in the bibliography) or in a manner that deviates from the 'normal' form, i.e., in a particularly marked way. (Griffig 2006: 154)

> Such deviant naming also includes deonomastic adjectives (such as the Gricean maxim, example from Richter 2015: 145) and name dropping (cf. White 2004). While the former can be recognized by the suffix without further analysis, determining whether *name dropping* or a conventional marking is present is not possible without further information about the cited author. *Name dropping* only works if the cited author has the corresponding prestige: "*name dropping* as part of dark persuasion [...] depends on the reputations of the citees" (White 2004: 98). By collecting 'reputation signals', Richter provides an approach for the empirical evaluation of reputation citations. Such analytical tools are not found in this form for the other functions in the relevant research.

4. The fourth question that can be directed at the use of quotations for functional analysis is *how often* citations occur. Unlike questions 1, 2, 3 & 5, this question does not refer categorically to the individual citation, but to the total number of citations and sources in a text. The usefulness of quantitative approaches for capturing the authority of a source has already been described. Quantitative approaches also make it possible to capture the weighting of a source in a citing text: the more frequently a source or source category is cited, the more it is prioritized. Following this, Pfister's analytical grid for the intensity of intertextual references (1985: 30; also proposed by Richter 2015: 149) can be used to assess weighting. As quantitative criteria[10] of intertextual intensity, Pfister lists the density and frequency of intertextual references as well as the number and distribution of the referenced pretexts. If the values are correspondingly high, a correspondingly high weighting of the references or the respective pretext can be inferred.
5. Thus, the assessment of a pretext by a citing text proves to be particularly revealing overall. This idea is also central to the proposed analysis of embedding contexts, which is the focus of the fifth guiding question, 'How is citation carried out?' Citation, by embedding in another context, always implies the creation of new relations with new textual environments. These relations between the citing text and the pretext can be located between affirmation and negation, from which conclusions can in turn be drawn about the respective functionalization of a citation. For economy as a shortcut for one's own argumentation,

[10] In addition, qualitative criteria are also cited, such as the degree of awareness of intertextuality on the part of the recipient in the case of non-marked references. However, these are more suitable for the study of literary texts, in which marking is not mandatory.

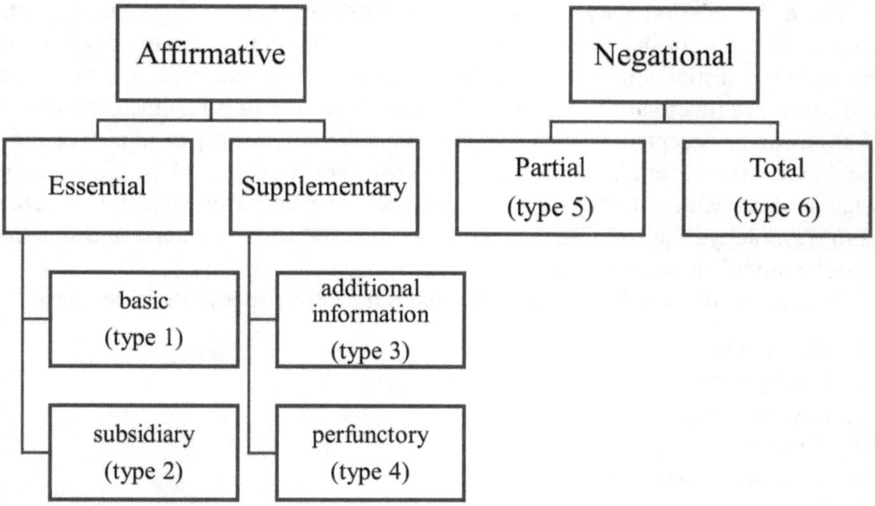

Fig. 3.1 Typology according to Chubin/Moitra (1975)[11]

for example, a source must be chosen that corresponds to or at least resembles one's own line of argument. The use of citations for purposes of economy, at least in the sense of the criticized shortcutting of one's own reasoning in judgments, presupposes affirmative citation. The rejection of a source means additional argumentative effort, which authors might avoid if they are primarily interested in economical text production.

The idea of considering intertextuality within the tension between affirmation and deconstruction goes back to Bakhtin's concept of dialogism (1979: 120). In his understanding, following a broad interpretation of intertextuality, these terms do not primarily refer to the handling of a specific pretext, but rather to literary forms that are to be deconstructed. Nevertheless, this opposition has significantly contributed to the development of functional models for describing intertextuality in the narrow sense (Schulte-Middelich 1985: 199 ff.): Whether a quoting text positions itself affirmatively or negatively toward a pretext is at the core of Genette's evaluative opposition (1982) of "valorisation" and "dévalorisation," that is, the upgrading or downgrading of a pretext. Both pairs of terms are literary studies designations that have not become established in the analysis of utilitarian texts. For the analysis of scientific citations, the citation typology of Chubin/Moitra (1975) has become established, which is essentially based on the same opposition as Genette's pair of terms *valorisation* and *dévalorisation*. However, Chubin/Moitra make more fine-grained distinctions (Fig. 3.1):

[11] Representation based on the diagram in Swales (1986: 42).

The differentiation shows a total of 6 types of affirmative and negative text–pretext relations. In the category of affirmative positioning, aspects of weighting are added; a distinction is made between indispensable "essential" citations and additional information offerings. What is essential above all is that the content of a citation can be accepted or rejected—and this either completely or in part (a comparable approach can also be found in Moravcsik/Murugesan 1975). To describe what is done with a text after a fundamental affirmation or negation, Lipetz's (1965) typology is suitable, as it captures not only the acceptance and rejection but also the modification of content:

Disposition of the scientific contribution of the cited paper to the citing paper

1. Noted only
2. Distinguished
3. Reviewed or compared
4. Applied
5. Improved or modified
6. Replaced
7. Changed the precision
8. Changed the scope of applicability
9. Questioned
10. Affirmed
11. Refuted

Lipetz himself does not associate his categories with the poles of affirmation and negation, but the actions he names presuppose acceptance or rejection of the pretext. For example, the application of a theory or method (category 4 "applied") must be based on a fundamentally affirmative position; the act of improvement (category 5 "improved"), in turn, on at least a partial negation.

Both typologies offer a valuable foundation for the analysis of authoritative citation: If a citer wishes to appropriate authority, they must acknowledge the authority of the cited by means of affirmation; if they deconstruct it, they cannot project it onto themselves. Conversely, however, negative citation does not preclude the presence of authoritative functions. A citer who uses a citation and then questions or rejects it does not attribute authority to the cited text, but may be attempting to demonstrate their own authority: The ability and expertise to deny a text validity, to modify it, or to improve its content, places the citer (at least ostensibly) *above* that text. In this context, a graduation of the demonstrated authority is also conceivable. By negating an author who is regarded as respected and authoritative, a citer can ascribe more authority to themselves than by negating an author/text to whom little or no authority is generally attributed.

The typologies of Chubin/Moitra and Lipetz do provide an initial impetus for such analysis regarding the relevance of how a citer positions themselves toward a citation. However, they do not offer a tool for demonstrably capturing affirmation and deconstruction. It is conceivable that reference labeling (see also Sect. 2.1.2.4) may provide clues as to how a citer wants a cited source to be classified. For example, in court decisions, the reference label "a.A." for "andere Ansicht" ("different opinion") is often found, which indicates negation.

3.5 Interim Conclusion II

Within law itself, citation functions have been little researched. Taking into account the insights of ancient rhetoric and findings on academic citation, the following foundations for the analysis of citation functions in judicial decisions have nevertheless been established.

- Since citation functions depend on the motivation of the citer, Sect. 3.1 adopted a broad concept of function, which includes both intentions encoded in the text and authorial intentions that transcend the text. This concept of function thus encompasses text-related functions such as substantiation, as well as functions that transcend the text, such as authority, and the potentially even more overarching persuasive intentions. Citations can therefore contain various functional subcomponents; each function can serve as an end in itself or as a means to a higher purpose.
- Sect. 3.2.2 introduced the functions of ornamentality and authority. When used ornamentally, a citation can embellish both a text and its citer. In the latter aspect, it is closely linked to authority, which can be regarded as the most multifaceted function of citation: authority can be attributed to a text or to an author. When a citer refers to an authoritative text or an authoritative author, they can confer authority upon themselves. This is a kind of interaction, since by borrowing authority, a citer in turn confers authority upon a source. In addition, authority can be demonstrated not only through projection, but also through one's own positioning; those who are able to criticize external content demonstrate their own competence. These two uses can be described as qualitative demonstrations of authority. Regardless of the authority of the source, a quantitative mechanism also comes into play; so-called *string citations* can signal an apparent majority opinion, thereby minimizing the contestability of a statement. Both ornamental and authoritative citations can be used for persuasive purposes.
- While authoritative and ornamental citation can be considered 'optional', the use of citations for purposes of economy and coherence (depending on the discourse) is obligatory (Sect. 3.2.3). In judicial decisions, citation is required for the sake of coherence. Citation can both signal and construct coherence. Every citation connects to an existing discourse and can, depending on the manner of connection, further develop it. Discourse networks are the prerequisite for the function of economy, which can facilitate both substantive work and the work of formulation.
- Sect. 3.3 has shown that the functions can be assigned to different levels; following Helbig (1996), they can exhibit four different orientations. These are recipient-, reference text-, text-, and producer-oriented functions. Another approach that enables the classification of citation functions and can also be used for the systematization of 'function bundles' is Von Thun's four-sides model of communication psychology, which Hamann (2014) applies to the functions of footnotes in legal scholarship.

- The attempt to classify the functions has shown that the functions cannot be separated and, among other things, are therefore difficult to identify. Sect. 3.4.1 has addressed the problematization of functional demarcation, as well as the reconstruction of intentionality and the ordering of functions.
- Sect. 3.4.2 has attempted to establish foundations for empirical analysis. Five promising criteria for analysis were identified: 1. the choice of citation type, 2. the author of the pretext or the nature and status of the pretext itself, 3. the placement of the author or source, 4. the frequency, and 5. the embedding of the citation. Overall, what proves decisive is what a citer does with a citation. Clues to this are found primarily not in the citation itself, but in its textual environment. The typologies presented for this purpose do describe which relations can be established between citation and citer, but neglect to specify in what these relations are manifested or by which linguistic features they can be concretely identified. For this reason, the following Chap. 4 delves into the nuanced and sometimes subtle possibilities for positioning by citers.

Chapter 4
Citing and Positioning: Modality and Evidentiality

If one wishes to reconstruct the purpose for which a citation is used, analyzing only the cited content and the cited wording yields little insight. The following two examples demonstrate that it is only the embedding context in the quoting text that provides information about possible functionalizations of the citation:

(1a) *In my opinion,* Professor Charles Belleau provides a *good* description of the plaintiff's burden at this preliminary stage: [translation] All in all, the question of admissibility involves inquiring into whether, independently of the substantive issues, the right of action a litigant claims to have meets fundamental criteria that give the court the authority to consider it. (Brunette v. Legault Joly Thiffault, s.e.n.c.r.l. 2018 SCC 55 - 07.12.2018, emphasis by J.S.)

(1b) *In my opinion,* Professor Charles Belleau provides a *problematic* description of the plaintiff's burden at this preliminary stage: [translation] All in all, the question of admissibility involves inquiring into whether, independently of the substantive issues, the right of action a litigant claims to have meets fundamental criteria that give the court the authority to consider it.

Example 1a is an authentic excerpt from a decision of the Supreme Court of Canada. The quoting instance explicitly evaluates the content of the quotation as "good"; the quotation is thus introduced affirmatively and in support of the argument. In contrast, the strikingly manipulated quotation introduction in Example 1b attributes problematic content to the quotation; the quoter positions themselves in a distancing manner. By labeling it as problematic, an argumentative-supportive functionalization of the quotation can largely be ruled out. As the manipulation of the quotation introduction has shown, the meaning of a quotation in the quoting text only unfolds in interaction with its specific embedding. In this sense, the present chapter is to be understood as a plea for the analysis of context-specific functionalizations of quotations.

© The Author(s), under exclusive license to Springer-Verlag GmbH, DE, part of Springer Nature 2025

J. Steigler-Herms, *How and Why Do Courts Cite?*,
https://doi.org/10.1007/978-3-662-71934-3_4

Between citation and source—according to the succinct formulation in Berkenkotter/Huckin (1995, cited in Yang 2013: 126)—there is a fundamental identification: "[Y]ou are what you cite." However, if a quoting or citing text wishes to nuance, restrict, or reject this identification, they must use various means of embedding quotations to establish semantic relations. Determining the relation between citation and citing text along the poles of affirmation and negation is crucial insofar as the act of citing *per se* contains a moment of reconstitution: The meaning of every proposition unfolds in the interplay of all (con)textual factors. In the act of quoting, the extraction and insertion into a new textual environment introduces *new* factors into this interplay and thus into the overall meaning; the original meaning of the quoted content is modulated and evaluated. The new contextual factors influence the meaning of citations so substantially that "by embedding [the referenced utterance] in a—broadly defined—modal context, the very basis for even a potentially literal interpretation is removed from the outset" (Gather 1994: 344).

In general, non-evaluative and objective citing, which at least largely allows for potentially literal interpretations, is possible but not common: Depending on the domain and text type, a discursive, critical, and evaluative handling of citations is established and intended. The concept of modalizations offers a suitable set of tools for describing positioning. Modalizations, that is, a writer's statements regarding the factuality of an utterance, enable the quoter to assign concrete, subject-bound functions to citations:

> For where the referencing of other texts serves to provide argumentative plausibility for one's own validity claims, modalization—here understood as the epistemic qualification of the referenced utterances and statements—becomes a critical factor. Its validity must be affirmed where it supports one's own statements; it must be restricted or rejected where it contradicts them. Corresponding modalizations are primarily made through epistemically qualifying expressions in the framing formulations, [...]. (Steinseifer 2019: 207)

Considering citation embeddings in the context of modalizations offers, in comparison to the typologies of acceptance and rejection of cited content presented in Chap. 3 (see especially Sect. 3.4.2), the decisive advantage that the relationship between citation and source can be empirically described and measured on the basis of linguistic means. With the aim of compiling such relevant means, the following discussion begins with an introduction to stance-taking theory, which can be regarded as a framework theory for acts of positioning (Sect. 4.1). A detailed treatment of the concept of modality and of linguistic means that can be used as modalization procedures (e.g., so-called boosters and hedges) can be found in Sect. 4.2. For some linguistic means, such as the subjunctive, it is disputed whether they serve as modalizations or merely signal the act of citing. A discussion of the interface between markers of objective citing and markers of subjective, evaluative quoting can be found in the presentation of the so-called evidentiality concept (Sect. 4.3), which deals with the totality of sources that prompt writers to make a statement and is closely related to the concept of modality.

4.1 Stancetaking as a Framework Theory

Analyses of the linguistic expression of positionings and evaluations fall under the so-called *stance* concept (the German translation as 'Haltung' is rarely found). Stance can be regarded as the background theory for the central concepts of this chapter, 'epistemic modality' and 'evidentiality' (although the status of the latter and its relation to stance and modality is disputed; not every evidential contains an element of positioning, see Sect. 4.1). Haßler (2015: 183) defines stance as a collective term for all positioning strategies:

> By speaker's stance we understand linguistic and non-linguistic forms and strategies that show a speaker's commitment to the status of the information that he is providing. Stancetaking causes the speaker, among other things, to specify the sources of his knowledge, whether it be to give the utterance more weight or to reduce his own responsibility for the contents.

As the term stancetaking implies, the linguistic analysis of stance is less interested in 'internal' attitudes (such as the psychological concept of *attitudes*), and more in the linguistic act of evaluating and positioning as a verbalized social act (cf. Du Bois 2007: 171). For Stubbs (1966: 202), the encoding of attitude and the adoption of stances, that is, stancetaking, is present in all utterances:

> Whenever speakers or writers say anything, they encode their point of view towards it: whether they think it is a reasonable thing to say, or might be found to be obvious, questionable, tentative, provisional, controversial, contradictory, irrelevant, impolite or whatever.

In principle, any referential object can be the subject of stancetaking, i.e., a writer[1] can evaluate both non-linguistic and linguistic elements, as well as their own and others' content. The present study is concerned exclusively with the latter, i.e., with intertextual references as stance objects. Du Bois (2007: 140) emphasizes the role of dialogicality (cf. Bakhtin 1934, among others) in so-called interactional stancetaking:

> Dialogicality makes its presence felt to the extent that a stancetaker's words derive from, and further engage with, the words of those who have spoken before—whether immediately within the current exchange of stance utterances, or more remotely along the horizons of language and prior text as projected by the community of discourse.

The existence of a "prior text" cannot be considered a prerequisite for stancetaking—as it is for intertextuality, whose defining feature is the existence of a pretext; both one's own and others' content can be evaluated.

Nevertheless, the necessity of positioning oneself is above all an expression of textual interaction (cf. Hyland/Jiang 2015: 548) and engagement with the other.

[1] The same applies to speakers and oral communication. However, since the present study analyzes a written language corpus, the term 'writer' will be used hereafter.

Especially in the act of quoting, at least two stances come into contact: the stance expressed in the citation by the original author, and the stance communicated by the citing text through the embedding of the citation (see also "What stance is the stancetaker responding to?" Du Bois 2007: 142). The following chapter deals with two sub-concepts for the explicit identification of stance—modality and evidentiality—as well as their respective linguistic means.

4.2 Epistemic Modality and Modalization Procedures

Modality itself is an umbrella term for two fundamentally different subtypes, whose commonality hardly extends beyond the central role of modal verbs: deontic modality (also called root modality) and epistemic modality must be distinguished. *Deontic modality* (derived from Ancient Greek *deon,* 'duty') refers to a "world-perspectivity" (Abraham/Leiss 2013: 5), which—depending on the modal verb—expresses possibility, ability, or necessity. The determination of what one may, can, or must do is indeed central to the action dimensions of law in general, but can be neglected for the analysis of evaluative citation contexts.

For the analysis of evaluative moments, it is above all the concept of *epistemic modality* that must be drawn upon. There is broad consensus on the definition of epistemic modality as "assessment of factuality" (Horváth 2013: 131). The term factuality here refers to the "being-a-fact of the […] proposition" (Helbig/Buscha 1986: 506) from the communicator's perspective. The latter is particularly important, as it does not concern objectively true facts, but exclusively a degree of factuality attributed by the writer. The concept of epistemic modality as an assessment of factuality is thus more narrowly defined than stance, which includes evaluations that may concern not only factuality but also other properties of a proposition. Since the writer's positioning toward the proposition forms the starting point of modalization, numerous definitions characterize epistemic modality as "speaker's attitude" (Narrog 2005: 680). This interpretation is also central to Diewald's (1999) terminology, who describes epistemic modality as a deictic process. Drawing on Bühler's theory, Diewald (1999: 167) calls deixis a "semiotic process by which the connection between language and speaker is established." The starting point, or the "coordinate zero point of the speaking 'ego'" (ibid.: 168), is always the origo, i.e., the speaker as the deictic center. As a simple example of this, especially for personal deixis, personal pronouns can be cited: the personal pronoun 'I' only acquires its concrete meaning and reference in relation to its user. According to Diewald, the same applies to epistemic modality: the assessment of factuality, as effected by epistemic modalizations, is not inherent to the represented state of affairs, but, like all deictics, represents the relation between what is represented and the speaker (Diewald 1999: 14).

4.2.1 Hedging and Boosting

Hedging and boosting are umbrella terms for those linguistic means by which epistemic modalizations can be carried out. Within this continuum, the two categories are opposed in that *hedges* represent distancing from the content, while *boosters* represent alignment with the content. In taxonomies, they are therefore recorded separately (e.g., Hyland 2005).

If a writer qualifies their content with "possibly," "in my opinion," "apparently," "to a large extent," or "approximately," they weaken the definiteness and factuality of their statement with the help of (here, five) hedges.

According to most functional definitions, hedges (cf. Bußmann 1990: 304) are epistemic modalization procedures or, in Hyland's (1998: 5) words, "the means by which writers can present a proposition as an opinion rather than a fact." As a rhetorical strategy, they allow the writer to distance themselves from content; by limiting "the writer's commitment" (Vázquez/Giner 2008: 173), hedges attenuate a claim. Such distancing may be desirable—again, for various reasons—both with regard to the writer's own propositions and especially when reproducing others' content. Vass (2015a: 151) therefore also refers to hedges as "marker of intertextuality and interdiscursivity"; Fløttum (2005) calls them "polyphonic markers."[2] A frequently cited example of hedge expressions are epistemic modal verbs (e.g., the epistemic function of 'must'), which in their epistemic reading reduce facts to possibilities. Whether modal verbs are to be understood as hedge expressions or not is inextricably linked to the context of their use; they do not inherently possess a 'hedging' function. With this context-dependent development of meaning, the analysis of hedges falls within the domain of pragmatics.

The currently widespread, pragmatic interpretation of the concept differs significantly from its original introduction by Lakoff (1972). As an essentially semantic and not pragmatic category, Lakoff describes the function of hedges as "to make things fuzzier or less fuzzy" (1972: 195). He demonstrates the effect of linguistic means that lead to 'semantic fuzziness' with the prominent example of the penguin, whose category membership is made "fuzzy" by means of a hedge expression: "A penguin is a sort of a bird" (ibid.). Hedges in Lakoff's sense thus scale a kind of membership to prototypes: "From the fact that (each relative to a specific cultural background) some exemplars are regarded as better/more typical examples of a category […] arises a need for […] hedges" (Gippert 1993: 243).

The original definition of hedging is less relevant for the present study, insofar as hedging-expressions are to be considered in their discursive function as markers of opinion and factuality in the use of external content, and not with regard to their function in prototype categorization. Nevertheless, a comparison of the current and original definitions of hedge expressions is useful, as it helps to explain

[2] However, Fløttum does not restrict the term to hedges, but applies it to all signals of "other voices present" (ibid.).

the terminologically complex relationship between hedging and modality. Palmer (1986), for example, argues for a conceptual subordination of *hedging* to modality, which in turn is understood in a very broad sense as a collective term for a set of positioning instruments. However, there are also opposing views that assume a reversed conceptual hierarchy. If, for example, one follows a narrow interpretation of epistemic modality, according to which writers can use modalizations to position themselves *only* between the poles of *true* and *false,* then hedges, with their function that sometimes goes beyond marking factuality and, among other things, signals opinion, cannot be considered a subcategory. Vázquez/Giner (2008: 172 f.) summarize both variants:

> It seems possible to see the relationship between modality—mostly of the epistemic type—and hedges in two ways: either modality is the wider concept and includes hedges or the other way round, hedging is the umbrella term and epistemic modality a part of it.

A comprehensive terminological analysis regarding the relationship between modality and hedging is still a desideratum in current literature. For the purposes of this study, hedging is understood as a linguistic expression of epistemic modality. The concept of epistemic modalization procedures largely covers the functional spectrum of hedges. However, it should be noted that some hedges, such as *approximately,* which is used for estimations, do not represent assessments of factuality—thus, hedges and epistemic modality (if the latter is defined as an assessment of factuality) are not entirely congruent.

By contrast, the broad functional spectrum of hedges has received far more attention than terminological clarification. Some functional dimensions have already been mentioned in the preceding definitions, which will be made explicit below: The primary function of mitigation is not the ultimate purpose of hedging, but is itself only a means to higher-level communicative purposes.

Hedges allow speakers and writers to subjectivize, evaluate, and qualify their own or others' statements. One of their overarching purposes is to reduce responsibility for the content of a statement. By distancing themselves and building a "protective 'hedge' around themselves" (Schröder 1989: 269), a writer anticipates possible criticism. In this sense, it is a form of "risk minimization" (Niemann 2018: 49) as a defensive strategy (cf. ibid.). By demonstrating a "potential negatability of claims" (Hyland 1998: 354) and avoiding absolute statements (cf. Rolek 2019), interpersonal relationships can also be protected. Niemann understands this as an offensive function, more precisely as the preservation of politeness. Whenever, for example, the content of another person is criticized, it may be considered a matter of politeness not to present this criticism as indisputably factual. Hedges can thus be regarded, among other things, as a means of avoiding so-called *face threatening acts,* which refer to the unmitigated expression of criticism (see also Niemann 2018 on the politeness of hedges).

The specific intention of hedging depends, on the one hand, on the context of use, but on the other hand also on the type of hedge in question. The functional spectrum as a whole—summarized in abstract terms—ranges from *content-oriented hedges* (for the purpose of specifying meaning), to *writer-oriented* (which are intended to 'protect' in cases of uncertainty about content), to *recipient-oriented (politeness) hedges.*

In view of the wide functional spectrum, it is useful to differentiate, for example, between *first-order and second-order functions.* First-order functions refer to the immediate effect of the hedge/booster on the modalized proposition (e.g., statement of probability) within the text; second-order functions refer to intended effects outside the text (e.g., avoidance of overly direct criticism).

To realize these functions, different types of hedges (and boosters) are used, which Salager-Meyer (1995) divides into five groups using English as an example:

1. *shields:* e.g., modal verbs such as "könnte" ("might")
2. *approximators:* estimations and roundings for degrees, frequencies, and quantities such as "rund" ("approximately")
3. *expressions of personal doubt and involvement:* e.g., "ich glaube" ("in my view")
4. *emotionally-charged intensifiers:* e.g., "extrem wichtig" ("extremely important")
5. *compound hedges:* e.g., "könnte verstanden werden als" ("could be suggested")

While Salager-Meyer's classification is primarily based on functional criteria (with the exception of *compound hedges*), the widely adopted approach of Hyland categorizes according to word classes (and word combinations). He distinguishes between *modal auxiliaries* ("may"), *modal adjuncts* ("probably"), *modal adjectives* ("possible"), *epistemic verbs* and *circumstances* ("in my view").

The studies by Hyland (e.g., 1998) are among the few investigations that, in addition to hedges, also address the phenomenon of boosters; even though, in terms of their intensifying function, these can be seen as the immediate antagonists of hedges, they have received far less attention in the relevant research.

As the term booster, 'intensifier', suggests, boosters intensify the validity of propositions. Boosters "allow writers to express conviction and assert a proposition with confidence, representing a strong claim about a state of affairs" (Hyland 1998: 350). They express the writer's unassailable conviction in their proposition and thus (anticipatorily) leave no room for other positions. The intensification of content can be achieved by means of amplifying adverbs ("definitely"), emphatic verbs ("demonstrate"), emphatic adjectives ("it is evident that"), as well as so-called *emphatics* ("in fact"). In the case of citation, a writer can use *boosters* to increase the degree of identification with the quotation.

Both hedges and boosters can, according to Hyland's model (2005), be understood as traces of metadiscourse. Hyland (2005: 37) defines this as "the cover term for the self-reflective expressions used to negotiate interactional meanings in a text, assisting the writer (or speaker) to express a viewpoint and engage with readers as members of a particular community." Both procedures are used to communicate statements *about* content, including quotations. In doing so, metadiscursive procedures and quotations manifest two different instances: "[M]etadiscourse and hedging are examples of *explicit* manifestation of the self; bibliographical references and citations are examples of *explicit* manifestations of the other" (Fløttum 2005: 30).

Thus, it can be assumed that hedges and boosters allow conclusions to be drawn about the position of a citer towards the cited content and thus, at least indirectly, also about the functions of citing.

4.2.2 *Adverbs as an Example of Modalization Procedures*

It has already been shown that modalization procedures are not tied to specific parts of speech. One part of speech that has received particular attention in studies surveying hedges is adverbs. Even though some examples from this category have already appeared in the discussion of hedges and boosters, it will therefore be examined in more detail below.

What is particularly interesting about adverbs classified as hedge or booster is that their evaluative function is 'readable' independently of context. While the epistemic dimension of modal verbs only unfolds in their context, for adverbs such as "möglicherweise," "certainly," and "possibly," it is evident from the word itself without major interpretive effort. The adverbs "certainly" and "possibly" (along with "indeed," "perhaps," "clearly," "of course," "arguably," and "reportedly") are among the most frequently used adverbial hedges/boosters in English academic articles. However, there are striking differences in their distribution across disciplines—the fewest epistemic adverbs are found in medical discourse and in scientific articles in physics. By contrast, their use is comparatively high in the humanities and social sciences (Rozumko 2017).

For the category referred to here as epistemic adverbs, the term "content disjunct" (Biber et al. 1999: 855) is also used, among others. Such a specification suggests that these adverbs primarily have a content-related function. As "propositional hedging" (Pic/Fumaniak 2012: 19), epistemic adverbs are indeed particularly close to the evaluation of content, but they can also be used in relation to the addressee and thus for relational orientation. An example of this is the English "perhaps," which is used "to soften a suggestion" (ibid.; on the function of "perhaps" see also Fraser 2010: 22). Celle (2009: 25) argues—again, more content-oriented—for considering epistemic adverbials as evidentials. Adverbials would indicate the manner in which knowledge is obtained. For some—undoubtedly including *reportedly*—the designation as evidential seems obvious. Whether this actually applies to all epistemic adverbials, however, is questionable.

From a classificatory perspective, two main criteria are used to characterize epistemic adverbs: the implied 'degree of certainty' (cf. Huddleston/Pullum 2002: 768) and the functions according to the taxonomy of Salager-Meyer (1995). The adverb "maybe," by its inherent semantics, expresses a lower degree of certainty than "probably". According to Salager-Meyer's taxonomy, however, both would fall into the class of *shields*. In addition, adverbs also appear in the other subclasses of the taxonomy, for example as emotionally charged intensifiers, such as "extremely relevant," or as *approximators* like "approximately" and "about".

The example "extremely relevant" also demonstrates the possibility of combining epistemic adverbs with other epistemic procedures: the modalizing forces of different procedures can be 'summed up.' For instance, if one explains the absence of a colleague in the office by saying "he must be ill," one can give even more weight to this assumption by adding "definitely" (on the combination of adverbs with other modalizations, see also Celle 2009). Both modal verbs, as in the example, and adjectives that are already modalizing can be epistemically extended with the help of adverbs.

The study of epistemic adjectives, in comparison to the numerous surveys of adverbs, is less common. This may be because the formulation of an epistemic evaluation using an adjective is sometimes very close to the adverbial version (e.g., "probably"—"probable"). However, the semantic proximity between an epistemic adverb and its (supposedly) adjectival counterpart is not always present. This is particularly evident in the comparison of the pair "es ist sicher, dass" *vs.* "sicherlich" (cf. Krifka 2020), which do not express entirely identical degrees of probability. Whether an epistemic adverb can be paraphrased by an adjective must therefore be examined on a case-by-case basis.

4.3 Evidentiality and Evidentiality Markers

Evidentiality describes the entirety of the "sources of information speakers have for expressing statements" (Diewald/Smirnova 2010: 2; see also Hart 2011: 758). The umbrella term *sources* is to be understood broadly in this context. In statements and argumentation, a writer can refer both to what has been seen or read and to what has been surmised. Evidentiality is therefore closely related to providing evidence and, more broadly, to the justification of one's own statements.

Aikhenvald (2004: 63 f.) distinguishes between five different sources of evidence, including, among others, visual and audio-visual perception, knowledge gained through inference, and so-called *quotative evidentials.* Quotative evidentials are understood as all statements that refer to quoted or cited content with source references. In a traditional subclassification (cf. Cornillie 2009), citations are considered an expression of indirect acquisition of information and are thus classified as *indirect evidentials*, which can be distinguished from those directly received by the writer, e.g., based on visual perception, the *direct evidentials.* The present work focuses exclusively on quotative evidentiality and the relevant linguistic evidentiality markers in this context. Considering the quotation against the background of the evidentiality concept is fruitful in at least two respects: *First*, the findings of evidentiality theory can be applied to quotations. If every citation is an evidential, then the functions of evidentiality also apply to citations. In their study on the argumentative use of evidentiality, Dalbergenova/Zharkynbekova (2020) identify two communicative-pragmatic functions. Naming the source of an utterance, first, limits the truth claim of a statement and can thus be instrumentalized as a safeguard in argumentation:

> Evidentiality markers enable the speaker not to commit to the truth of their arguments and to avoid responsibility. The argumentation does not lose credibility through the evidentiality markers. Moreover, they help the speaker to save face, even if their statement should turn out to be false. (ibid., 142)

Second, especially epistemically modalized evidentiality markers, as will be presented below using the example of the quotative subjunctive and citation-accompanying phrases, offer the possibility of making positioning transparent.

Whether evidentiality markers actually contain an epistemic-modalizing element is, however, highly disputed. Mori/Okano (2013: 189) summarize this as follows:

> Some researchers derive evidentiality from modality, others, conversely, locate the latter within the former [...], and still others assume a superordinate term for both categories [...]. But there are also those who consider both as distinct categories [...].

The conflict can be illustrated by two examples: If one thinks of at least seemingly objective evidentiality-citation markers such as the verb "say," it is initially reasonable to deny an epistemic content to evidentiality; the verb 'say' alone does not reveal any position or evaluation of the citing instance The modal verb 'wollen' in quotative use, with its property of referring to a source, is definitely and primarily an evidential, but it also affects the assessment of factuality and thus epistemic modality (Haßler 2015: 182). Some positions therefore emphasize the inseparability of the two concepts by integrating an evaluative element into the definition of evidentiality. According to these approaches, evidentials metadiscursively assess the reliability of communicated knowledge: "Evidentiality refers to the status of the knowledge contained in propositions and concerns its reliability, implying its source, how it was acquired, and the credibility we can invest in it" (Hyland/Jiang 2016: 252).

The present study assumes (in accordance with the Western research tradition, cf. Cornillie 2009: 49) a partial overlap of both concepts: Not every evidential marker can be regarded without restriction and independent of context as an epistemic modalization procedure (cf. 'say')—however, a large proportion of evidential markers do contain evaluative elements. In the context of citations, it is above all the *citation-accompanying expressions* to be discussed below as markers of *lexical evidentiality* (cf. Xu 2015) and the subjunctive as *grammatical evidentiality* (ibid.), in which subjective evaluations, that is, epistemic modalizations, become apparent.

4.3.1 The German Subjunctive: An Epistemic Quotative?

The subjunctive is closely connected to citation, more precisely to indirect and mixed citation. Regardless of the functional and morphological differentiation between Subjunctive I and Subjunctive II, one of the central functions of both modes[3] is the marking of non-original content. Reflecting this functional aspect terminologically, the evidential subjunctive is also referred to as "reportative subjunctive," "indirectness subjunctive" (Fabricus-Hansen/Solfjeld/Pitz 2019), and as "quotative" (Diewald 1999: 182). However, the subjunctive can have not only a report-signaling but also a modalizing function, as is evident from the definition of the IDS Grammar (1997) of the subjunctive as a marker in "contexts of indirectness" and "contexts of modality." To what extent the subjunctive modalizes, and whether it thus has an epistemic component, is, however, highly contested.

As is particularly evident from the term 'indirectness subjunctive,' the subjunctive signals the 'mediatedness' of content. It cannot be used in the context of direct quotations, among other reasons because direct quotations block any kind of intervention *salva veritate* and thus the mode of the verbs contained in the original utterance may not be changed. In indirect and mixed citation, the subjunctive *alone* is sufficient to signal the act of citing. Combination with other citation markers, such as citation-accompanying expressions, is possible but not strictly necessary.

This self-sufficient marking potential applies equally to Subjunctive I and Subjunctive II. One of the reasons why *both* morphologically very different forms are nevertheless used in the same function as markers of indirectness is the partial syncretism of forms between Subjunctive I and the indicative. Only half of the Subjunctive I conjugation forms (2nd person singular, 3rd person singular, and 2nd person plural) differ morphologically from the verb endings of the indicative.[4] The other half has no morphologically distinctive features that would allow a distinction between Subjunctive I and the indicative. In the case of ambiguous Subjunctive I forms, therefore (at least from a prescriptive linguistic perspective), Subjunctive II must be used instead (Duden[5]). Schecker (2002), however, counters this rule with the observation that Subjunctive II is also used in cases where, in theory, an unambiguous Subjunctive I is available.[6] As a possible explanation, he cites, among other things, euphonic reasons (ibid.: 26). In addition, the frequency of forms, which also significantly contributes to their establishment, should be mentioned. This also explains the preference for the analytic Subjunctive II over the synthetic variant.[7]

---

[3] The use of Subjunctive I as a jussive (imperative form, example: man koche…) and as an optative (wishing form: lange lebe…) is rare and uncommon in contemporary language use. The various usage contexts of Subjunctive II, including as irrealis or as a form of politeness, are by contrast very widespread and common.

[4] For quotation contexts, the 3rd person singular and 3rd person plural are usually used.

[5] https://www.duden.de/sprachwissen/sprachratgeber/konjunktiv-1-oder-2.

[6] An example of this is the 2nd person singular: The Subjunctive I form 'du habest' is clearly different from the indicative conjugation 'du hast'. Nevertheless, the Subjunctive II form 'du hättest' is far more common.

[7] The synthetic paradigm of Subjunctive II (also preterite subjunctive) is comparatively rare in current language use and is only common for a few verbs, e.g. "ich fände" ("I would find"), "es wäre" ("it would be"), "wir hätten" ("we would have"); usually the analytic form with 'würde' is used, e.g. "ich würde kochen" ("I would cook").

Thus, the choice between indicative, Subjunctive I, and Subjunctive II is influenced not only by grammatical factors but, more interestingly, above all by factors that can be subsumed under the aspect of social conventions: Whether a subjunctive is used as a marker of reported speech, and if so, which one, depends crucially on the differing requirements of orality and literacy. The range of requirements for how an indirect/mixed citation is to be marked also arises essentially from the domain of its use and the language forms characteristic of that domain, i.e., the register.

The question of the appropriateness of subjunctive use arises particularly in the discussion of possible epistemic dimensions. Older works in particular argue against an epistemic potential of the subjunctive: According to this position, the subjunctive (I) is the normal mode of indirect speech. Its use is—regardless of the communicative function to which the use of the citation is meant to contribute—always correct. The subjunctive thus does not imply any doubted factuality and is to be interpreted as a neutral quotative. As an example, Diewald (1999: 183) cites academic texts in which Subjunctive I "is used as an economical means of marking the origin of statements that are reproduced without any doubt as to their correctness." Depending on the context, however, Diewald (ibid.) does not rule out the possibility that "doubts of the speaker about the quoted evaluation are also implied or understood." The evaluation of factuality lies with the cited and not the citing speaker, since it is a case of "origo shift or displacement deixis"; the quoter "points to the quoted speaker as the origo of the quotation and presents the relation between quoted speaker and quotation as factual" (Diewald 1999: 182). According to this argument, the subjunctive does not contain any evaluation of the factuality of the cited content. If one agrees with Diewald's argument, the subjunctive is a quotative that does not normally lead to an epistemic interpretation of the cited content.

This assessment is contrasted by a pragmatic perspective: Depending on the validity claim that is ascribed or denied to a quotation, the use of the subjunctive can in fact be inappropriate. Steinseifer (2019: 206–208) presents this particularly convincingly in his discussion of the conditions of appropriateness and inappropriateness of subjunctive use. When validity claims of non-original content are being negotiated, the subjunctive can be an instrument of rejection. In rejecting usage, its use is unproblematic. In usage with affirmatively functionalized citation, however, content-related tensions can arise—an important indication of epistemic modalization through the subjunctive:

> The contextually expected modalization [by the subjunctive] leads […] to the result that wherever the argumentative appropriation of the validity claim of a statement referred to as a paraphrase is at issue, the epistemically qualifying dimension of the subjunctive conflicts with this appropriation and the use of the indicative appears more appropriate.

The conflict between the subjunctive and affirmative citations, which serve the purpose of content appropriation, can be tested by means of substitution, here following Steinseifer (2019):

> As Peter Kappel rightly emphasizes, the influence of written language on the spoken standard is much greater than on non-standard varieties of spoken German (cf. Kappel 2007: 220 f.; see also Eisenberg 2007a). We can therefore assume clear affinities between the two standards, the spoken and the written. (Schneider 2011: 172, example cited after Steinseifer 2019: 208) / German original: Wie Peter Kappel zu Recht betont, ist [sei] der Einfluss der geschriebenen Sprache auf den gesprochenen Standard weitaus größer als auf standardferne Varietäten des gesprochenen Deutsch (vgl. Kappel 2007: 220 f.; vgl. auch Eisenberg 2007a). Wir können also von deutlichen Affinitäten zwischen den beiden Standards, dem gesprochenen und dem geschriebenen, ausgehen. (Schneider 2011: 172, Beispiel zitiert nach Steinseifer 2019: 208)

As illustrated by the replacement of the indicative 'ist' with the form 'sei', the subjunctive conflicts with the identification of the citer with the citation. The citing instance Schneider designates Kappel's assertion as legitimate; the distancing effect of the subjunctive appears inappropriate in this context (Steinseifer 2019: 208):

> The pragmatic acceptability varies. To the extent that the degree of appropriation of the reported content increases, [...] the use of the subjunctive appears less appropriate. If, in the context of reporting, the subjunctive were solely to indicate the indirectness of the reproduction, this would not be expected.

From a pragmatic perspective, the subjunctive thus belongs to the potential forms of epistemic modalization. For the reconstruction of possible intended modalizations, however, the analysis of subjunctives remains a problematic feature, since whether a writer uses the subjunctive for distancing modalization or as a non-modalizing evidential due to conventions of reproduction can be surmised with the help of semantic relations, but cannot be irrefutably proven.

4.3.2 Citation-Accompanying Expressions

Citation-accompanying verbs belong to the optional and at the same time explicit repertoires for marking external content:

> The use of a reporting verb is one of the most explicit ways of attributing content to another source and represents a significant rhetorical choice. The wide range of verbs that can be used to introduce reports allow writers to convey both the kind of activity reported and whether the claims are to be taken as accepted or not. (Hyland 2002: 4)

As Hyland's description shows, citation-accompanying verbs do not only serve to mark citations, but—more interestingly from a functional perspective—also open up a wide spectrum of attitudinal nuances for the citing instance. The richness of possibilities for expressing stance with these verbs is illustrated by the quantitative compilation by Michels (1966: 2018), in which he identifies "400 different speech-introducing verbs" based solely on the example of contemporary prose works.

Before discussing some examples from different (mostly academic) corpora and related classification proposals, a terminological discussion is necessary: The verbs previously referred to as 'quotation-accompanying' are traditionally subsumed under various terms. Particularly widespread are the designations *'verba dicendi'* and 'speech-introducing verbs'; the English-language research canon refers to the same phenomenon as *'reporting verbs'*.

For the following reasons, all three terms are to some extent to be rejected for the purposes of analysis in connection with quotations in court decisions:

- The designation *verba dicendi* is inadequate or at least misleading in view of the basic understanding of quotations as the reproduction of language and thought in general, and not only as the reproduction of *speech*. Citations can be accompanied not only by *verba dicendi* but also by *verba sentiendi* and *verba scribendi.*[8] In its broadest definition, the group of *verba dicendi* also includes verbs that, as general communication verbs, refer to the act of verbalization, but do not necessarily have anything to do exclusively with the act of citing. Moreover, as will be further elaborated below, citation-introducing and -concluding expressions are not always verbs. Citations can, for example, also be accompanied by prepositional phrases (e.g., "according to the defendant's statement") or nominal constructions.
- The same applies to *speech-introducing verbs:* If the concept of *speech* is understood in the narrower sense as a verbal and not a written act of utterance, the term is unsuitable for the analysis of written citation. Furthermore, a speech-*introducing* use is only one of three possible positions: they can be used as introductory, parenthetical, or concluding.
- The terminological objections described above do not fully apply to *reporting verbs*. However, the act of reporting or the specification '*reporting*' appears objective. The semantics of reporting may therefore conflict with the potentially subjective and evaluative force of what, in the following, will be referred to as 'citation-accompanying expressions' (following Lenk 2008).

The terminological discussion has already suggested that citation-accompanying expressions can not only refer y to acts of verbalization, but also, for example, to acts of thinking. Citation-accompanying verbs can include—just to name a few examples—verbs such as "say," "think," "wonder," "emphasize," "criticize." Traditional categorization approaches subdivide the various citation-accompanying verbs according to the syntactic feature of valency.[9]

[8] See also Gansel (2002: 1564): "Content-related delimitations of verba dicendi are indeed problematic, as they fluctuate between an extension to any speech-introducing verbs and a restriction to informative verbs of saying […] The equation of verba dicendi with speech-introducing verbs is increasingly pushed back by narrower content-related definitions, especially since verbs such as laugh, shake one's head, sigh can also function as speech-introducing."

[9] Valency grammar deals, among other things, with verb-dependent (optional and obligatory) complements; for further definition and justification of the approach, see Tesnière (1959). While the verb 'say,' for example, necessarily requires an object, complements for the verb 'speak' are optional. These syntactic conditions significantly restrict the choice of the respective quotation-accompanying verb in relation to the choice of quotation type. Due to valency-grammatical properties, not every verb can be used for every type of quotation.

In addition to syntactic perspectives, categorial descriptions from semantic-functional viewpoints are particularly important. Thompson/Ye (1991) make a threefold distinction and identify *research/real world acts* (such as "analyze" and "observe"), *cognition acts,* which denote mental processes (such as "conceptualize" and "believe"), and *discourse acts.* The latter, which includes verbs such as "describe" and "claim," serves as a collective term for acts of verbalization.

A further differentiation of *reporting verbs,* though with a focus on possible dimensions of evaluation, is provided by Hyland (1999: 350): A writer can accept the cited content, reject it, or position themselves neutrally or ambiguously towards it.[10] In the case of a neutral positioning by the citing instance, Hyland (ibid.) suggests consulting the stance of the cited author. Stances *in* a cited proposition can themselves (at least for discursive academic texts) be "positive, neutral, tentative [or] critical" (ibid.). If the citing instance does not otherwise position themselves, identification with the cited content is to be assumed.

Lenk (2008) adopts a comparatively broad approach, who in his classification scheme (ibid.: 104 f.) also orients himself towards *processes, states*, and *actions*. For each class, he again makes detailed subcategorizations, so that he documents a total of 27 "verbs and expressions for embedding citations" (as the subtitle of the article puts it). In the subcategorization of verbs and expressions that express mental processes and states alone, Lenk distinguishes between six different types, including epistemic attitudes (e.g., "estimate"), doxastic attitudes (e.g., "to be of the opinion," "to be convinced"), and evaluative attitudes (e.g., "consider to be" + evaluative adjective). With this comprehensive inventory, Lenk offers a very valuable extension of the perspective otherwise primarily limited to the consideration of verbs: not only verbs, but also nominal and adjectival *expressions* are used for embedding citations. This is particularly noteworthy in view of the nominal style prevalent in legal discourse. Intertextuality is therefore not necessarily signaled in the verbal complex, but can, as in the following example, also be marked in a noun phrase:

(2) *According to the prevailing opinion*, the obligation to register in due time does not apply to spontaneous demonstrations that form instantly due to a current occasion (see e.g. [...]). (14.05.1985 1st Senate BVerfG 69, 315; emphasis by J.S.)

A stronger focus on nominal-based structures in stance research in general is also called for by Jiang/Hyland (2015: 529):

> A relatively overlooked means of expressing a stance, however, is through a Noun Complement structure, where a stance head noun takes a nominal complement clause. This pattern allows a writer to front-load attitude meanings and offers an explicit statement of evaluation of the proposition which follows [...].

[10] Designation of the possibilities in the original: *factive/ writer's acceptance—non-factive/ no clear signal—counter-factive/ writer's disagreement.*

It is also striking that none of the many examples in the classifications presented contain passive constructions. However, considering the prominence of the passive in legal discourse, it is necessary to be aware that the verbs accompanying citations can occur in both their active and passive forms. This is demonstrated by the following passage from the already quoted BVerfG decision:

(3) *In the literature,* the stabilizing function of freedom of assembly for the representative system is aptly *described* as allowing dissatisfied individuals to publicly express discontent and criticism [...]. (14.05.1985 1st Senate BVerfG 69, 315; emphasis by J.S.)

The choice of expressions embedding citations (as well as the practice of citing itself, e.g., the preference for certain types of citations and their quantitatively appropriate use) depends greatly on the domain. Hyland (1999: 341) notes that in the humanities and social sciences—depending on the "epistemological and social conventions"—more "discourse reporting verbs [...] to represent cited authors as adopting a stance to their material" are used than in engineering and the natural sciences.

How formally and semantically diverse these *stance*-signalingcitation embeddings can be is shown especially in Yang's (2013) discussion of *reporting evidentials.* Using the example of English academic articles, Yang demonstrates a wide variety of lexico-grammatical realizations and phraseological patterns of citation. Yang's inventory-based classification—with the aim of accounting for all forms of marking *reporting evidentials*—is even broader than that of Lenk (2008), who had already moved beyond the traditional focus on verbs by including expressions embedding citations. Accordingly, Yang (2013) also considers 'minimal markings' such as the conventionalized parenthetical reference to the source including author and year of publication. Including this form of marking under evidentiality categories is, on the one hand, of course, reasonable; the parenthetical source reference explicitly proves the origin of information.[11] On the other hand, this again highlights the terminological weaknesses and conflicts regarding the relationship between *stance,* modality, and epistemicity. If, as presented in Sect. 4.3, evidentiality is subsumed under epistemicity and source references are in turn counted as evidentiality, then source references would be epistemically *stance*-marking and would therefore contain a subjective nuance. A source reference *can* certainly be supplemented with epistemic features—for example, in the form of reference labels (see also Sect. 2.1.3.4)—but for its 'classic' variant, consisting of author and year (possibly also page numbers), it remains to be discussed whether there is room for the subjectivity of the citer in such a mandatory and standardized mention.

[11] Furthermore, Yang (2013: 122) defines the terms evidentiality and evaluation very broadly for the purposes of her study, so that even the selection of the cited source already contains an evaluative element.

As further evidentiality markers, Yang (2013) names, in addition to verbal and nominal realizations, also adjuncts accompanying citations(e.g., *according to*). This again confirms that the focus on *verba dicendi* is insufficient for the analysis of citation embeddings. If Yang's findings are transferred to German, it can be concluded that prepositions can also function as important means of embedding quotations. The preposition *gemäß* is found in abundance in legal texts:

(4) The operative part of the decision has the force of law pursuant to §31 para. 2 BVerfGG. (15.01.1985 2nd Senate BVerfGE 69, 92)

Yang (2013: 123) attributes a potential evaluative force to all forms of evidentiality marking with regard to the cited content. The markings "help the writer to differentiate his various degrees of commitment to the cited messages, which at the same time demonstrate implicitly the writer's personal stance towards the cited author."

4.4 Stancetaking Repertoires in Cross-Linguistic Comparison

Just as the manner of citing depends on the distinct language, so too does the use of stance-marking devices. For citations, it is highly regulated which operations, for example, must be performed to transfer a direct quotation into a context of indirectness. For instance, English grammar requires, depending on the tense of the verb accompanying the citation, a temporal shift within the citation(see also the characterization of indirect citation in Sect. 2.1.3.2).[12]

For stance-marking, there are also grammatical norms on the one hand, but on the other hand, it is above all sociocultural conventions that determine the appropriateness or inappropriateness of using these markers. The resulting cross-linguistic differences are discussed below.

The problematization of these differences constitutes an important foundation for comparative studies that—like the present investigation—compare corpora from different languages. The analysis of which stance-marking devices a writer chooses when embedding a citation can only be conducted with consideration of the stance repertoire available to them in a given language. An obvious example of differing stance repertoires in German and English is the subjunctive. The use of the subjunctive as (potentially epistemic) evidential marking in German has already been explained. The English *conditional*, which is at least in some dimensions of use similar to the German subjunctive, cannot, however, be employed as

[12] The requirements of individual languages can also affect the choice of reporting expressions themselves; see further the cross-linguistic (German vs. French) approach of Sabban (1978).

such a resource.[13] In a comparison of modality in German and English, Abraham/Leiss (2013: 1) therefore state that

> Modality […] in German is encoded in a much more overt and thus more transparent way in cross-linguistic comparison than in most other languages. […] In addition, the system of modal verbs in German is far more systematically organized than, for example, in English, where the system is in a state of dissolution and reorganization.

From a contrastive linguistic perspective—here, German and English—the analysis of modal verb usage proves to be particularly delicate; other categories, such as stance-marking adverbs, behave similarly (at least in comparison between Romance languages and German) (see Haßler 2015: 192).

The potentially divergent meaning or even the partial impossibility of a literal transposition of modal verbs into another language is illustrated by the following German-English translations:

(5a) Der Richter will den Fall fair entschieden haben.
(5b) *The judge wants to have decided the case fairly.
(5c) The judge claims to have decided the case fairly.
(6a) Der Richter soll den Fall fair entschieden haben.
(6b) The judge should have decided the case fairly.
(6c) The judge is said to have decided the case fairly.

Attempts at literal translation either result in *ungrammatical constructions (*5b) or in a loss of the original sentence meaning (4b), that is, ultimately, in an incorrect translation. Since the modal verbs "should" and "want" (as supposed translations of "wollen" and "sollen") are not used in a reportative/quotative sense in English, one would likely opt for a deontic reading in translating sentence (5a) into English and render it as "The judge wants the case to be decided fairly." Such a deontic interpretation of the sentence would also be possible in German depending on the context; however, it is probably less likely than the interpretation of "will" as quotative.[14]

A particularly noteworthy study with a contrastive linguistic approach is Kranich's (2011) comparison of German and English epistemic modal

---

[13] For the use of the reportative subjunctive in Romance languages, differences in its frequency of use, and its role in signaling stance, see Guentcheva (2018).

[14] Although it does not belong to the core area of *stance* analysis, it is at least worth mentioning in passing that not only quotative/reportative modal verbs behave problematically in translation. Deontic modal verbs also run the risk of meaning distortion in translation. Jaskot/Wiltos (2017), for example, reach such a conclusion in their study of Polish and English translations of the Charter of Fundamental Rights of the European Union. Jaskot/Wiltos (2017: 11) record "possible differences in meaning between functors expressing obligation, *musi, powinien, nalezy* (in Polish) and *shall, must* (in English)." As a result, according to their interpretation of the relevant Polish translations, ambiguities arise in the expressed modality: "The lack of a clear modal functor leaves ample room for possible interpretations" (ibid.; for further contrastive linguistic considerations on modal verbs, see also Mori/Okano 2013 and Mortelsmans/Vanderbiesen 2013).

expressions. In her study, using a popular science corpus, she demonstrates both quantitative and qualitative differences in "English texts, English–German translations, and German original texts" (ibid.: 77) with regard to epistemic expressions. In terms of frequency, she finds that the English texts contain significantly more epistemic expressions than their German counterparts. In addition, English texts qualitatively prefer "[m]arkers expressing mere possibility (e.g. maybe)"; German texts, by contrast, prefer "markers of high probability (e.g. probably)" (ibid.). Kranich interprets these different preferences as reflecting different orientations of the writers: while English-speaking writers orient their choice of epistemic markers toward the addressee, German-speaking writers orient their epistemic markers toward the content.

From Kranich's interpretation of the results, one can further infer that the use of hedges in English serves the relational aspect more than the nuanced expression of factuality. This thesis is also supported by the observation that the use of many hedges produces a comparatively 'more dialogic' text; a text with few hedges, in turn, is more monologic and thus more authoritative (see Kranich 2011: 94).

In a second step, Kranich analyzes how translators handle *hedges* and arrives at another interesting result: bilingual translators sometimes omit the epistemic markers used in the original when translating from English into German; the translators "find it inappropriate to use such a marker in a functionally equivalent German utterance" (2011: 93). The omission of hedges can be seen as evidence of at least implicit knowledge of the appropriateness and usage of modalization. Despite this awareness, cross-linguistic influences still seem to occur: in Kranich's study, German texts that were translations from English contained up to three times as many modalization procedures as 'original' German texts (2011: 13). Schröder (1989: 174) also cautions that special attention should be paid to hedges in translation: "[…] the conventions of hedging may be different in the two cultures involved." Even though the corpus in this study does not consist of translations, reflection on language-specific influences is relevant insofar as the influence of the legal system, rather than that of linguistic conventions, is to be measured.

As another factor influencing the choice of modalization devices, Fløttum et al. (2006: 54) also mention knowledge of appropriateness in the respective writing domain (e.g., in the academic discipline). According to Fløttum et al., disciplinary conventions are even more decisive than a writer's native language, as writers adapt their use of modalization procedures to the respective text type, even if this requires a different approach than in their native language. Whether the conventions of a discipline can be met, however, is of course also a question of linguistic competence.

The process of selecting stance-marking devices is thus, as Kranich's (2011) study in particular shows, not only dependent on the resources provided by the language; the selection also passes through a "cultural filter" (ibid.: 78). This 'filter' also seems to function—on a smaller scale—as a disciplinary-cultural filter.

4.5 Modality and Evidentiality in Legal Discourse

Continuing the fundamental assumption of intertextuality as a constitutive element of law, Cheng/Sin (2011: 126, emphasis by J.S.) highlight the dialogic character of law using the example of common law decisions:

> The court judgments in the common law system are in fact the dialogue among judges, the inter-judge dialogue or institutional dialogue (Cheng and Sin 2008), *which necessarily involves interpersonal indicators including modality.*

Since the act of engagement (e.g., of a quoter with a quotation) in turn brings about the necessity of positioning, the fundamental dialogicity and intertextuality of law also underlie the presence of subjectivizing and modalizing procedures: "Modality in legal settings [...] is of crucial importance" (Cheng/Sin 2011: 124). The concept of modality should be understood broadly here, as both deontic and epistemic modality are of particular significance in the context of law. It is hardly surprising that the use of deontic modal verbs is frequent in legal language. After all, determining what one *can, may, must* or *should* do is among the central tasks of law—deontic modal verbs express permissions, obligations, prohibitions, and requirements (see also Cheng 2017: 20). As necessary and established as the use of modal verbs in this function is in legal texts, their interpretation is equally problematic. Due to their polyfunctionality, the interpretation of modal verbs can be ambiguous.[15]

In addition to deontic modality, legal texts also contain markers of stance, that is, of epistemicity and evidentiality. These markers appear both in the form of citation-accompanying phrases and in the form of adjectives and adverbs. For the latter, Rozumko (2017) notes a frequent use of the adverb "reportedly" in legal discourse. From this, one could hypothesize that the signaling of evidentiality in legal discourse is weighted more highly than the nuance of probabilities—Rozumko, for example, finds far fewer occurrences of the adverb "probably" (for the frequency of individual occurrences, also in interdisciplinary comparison, see 2017: 83). The occurrence of *reporting verbs* is examined by Yu (2020) using the example of their use in the construction of argumentation in common law. Yu refers to the practice of referencing in common law as a "combination of various voices" (2019: 526). In dealing with the many 'voices', both speech act verbs and verbs denoting mental processes are used—in different functions:

[15] The problem of this ambiguity can be particularly illustrated by the example of the English modal verb *shall*: Garner (2009) attests the "biggest troublemaker" (Garzone 2013: 72) *shall* to have eight different dimensions of use in legal contexts—including, for example, the use to establish obligations, but also to stipulate actions to be performed in the future (see also Goga-Vigaru 2012). In addition to the various readings within a single language, modal verbs can also pose a major challenge, especially in the translation of legal texts into other languages. Whether a modal verb is read deontically or epistemically undoubtedly has a significant impact on the interpretation of the law (see further Jaskot/Wiltos 2017).

> Judicial speech act verbs and judicial mental verbs are applied differently to enhance the authority of the reporters and externalise the individuals' reasoning process. Therefore, speech and thought are presented differently in judicial contexts. The two types of reporting verbs embody significant degrees of dialogicality. The construction of judicial arguments is highly goal-oriented, constructing legal facts or statements. Judicial speech act reporting verbs enhance the authority of the sentencing, whereas judicial mental reporting verbs are more likely to present the personal reasoning process of the decision making.

The study of stance markers in legal discourse is, overall, a comparatively under-researched field. Studies that provide particularly comprehensive sets of analysis categories for potentially subjectivizing linguistic means in law include those by Vass (2015) and Szczyrbak (2014). Comparing *Law Review* articles and *Supreme Court* decisions, Vass (2015) uses a concordance analysis to examine a small corpus of lexical hedges (a detailed list of potential hedges in Vass 2015: 29, including epistemic modal verbs (e.g., "might"), other epistemic verbs (e.g., "doubt, think, believe"), epistemic nouns (e.g., "likelihood"), epistemic adjectives (e.g., "questionable"), and epistemic adverbs (e.g., "maybe", "possibly")). The comparative approach shows a significant difference in the use of hedges between the two text types: In *Law Review* articles, about 25% more hedges are used compared to Supreme Court decisions. In addition to this quantitative difference, qualitative differences can also be observed regarding the preference for certain hedge types. The range of hedge types used in the articles is broader than in the decisions, in which only a small number of epistemic nouns and epistemic adverbs are found; the Supreme Court relies comparatively more often on epistemic adjectives (Vass 2015: 33).

Which and *how many* hedges are used thus depends, according to Vass, on the specific text type of legal discourse and its associated function—for example, discursive engagement in scholarly articles or determination in judgments. Szczyrbak (2014) examines "evidence from US Supreme Court Opinions" with regard to "stancetaking strategies in judicial discourse" (as the title of the study puts it). In her comprehensive *stance analysis framework* (ibid.: 102), she operationalizes the various manifestations of stance as well as the corresponding linguistic features in a step-by-step manner. Szczyrbak's overall findings diagnose a diverse set of tools for marking *stance:*

> […] the repertoire of linguistic resources which US Supreme Court Justices use to convey stance is quite varied, with the justices employing a wide range of linguistic markers and their combinations to express personal feelings and subjective assessments.

The frequency of stance markers varies remarkably depending on whether it is a majority opinion, a dissenting opinion (*dissenting*), or a *concurring opinion* (ibid.: 116 f.): When a justice holds a view different from the majority opinion or arrives at the same decision as the *majority opinion* but for different reasons, they use more stance markers.

4.6 Interim Conclusion III

The preceding chapter has shown how those who cite can linguistically realize their positioning toward cited content. Especially when a citer does not fully identify with the content of their citation (recall here the memorable observation by Berkenkotter and Huckins [1995]: "you are what you cite"), they can use evaluative citation embeddings to express differentiated and nuanced attitudes toward the content. The linguistic repertoire available for evaluative citation embeddings and its functional qualities, as the survey has shown, are diverse.

- For the analysis of positioning, the concepts of stance, modality, and evidentiality can be employed. The classification and subordination of the categories modality, epistemicity, and evidentiality have proven terminologically challenging. Boundaries—such as when a marker is a non-evaluative, 'objective' indication of a citation and when it constitutes epistemic marking—cannot always be clearly drawn. Broad, expansive subcategorizations, such as subsuming evidentiality under epistemic modality, are controversial—this became particularly evident in the later discussion about the epistemic quality of the subjunctive.
- The modalizing function of the hedges and boosters introduced in Sect. 4.2.1 is, by contrast, undisputed. In terms of analyzing citation functions, they are promising indicators insofar as their respective functions are richly documented. An example of a typical function of hedges is the avoidance of so-called *face threatening acts*.
- What can function as a hedge or booster at the word level was then explored using the example of epistemic adverbs. Since epistemic marking via adverbs operates through a single, inherently epistemic element—and not, as with modal verbs, through context-dependent constructions—these are comparatively simple positioning strategies to identify.
- Sect. 4.3.2, with its presentation of various citation-accompanying expressions, serves as an argument for expanding the 'traditional' perspective, which focuses on the use of *verba dicendi.* Verbs certainly play a significant role in introducing and concluding citations, but this function (as in judicial decisions, for example) can also be fulfilled by nominal or prepositional elements.
- Whether the subjunctive as an evidential in the context of citation reproduction has more than one possible interpretation is disputed. What is certain is that, as a quotative, it marks the indirectness of a statement and the act of citing. It is, however, controversial whether it also entails epistemic distancing. A strong argument for an epistemic quality is the inappropriateness of using the subjunctive in affirmative citation.
- Contrastive linguistic analysis forms an important basis when one wishes to interpret the use of modalizing devices. Using English and German as examples, it was shown that the use of hedges—even in the same genre and with the same content—varies depending on the language. The use of hedges also depends, among other things, on the cultural and social conventions of a language (and, for example, on genre conventions).

- In legal discourse, both deontic and epistemic modalities play a role. The frequent occurrence of the former embodies the functional logic of law—it determines what one *can, may, must* or *should* do. The epistemic modalities relevant to this study in law can—as has been shown for common law—be understood as expressions of judicial dialogue and intertextual engagement. Their use varies with the respective actions in the decisions; the act of questioning and rejecting leads to an increased frequency of modalization procedures. *Dissenting* and *concurring opinions* therefore contain more hedges.

A review of the surveyed theory highlights the following research desideratum in particular: Studies that deal with various forms of stance signaling mention the relationship of modalization procedures to intertextual references only in passing. Although this connection is indeed explicitly named in theoretical approaches (e.g., hedges as "marker of intertextuality and interdiscursivity" in Vass 2015: 135), it is not taken into account in the operationalization of studies. In all the studies presented, the results do not differentiate whether the identified modalization procedures occur in relation to the presentation of one's own or others' content. Previous studies have dealt *either* with the visibility of an author and their (explicit or implicit) stance signaling *or* with the manifestations of others' content; combinatory approaches are lacking.

> In many studies [...], the self (or the *I/we*) perspective and different types of self-mention constitute an important dimension [...]. The *other* (or *you/they*) perspective, studied for example through bibliographical references and citations, is another important dimension [...]. However, the self perspective in combination with the other perspective seems to have been examined less [...]. (Fløttum 2005: 29f.)

To capture the functionalization of citations, however, such a combinatory perspective is indispensable, because—as Fløttum's terminology puts it—the way the *self* of a text relates to the *others* fundamentally determines the functional potential of citations.

Chapter 5
Citation Practices Depending on Legal Systems: *Common Law* and *Civil Law*

Citations are required in judicial decisions—as already discussed in Chap. 3, citations serve a variety of functions in legal writing, which is characterized by a high degree of intertextuality. They can establish connections between decisions and statutes, or between different judicial decisions themselves, thereby contributing to the process of decision-making, the reasoning behind decisions, and the legitimacy of those decisions. However, this analysis requires further differentiation, since, as previously noted, the intended function of a citation can vary depending on the requirements and objectives of a particular text type or individual text. For judicial decisions, it is also true that they are shaped by the respective legal tradition. The legal system, as well as the interpretive methodology specific to each legal tradition, imposes certain requirements on the use of sources. These may, for example, concern the type of sources cited—such as the requirement in *Common Law* systems to cite precedents, which, in *Civil Law* systems, play a lesser role at least in terms of their legal authority. A central concern of this work is to examine whether patterns can be identified in citation practices that correlate with the respective legal tradition.

Although there are as yet no data-driven comparative analyses of citation practices in *Common Law* and *Civil Law* systems, this question has at least been addressed with regard to the selection of legal sources. The two legal traditions—beyond the sources that must be considered by law—tend to prefer different types of legal sources:

> In the Anglo-American judicial tradition, however, the favoured weapon in the explanatory arsenal of judges is a reference to the decisions (that is, to the logical arguments that have been given as reasons to explain the outcome) of other judges in previously decided cases in their own and other courts. This means that the citation patterns of individual judges and, therefore, of the courts that are the collegial aggregate of those judges are an important statement of judicial influence, all the more valuable for the fact that judges have explicitly acknowledged that influence as part of the rational process that explains and justifies their actions to their fellow professionals. The preference for judicial

© The Author(s), under exclusive license to Springer-Verlag GmbH, DE, part of Springer Nature 2025

J. Steigler-Herms, *How and Why Do Courts Cite?*,
https://doi.org/10.1007/978-3-662-71934-3_5

> citations in the explanatory process itself distinguishes Anglo-American judges from their continental European counterparts, who are more likely to build their own reasons for outcomes around academic textbooks. (McCormick 1995: 455f.)

This chapter (Chapter 5) explores what other differences exist, beyond the preference for certain legal sources. It begins with an introduction to the theory of legal traditions and a comparison of the two major legal traditions, *Common Law* and *Civil Law,* in Sect. 5.1. The discussion of both legal traditions includes, among other things, insights into their legal foundations and methods of interpretation.

Sect. 5.2 then focuses on two prominent representatives of each legal tradition—the *Federal Constitutional Court* and the *Supreme Court of Canada.* While the citation practices of these two courts have not yet been compared in previous studies, they have been examined individually. Sect. 5.3 discusses the findings of these studies.

5.1 Legal Traditions: *Common Law* and *Civil Law*

Common Law and *Civil Law* are two prominent representatives of the world's legal traditions. They exhibit remarkable differences in their approaches to decision-making, for even though "law seems to be a universal phenomenon," the "legal systems of the world differ significantly from one another in both substance and style" (Hilgendorf 2017: 30). The categorization of different legal systems, such as *Civil Law* and *Common Law,* is the subject of the theory of legal traditions (*Rechtskreislehre*). Legal traditions, also referred to as legal families or legal cultures, group legal systems according to their 'degree of kinship' and similarities (Kötz 2009). In addition to the Anglo-American and Continental European legal traditions, examples include the Islamic, Jewish, and Far Eastern legal traditions. In a rather undifferentiated manner, David (1992) groups these legal traditions under *autres systèmes* in contrast to the socialist and Romano-Germanic legal families. David's classification is based on the criterion of ideology, one of many possible typological criteria. The assignment of a legal system to a particular legal tradition can vary depending on the chosen criterion. Various typological criteria can be used to determine similarities and differences, including spatial classification, classification by ideology, and classification by so-called styles. The criterion of spatial classification proceeds by continent and thus refers, for example, to Continental European, African, and Asian law. Such broad groupings are sometimes considered meaningless in comparative law (cf. Glenn 2006: 421). Far more informative are multi-criteria approaches that use the concept of style as defined by Zweigert (1961). Here, style is a collective term for the prevailing ideologies and ways of thinking in a legal system, its characteristic institutions, its history, its methods of interpretation, and, not least, the types of binding and non-binding legal sources it employs. The last two criteria—legal methodology and legal sources—are often used to compare *Common Law* and *Civil Law.* The criterion of binding authority is reflected, for example, in the contrast between judge-made law and statutory law. Both aspects are discussed in more detail in Sects. 5.1.1 and 5.1.2. The approach to legal reasoning also distinguishes the two legal traditions. *Common Law* is characterized by an inductive approach, while *Civil Law* follows a deductive approach:

> Put simply: when a continental lawyer wants to find information on a particular legal question, they reach for a comprehensive legal treatise and consult the table of contents to locate the relevant information based on its systematic structure. In the case of a commentary, the structure is replaced by the statutory text. By contrast, a common law lawyer would start with the index. (Röhl/Röhl 2001: 3)

Reflections of this kind, as well as the identification and, above all, the comparison of legal traditions, are part of what is known as comparative law (*Rechtsvergleichung*). Comparative law, as a methodological sub-discipline of legal scholarship, deals with the comparison of statutes or, more generally, the law of different countries or legal traditions (Beck 2021: 81). The objectives of such research can vary, especially since comparative law as a methodology is not tied to any particular legal discipline; that is, comparisons are made in civil law, public law, and criminal law alike. Beck (ibid.) sees the "main incentive for comparative activity in the field of legal scholarship" in the "attempt to optimize one's own solutions to social conflicts."

5.1.1 The Continental European Legal System: The Civil Law

The continental European legal system is often referred to as *Civil Law*, especially in contrast to the *Common Law* and in the context of comparative law. Terminologically, two potential misunderstandings should be noted: The term *Civil Law* carries the risk of being mistakenly understood as the English translation of the German term "Zivilrecht" (civil law in the sense of private law). Conversely, the term "continental European legal system" may misleadingly suggest a purely geographical reference. This is also incorrect, as not all countries whose legal systems can be described as continental European are actually located in continental Europe (both terminological notes according to Kischel 2019: 389).

To characterize *Civil Law*, the criterion of the source of law is usually applied. Continental European law is statutory law, meaning that statutes are the primary source and are primarily used for decision-making (see ibid., 392). This presupposes the existence of a *codification*, that is, a systematic body of law that enables the assignment of cases to statutes. The term codification refers to "the comprehensive planning and structuring of law in a particular area […]. In terms of content, codification aims for simplicity, consistency, and completeness" (Kroppenberg 2004: col. 1918). In addition, the results of such systematization, such as the German Civil Code (BGB), are also referred to as codifications.

The practice of codification has its historical roots in the era of Roman law. In 528, Emperor Justinian commissioned a written compilation of Roman law.

The resulting *Corpus Juris Civilis* was initially not further received after the fall of the Western Roman Empire; however, it was rediscovered, taught, and disseminated in the 12th century. As the *jus commune,* the code was intended to be applied throughout the Western world, beyond the borders of Italy. By no later than 200 years later, reference to the code had become established in legal practice as well, so that, among other things, judicial opinions were based on the codified law of Justinian (Röhl 2001: 5 f.; Dainow 1966: 419–421). A comparable orientation toward codes has persisted to this day.

The establishment of codifications as binding sources of law in the continental European legal system presupposes a positivist understanding of law; *Civil Law* focuses on statutory texts and legal doctrine.[1] Other law outside the codes (e.g., legal concepts, sense of justice) is therefore not taken into account in practice:

> The practicing continental European lawyer, in searching for legal norms, consults the statute without concerning themselves with the possible existence of a general order of justice postulated by natural law, which could produce norms valid independently of human legislation. (Kischel 2019: 393).

To assign a specific case to legal norms in practice, *Civil Law* employs the method of *subsumption.* Subsumptive application of the law is based, among other things, on the formation of syllogisms; it examines whether and to what extent a concrete case can be assigned to an abstract norm (for further reading on the theory and technique of subsumption, see, e.g., Gröschner 2014). Against this background, the question of the judge's role also arises. Theoretically, *Civil Law* is not judge-made law; law is not supposed to be *created* by judges through case decisions, but rather *ascertained* objectively. In practice, however, due to the "creative element," it is more accurate to speak of the creation of law rather than its mere discovery (Czermak 2021: 20). In this context, the ideal formulated by Montesquieu (1748, cited after 1834: 296), who described the judge as "la bouche qui prononce les paroles de la loi," is often quoted and also criticized. According to him, judgments should never be more than "un texte précis de la loi" (ibid., 305). From a legal-linguistic perspective, this ideal is regarded as the "fiction of automatic subsumption" (Busse 1992: 18), since the "rhetorical façade of mere legal recognition" always involves "actual decision-making processes" (Christensen/ Jeand'Heur 1989: 9)—and thus judicial subjectivity.

Furthermore, the primacy of legal norms does not mean that no other sources besides binding statutory texts are or may be used in the process of legal decision-making or law creation. Established and legitimate sources of legal knowledge include, for example, precedents and scholarly writings. Although continental European law is not bound by precedent, it is common in legal education to engage

[1] This is a simplified account, which is open to challenge from a legal-philosophical perspective. Although adherence to codifications has become legally established, debates about the relationship between natural law and positivism remain unresolved. Furthermore, the law itself allows for the possibility of judging other laws as unjust and therefore void. Codified law is not unassailable.

with, for instance, the case law of the Federal Court of Justice when solving cases (Hilgendorf 2017: 31). The less a particular area of law is regulated and codified, the more frequently precedents are taken into account, and "in areas that are less strictly regulated by statute, such as constitutional law or labor law, the proportion of judge-made law is higher than, for example, in criminal law" (ibid.).

Such gaps in the law can also be closed by taking academic literature into account. Scholarship and law are closely intertwined in the continental European legal sphere. There is "a lively exchange between academic engagement with the law and its practical application. Not only do practitioners often act as authors and scholars occasionally work in practice. Both sides also enrich each other in terms of content" (Kischel 2019: 470). Hilgendorf (2017: 31) sees a close connection between legal scholarship and the judiciary:

> Legal scholars teaching at universities, that is, professors of law, in Germany, Switzerland, or Austria, for example, generally argue from the perspective of the practitioner, that is, from an internal perspective of the law. In this, they do not differ from judges, who also strive to apply the law systematically. Legal scholarship and the judiciary work closely together in most continental European countries. This is especially true in Germany, where it is more or less taken for granted that legal scholars and judges attend conferences together, publish in the same journals, and exchange arguments with one another.

Overall, legal practice in the continental European legal system is thus strongly shaped by scholarship. This is reflected, among other things, in the style of judicial decisions, which is characterized by systematic reasoning and, linguistically, by a scholarly tone. The style of judgments, especially those of the highest courts, resembles that of academic legal treatises. It is objective and depersonalized:

> A judgment of a German court is therefore typically clearly structured and considerably more detailed than its French counterpart. The writing style is factual and impersonal, meaning that it is not the judge as an individual who speaks, but the court in the name of the people; the pronoun "I" is not used. In terms of content, the judgment follows the basic principles of subsumption, that is, it explains which legal norms are fulfilled or not fulfilled by breaking them down into their components, defining these, and applying the definitions and, where applicable, sub-definitions to the facts. In doing so, it usually not only addresses the opposing views of the losing party, but also analyzes case law and academic literature, which, outside of routine cases, are often cited extensively. (Kischel 2019: 468)

A more detailed discussion of the last aspect, namely citations, is provided in Sect. 5.3.

5.1.2 *The Anglo-American Legal System: The Common Law*

The *Common Law* legal system prevails in many English-speaking countries, such as the USA, Australia, and—particularly relevant for this study—Canada. Before discussing this legal system, a few terminological remarks should be made. The perspective of this study is based on a legal-systematic definition of

Common Law, using the term to refer to the entire Anglo-American legal system. In the doctrine of legal sources, however, the term is defined more narrowly as pure case law, which is to be distinguished from statutory law (*Statute Law*) (Handschug 2003: 12).

Common Law has its roots in twelfth-century England. With the establishment of a royal court (*Curia Regis*), King Henry II created a supreme court that was superior to the local courts. In cases of disagreement in judicial decisions, the local courts were required to follow the decisions of the royal court. In this way, he not only strengthened his own power but also promoted the uniformity of judicial decisions and, at the same time, legal certainty through a certain predictability of rulings. Today, the term *Common Law* refers to countries whose legal systems have been influenced by the English legal system of that time (Byrd et al. 2021: 3 f.).

Whenever a court is required to take into account the decisions of another court in its own decision-making process, there is a binding effect of precedent. On this basis, judges identify right and wrong (so-called judge-made law). The role of precedent is considered the central characteristic, which is used not only to describe *Common Law* in more detail, but also to distinguish it from the *Civil Law* system. Precedents, defined as "prior decisions that function as models for later decisions" (MacCormick/Summers 1997: 1), support both the decision-making process and the reasoning behind decisions. The binding effect of *precedents* is also referred to as the *stare decisis et non quieta movere* doctrine—judges in the *Common Law* system are to "stand by what has been decided and not disturb what is settled" (Vogenauer 2009: 1304). By means of analogical reasoning, an attempt is made to inductively extract a general guiding principle from a decision and to apply this principle to the case at hand (Handschug 2003: 13). The binding effect applies only to this "guiding principle," which does not necessarily coincide with the entire content of a decision: The *stare decisis* doctrine refers to the *ratio decidendi* of a decision and not to *obiter dicta:*

> In common law countries, the doctrine of stare decisis has been firmly established in legal theory. The doctrine has been developed over many centuries and is based on a distinction between ratio decidendi and obiter dicta, where ratio decidendi is defined as the reasoning that decides a case, and obiter dicta is defined as non-binding remarks made in the judgment, but which is not directly linked to the reasoning that determines the case. (Palmer/Christensen 2021: 18)

The *ratio decidendi* contains the reasoning for the decision, whereas *obiter* are irrelevant in terms of binding effect. The inclusion of non-binding *obiter dicta* in decisions is sometimes viewed critically, since, in contrast to the *rationes decidendi,* they "have no significance for the decision of a specific case and no binding force for other panels or courts. They state what would be the case if things were as they are not. This is usually superfluous and sometimes dangerous: The next time it really matters in a case, entirely different judges may be involved or different opinions may be held. Obiter dicta therefore do not have a good reputation: 'They puff up their cheeks where there is nothing to whistle.'"[2] (Schulz 2018: 403).

Characterizing *Common Law* by its binding effect of precedent is common and allows for a distinction from the codification of *Civil Law,* but at the same time carries the risk of a narrow perspective on Anglo-American jurisprudence (cf. Röhl 2008: 3) and of neglecting its statutes: In Canada, both *cases* and *statutes* are used as sources of law (see also Sect. 5.2.2). *Statutes* are laws to be interpreted objectively, according to the intent of the legislature:

> A statute is the will of legislature, and the fundamental rule of interpretation, to which all others are subordinate, is, that a statute is to be expounded, according to the intent of those who made it. [...] The fundamental maxim of sound interpretation is: ita scriptum est, and it is not the business of courts to be wiser than the laws and to mould them with judicial views of what is just or unjust. The letter of the law is the law itself. (Maxwell 1946: 1f)

It is not always clear whether a case should be decided on the basis of *statutes* or *cases.* Handschug (2003: 16) therefore points to a complex relationship between statutory law and case law in Canada; thus, precedents can also be incorporated into formal statutes and codified.

5.2 Two Representatives of the Legal Systems: BVerfG and SCC

With a research corpus consisting of decisions from the Federal Constitutional Court and the Supreme Court of Canada, this comparative study focuses on two courts that, among other things, exhibit significant differences due to their affiliation with different legal systems. This concerns the categories already presented in Sects. 5.1.1 and 5.1.2, such as the binding force of different sources of law and methods of interpretation, but also other characteristics of the courts that may influence their citation practices. These include, for example, the special role of judges as individual decision-makers at the Supreme Court of Canada, as well as the specific structure of decisions at the Federal Constitutional Court. The following Sects. 5.2.1 and 5.2.2 address these and other fundamental features of the two courts.

[2] The *ratio decidendi* and *obiter dictum* are not concepts unique to decisions in the *Common Law* system; the criticism cited from Schulz was originally made in reference to German law. However, the distinction between the two is far more relevant for *Common Law* than for *Civil Law,* because the *ratio decidendi* forms the core of the *stare decisis* doctrine.

5.2.1 The Federal Constitutional Court

As the "guardian of the constitution," the Federal Constitutional Court (BVerfG) occupies an outstanding position in the legal system and is vested with extensive powers. It is the highest court in Germany and a prominent representative of the *Civil Law* legal system.

Constitutional jurisdiction, defined as "jurisdiction exercised directly in constitutional matters" (Eichenberger 1983: 437), is exercised in Germany by the Federal Constitutional Court (BVerfG). Its extensive powers are guaranteed, among other things, by Article 93 of the Basic Law. The first paragraph of this article stipulates that the Federal Constitutional Court "shall decide on the interpretation of this Basic Law in the event of disputes concerning the scope of the rights and duties of a supreme federal body or other parties vested with their own rights by this Basic Law or by the rules of procedure of a supreme federal body." Further details regarding the jurisdiction of the BVerfG are governed by the Federal Constitutional Court Act (BVerfGG) according to the principle of enumeration. Section 13 of the BVerfGG contains 15 paragraphs outlining the decision-making powers of the BVerfG, which—just to name a few examples—range from decisions on the forfeiture of fundamental rights (BVerfGG § 13 para. 1, see also Art. 18 GG[3]) to the unconstitutionality of political parties (BVerfGG § 13 para. 2) and the compatibility of laws with the Basic Law in cases of disputes (BVerfGG § 13 paras. 6, 6a, 6b).

The types of proceedings differ in terms of their subject matter and possible consequences, but they have at least two things in common: the BVerfG always bases its decisions on the Basic Law, and the court acts only upon application; it is not a court of super-appeal. A summary classification of the types of proceedings assigned to the BVerfG by law can be found in Schlaich/Korioth (2018: 7):

1. Judicial review of statutes
2. Constitutional complaint
3. Proceedings for the protection of the constitution and proceedings for the review of elections and mandates
4. Federal disputes
5. Disputes between constitutional organs

[3]Article 13 GG explicitly designates the BVerfG as the decision-making body in cases of forfeiture of fundamental rights: "Anyone who abuses the freedom of expression, in particular the freedom of the press (Article 5 para. 1), the freedom of teaching (Article 5 para. 3), the freedom of assembly (Article 8), the freedom of association (Article 9), the secrecy of correspondence, posts and telecommunications (Article 10), property (Article 14), or the right of asylum (Article 16a) to fight against the free democratic basic order, forfeits these fundamental rights. The forfeiture and its extent shall be pronounced by the Federal Constitutional Court."

Constitutional complaints make up a significant majority of all proceedings before the BVerfG. In its 2021 annual report[4] the BVerfG therefore refers to itself as a "citizens' court":

> Even in the anniversary year 2021, the number of new cases registered remained consistently high at 5,352. The fact that constitutional complaints accounted for an overwhelming majority of 95% of proceedings underscores the character of the Federal Constitutional Court as a citizens' court. The total of 10,265 entries in the General Register also shows that the low-threshold access to the court was actively used.

A constitutional complaint, recognizable in the BVerfG's case numbers by the abbreviation BvR, can in principle be filed by any person, since, as provided in Article 93 para. 4 of the Basic Law, the BVerfG decides "on constitutional complaints that may be filed by anyone claiming that one of their fundamental rights or one of the rights contained in Articles 20 para. 4, 33, 38, 101, 103, 104 has been violated by public authority." In this sense, the constitutional complaint is a procedure for the protection of fundamental rights and serves as a form of individual legal protection. Prerequisites for the acceptance of a constitutional complaint before the BVerfG include, among others, the fundamental constitutional relevance of a case and the exhaustion of legal remedies. Before a constitutional complaint can be filed, all ordinary procedural remedies (e.g., appeal, etc.) before the hierarchically subordinate specialized courts must have been exhausted.

The Federal Constitutional Court consists of two panels, the First Senate and the Second Senate. They differ in terms of their jurisdiction: the First Senate of the BVerfG is primarily responsible for judicial review proceedings and constitutional complaints (BVerfGG § 14 para. 1). The jurisdiction of the Second Senate includes, for example, the unconstitutionality of political parties (BVerfGG § 14 para. 1), complaints against decisions of the Bundestag (BVerfGG § 14 para. 3), and disputes concerning the rights and duties of the Federation and the Länder (BVerfGG § 14 para. 7). In some cases, it is not clear whether jurisdiction lies with the First or Second Senate; in such cases, a committee decides (BVerfGG § 14 para. 5). Each Senate is composed of eight judges. The procedures for appointment, selection criteria for qualification, and terms of office are governed by §§ 2–12 of the BVerfGG.

In principle, the BVerfG must observe the same methods of legal interpretation as other courts. These may include interpretation according to the wording of the law, systematic interpretation, teleological interpretation, or the so-called historical interpretation (see Czermak 2021: 20). Despite this differentiated methodology, problems of interpretation may arise due to the indeterminacy of legal norms.

> The judges of the BVerfG must take into account specific problems of legal application and legal development. Fundamental rights are, to a large extent, highly abstract, so that it is difficult, if not impossible, to derive or develop practical principles from their text. For the legal details of practical cases, they usually provide little to no guidance. (Czermak 2021: 22)

[4] Available at: https://www.bundesverfassungsgericht.de/DE/Presse/jahresberichte/jahresberichte.html.

This makes the legitimacy of decisions all the more important, which is supported not only by the substantive reasoning but also by the structural composition of the decisions, as discussed below. Fundamentally, a distinction must first be made between judgments and orders: "A decision based on oral proceedings is issued as a judgment, decisions without oral proceedings as an order" (§ 25 para. 2 BVerfGG). Regardless, the written decisions of the BVerfG (judgments and orders) can structurally be divided into four sections; they begin with *unofficial guiding principles,* followed by the *rubrum.* Central are the *operative part* (decision formula) set out thereafter and the *reasons for the decision,* which can in turn be subdivided into the facts of the case (marked 'A'), admissibility ('B'), and the section on standards and subsumption ('C.I.' & 'C.II.') that contains the reasoning on the merits (see the presentation of the decision structure in Klatt 2020).

The *guiding principles* that open the decisions are not part of the decision-making process itself, but rather serve as a kind of summary of the statements in a decision considered central. The selection of these aspects, which are presented before the rubrum, can provide insight into which reasons the judges consider decisive (Klatt 2020: 70). In the well-known 'Esra decision' on the ban of the novel of the same name (BVerfGE 119,1 decision of 13.06.2007, case no. 1 BvR 1783/05), for example, the BVerfG sets out four guiding principles on the general issue of balancing artistic freedom and the right to personality.

The subsequent *rubrum* contains the factual key data of the case; these are the subject matter of the proceedings and the case number, as well as the names of all parties involved, i.e., the parties and also the judges.

The operative part, also referred to as the 'decision formula,' is central in that it contains the actual decision. In this section, the Federal Constitutional Court (BVerfG) determines the legal consequences it has decided upon. In the case of the previously mentioned 'Esra decision,' it states (in excerpts):

> The judgment of the Federal Court of Justice of June 21, 2005—VI ZR 122/04 –, the final judgment of the Higher Regional Court of Munich of April 6, 2004—18 U 4890/03—as well as the final judgment of the Regional Court of Munich I of October 15, 2003—9 O 11360/03—violate the complainant's fundamental right under Article 5(3), sentence 1 of the Basic Law, insofar as the judgments granted the second plaintiff the right to prohibit the complainant, under threat of a fine, from publishing or causing to be published, distributing or causing to be distributed, delivering or causing to be delivered, and advertising or causing to be advertised the book "Esra" in the version according to the declaration of commitment of August 18, 2003. The constitutional complaint is otherwise dismissed.

The reasons that led the Federal Constitutional Court to determine these legal consequences are explained in the section on the *grounds for the decision.* These are introduced by a presentation of the *facts of the case (A)* and the *admissibility requirements (B).* This is followed by the *standards section (C.I.) and the application section (C.II.),* which can be summarized as the *merits (C).*

At the end of a decision, dissenting opinions and separate votes may be presented; however, in the practice of the Federal Constitutional Court, this is rarely the case (for more on separate opinions at the Federal Constitutional Court, see Klatt 2023).

Lepsius (2006: 123) describes the structure of decisions, and especially the establishment of the court's own standards in the standards section, as a specific decision-making technique that has contributed to the court's high standing and acceptance by other courts:

> By developing its own standards, the material primacy of the constitution is transposed onto the institutional position of the court. Taken to the extreme, one could say: the court's success depends on its self-invention as a standard-setting authority. The guardian of the constitution can become the master of the constitution. (Lepsius 2006: 129)

Klatt expresses a similar view regarding the role of the standards section (2020: 79 f.):

> In the standards section (usually: C.I.), the Federal Constitutional Court acts as an interpreter of the constitution. Here, deliberately removed from the specific facts of the case, the content of constitutional norms is worked out objectively and in the abstract. [...] In this way, the court acquires an exceptionally high degree of substantive authority over constitutional interpretation.

The fact that the Federal Constitutional Court frequently cites passages from standards it has formulated in previous decisions, as an alternative to statutory sources, is sometimes criticized as a departure from the constitutional text (Czermak 2021: 122; see also Sect. 5.3.1).

5.2.2 *The Supreme Court of Canada*

The Supreme Court of Canada (SCC), also referred to as the Cour Suprême du Canada (CSC) due to its bilingualism, is the highest court in Canada. As the highest appellate instance in the Canadian legal system, it can alter or overturn decisions of lower courts (Rémillard et al. 2017). A distinctive feature of the Canadian Supreme Court and the entire Canadian legal system is so-called *bijuralism,* meaning that both the common law and civil law traditions coexist in Canada. Depending on the area of law, either civil law or common law procedures are applied (e.g., common law in criminal law and civil law in family law), so that the SCC, strictly speaking, cannot be described as a purely common law court (see also Brown-John/Pawley 2004).

The jurisdiction of the SCC is significantly broader than that of the Federal Constitutional Court, which acts exclusively in matters of constitutional relevance. The SCC makes decisions of public interest and deals with cases in the areas of *public law, private law,* and *criminal law:*

> As Canada's final court of appeal, the Supreme Court has jurisdiction over disputes in every area of the law. Judges answer a wide variety of important questions—from child support and corporate restructuring, to treaty and constitutional rights. (SCC Annual Report 2021[5])

---

[5] Available at: https://www.scc-csc.ca/review-revue/2021/index-eng.html.

Cases involving public law account for nearly 50% of all applications for decisions, making up the majority. The SCC's currently broad jurisdiction is particularly noteworthy given that it has only exercised constitutional jurisdiction since 1984—more than a hundred years after its founding in 1875:

> […] there has been a major transformation of the Court's role in Canadian law and politics, largely a result of the Charter of Rights. Most obviously, since 1984 the Court's agenda has undergone a radical revision. […] the court no longer concerns itself mainly with the resolution of private disputes between individuals and businesses and with routine, fact-driven public law cases such tax disputes; it is now a public law Court with a special interest in constitutional issues and the interpretation of widely applicable statutes. As one of the justices noted, the orientation of the current Court is that 'we won't take cases on which the law is well settled … and we are generally not interested in cases that are 'fact driven'—'who done it' is a question for the lower courts.' (Songer 2008: 239)

The Canadian Charter of Rights and Freedoms contains the fundamental rights, is part of the Constitution Act, and is the reason why the SCC can refer to itself as "the guardian of the Constitution" (see Annual Report 2021). The court is governed by the *Supreme Court Act (Loi sur la Cour suprême).* This act not only authorizes the court to conduct supervisions, but above all regulates all structural aspects of the court, such as the composition and appointment of the judiciary. The court consists of a total of nine judges, including "the Chief Justice of Canada" and eight "puisne judges" (*Supreme Court Act* 4,1). The role of the judiciary in the SCC is particularly noteworthy, as the court is often described in terms of its individual judges. For example, the entry on the SCC in the Canadian Encyclopedia (Rémillard et al. 2017) devotes nearly half its content to introducing individual judges (and, in some cases, other staff members). The importance of judges as individuals (unlike the Federal Constitutional Court, which tends to appear as a depersonalized court with a collective of judges) is also reflected in academic studies on the SCC, which analyze their items separately for each judge (an example is Rado's (2020) study on the SCC's citation practices, in which the citation frequency of each judge is determined individually; see Sect. 5.3.2). It is also not uncommon in academic studies on the SCC for the judges themselves to be quoted and for the review of academic literature to be supplemented by practical experience. This is the case, for example, in Songer (2008: 110), who describes the decision-making process: "Judging can be tough. Justice Dickson is quoted as saying that he 'sweated blood' to make his judgments as clear as possible. He often worked through ten drafts of an opinion before circulating it to his colleagues."

The prominent role of judges may be one reason for the subjective element that studies on the interpretive practice of the SCC assume. As a *Common Law* court, the SCC issues decisions that other courts are obliged to follow, and it is itself bound by precedent: "It (the SCC) is the final arbiter of law in a court system based primarily on common law (using judicial precedent) and on respect for the rule of stare decisis […] This principle of upholding prior judgments lies at the heart of the judicial system" (Rémillard et al. 2017: n.p.). Like the Federal

Constitutional Court (BVerfG), the SCC is confronted with vague language in indeterminate *statute* texts (Songer 2017: 110). This necessitates an interpretive method in which judges ideally act as "impartial arbiters" without "personal opinion" (Rémillard et al. 2017: n.p.). Proponents of the so-called *attitudinal model* (e.g., Segal/Spaeth 2002), however, are critical of this, arguing that ultimately, judicial decision-making is significantly shaped by the judges' subjective attitudes toward an issue. The model describes, among other things, the influence of political convictions: "[T]hough the Court's decisions prominently cite law and precedent, those decisions are actually framed by the political attitudes of justices. [...] In summary, the evidence that the political preferences of the justices have some influence on their voting choices seems to be extremely well established" (Songer 2017: 244). Ostberg/Wetstein (2007: 4) express a similar view: It can be assumed that "the written opinions of judges, which seem to follow the norms of precedent and the plain meaning of legal texts, simply act as a rationalization for advancing the justice's own beliefs and values in the cases they decide." This raises, on the one hand, the question of whether these *attitudes, beliefs* and *values*—that is, forms of subjectivity—can also be demonstrated linguistically, especially in connection with citations, and, on the other hand, may also explain the frequency of *minority reasons*: Particularly in comparison to the Federal Constitutional Court, where dissenting opinions are rare, the frequent occurrence of *minority reasons* is striking. More than half of SCC decisions (at least in the period from 1990 to 2007, according to McCormick 2009) contain *dissenting opinions,* in which judges argue for a different outcome, or *concurring opinions,* in which judges indicate that while they support the overall outcome of the majority decision, they consider reasons other than those advanced by the majority to be decisive (ibid.: 2009: 55).

Given the subjectivity attributed to the SCC's decision-making and the prominent role of judges as individuals, it is noteworthy that McCormick/Zanoni (2019) have identified unusual trends toward collectivization and anonymization in the delivery of judgments in recent SCC decisions and, more broadly, in the entire *Common Law* tradition. In particular, decisions in constitutional matters are now often delivered unanimously in the name of the court, rather than (any longer) in the name of specific judges:

> But within the large development [of the court's decision formats] is another story, one more than anyone seems to have realized—the emergence of a highly unusual and uniquely Canadian style of delivering judgments for a select but impressive list of its major decisions, specifically for decisions in important constitutional cases. That judgment delivery style is the anonymous, and almost unanimous, *By the Court style.* We consider it unusual because for Canada, as for all the comparable countries in the common law tradition, decisions of the court are typically attributed to a single specific judge—'the judgment was delivered by Justice X'—whether the decision itself is unanimous or delivered on behalf of a majority of the panel. Our own Supreme Court, however, has invented, repeatedly used, and (perhaps) recently begun to regularize a unique style for an important subset of its decisions, under the format 'the judgment was delivered by THE COURT.' (McCormick/Zanoni 2019: 20f., emphasis in the original)

The modern structure of decisions (McCormick 2009) can also be interpreted as a form of strengthening the judicial collective. SCC decisions generally consist of the following sections (summarized after McCormick/Zanoni 2019: 24).

- Name of the case, identification of the parties involved, as well as the participating judges
- *Headnotes,* summarizing the central issue of the decision and relevant aspects of the ruling
- Description of the case
- Outcome of the decision
- Reasons for the decision
- if applicable, *minority opinions*

From a diachronic perspective, this structure represents a radical departure from the *seriatim* format that was in use until around 1960 (see McCormick 2016). In the *seriatim* structure, the judges—one after another, in sequence and without explicit reference to each other—presented their reasons for the decision within a single judgment text. This 'judge-oriented' structure, which from today's perspective could be criticized as, among other things, uneconomical and labor-intensive (McCormick/Zanoni 2009: 50 f.), has been replaced in modern decisions by a content-oriented arrangement of arguments.

5.3 On the Citation Practice of the Federal Constitutional Court and the Supreme Court of Canada

The way citations are made in judicial decisions is subject to a wide range of influences. Using the example of the Federal Constitutional Court, Jestaedt (2009: 147 f.) warns against assuming that there is *a single* citation practice among courts:

> Once again: *The* Federal Constitutional Court, strictly speaking, does not exist. Not only are the decisions and citation practices significantly shaped by the reporting judge (and their socialization); the periodic personnel changes also play a role. Ultimately, there are neither reliable statistical data on the citation practices of the Federal Constitutional Court nor a binding internal citation code for the court.

Individual factors must not be neglected when attempting to capture citation practices. The following discussion will show that, despite these individual factors, legal-system-specific tendencies in citation practice can nevertheless be identified.

5.3.1 The Citation Practice of the Federal Constitutional Court

According to former Federal Constitutional Court judge Lübbe-Wolff, engagement with a variety of sources is a regular part of deliberations at the Federal Constitutional Court. She describes the decision-making process as follows (Lübbe-Wolff 2022: 32 f.):

> The draft opinion first presents the facts of the case, including any relevant procedural history—for example, in constitutional complaints, the proceedings the complainant has already undergone to exhaust legal remedies, and their outcomes—as well as the submissions of the parties, those entitled to comment, and any expert third parties who were given the opportunity to provide statements. It also systematically analyzes the questions raised by the case, in particular addressing all legal issues involved. This includes an analysis of all relevant case law, including the jurisprudence of international and supranational courts, and the legal literature. Case law from foreign national courts is also systematically considered, insofar as it is legally relevant to the legal situation applicable to German courts, which is especially the case with findings concerning customary international law. Otherwise, the inclusion of comparative legal material in the draft opinion long depended on how useful the respective reporting judge considered it. More recently, however, such inclusion is increasingly expected, especially since an internal court *newsletter* now regularly provides information on important decisions of transnational courts and foreign constitutional courts.

Despite the significant role of citation that can be inferred from this, only a few studies have focused specifically on the citation practice of the Federal Constitutional Court. The most comprehensive scholarly examination of citations in the Court's decisions is provided by Jestaedt (2009). Given the previously discussed indeterminacy of the constitutional text, the Court can hardly provide reasoning and justification "sola lege" (or, for constitutional judges: "sola constitutione") (ibid., 142). Constitutional law must be interpreted by the judges of the Federal Constitutional Court, and "for this purpose, other sources must be tapped, not to say: other authorities must be called upon. And in this, the citation plays a role that should not be underestimated" (ibid., 143). According to Jestaedt, the use of citations at the Court can be described on three levels: Functionally, citations in the decisions are highly pragmatic; they are not intended to embellish the judge as author or the decision as a text, but serve the aforementioned purpose of providing reasons for the decision (ibid., 148). Formally, intertextual references usually appear as paraphrases and/or source references in parentheses (ibid., 149). If one examines these sources more closely in terms of who or what is being cited, they are usually either citations of hierarchically equivalent or higher courts (ibid., 144) or self-citations. Especially in addressing constitutional law issues, the Court operates self-sufficiently—the "Court's own competence, authority, and reputation, in its own estimation, rarely require reinforcement through external borrowings" (ibid., 154).[6] The vast majority of citations are self-citations: "Most frequently and most extensively, the Federal Constitutional Court cites the Federal Constitutional Court itself" (ibid., 155). This practice of self-citation has not gone without criticism. On the one hand, the often unnecessary and lengthy self-citations make decisions less clear and harder to review (Czermak 2021: 122). On the other hand, the criticism concerns the distance this creates from the Constitution itself. Self-citations by the Court are usually taken from the standards section of its earlier decisions (Lepsius 2006: 124). As a result, the Basic Law is only indirectly referenced, the reasoning is based on the Court's *own* standards, and case-specific justifications are replaced in a patchwork fashion by generic "text modules," as Czermak (2021: 122) criticizes:

> This can easily lead to ossification, especially when the Court supplements its reasoning by almost constantly referring back to and frequently citing its own previous decisions. These self-citations are almost always taken from the standards section. In the long run, this means that constitutional law is derived not from the Constitution, but from the objectified standards formulated by the Court itself. Expectations regarding constitutional interpretation are shaped primarily by these standards, a *legal intermediate level.* This easily discourages renewed direct efforts to interpret the Basic Law. The standards encourage unreflective repetition through text modules. The Court thus becomes easily dependent on its own jurisprudence.

This criticism raises the question of whether, and to what extent, the Court's self-citations are compatible with the continental European concept of statutory law. In contrast, Jestaedt defends the legitimacy of self-citation (2009: 157 f.). Self-citations could only be dispensed with in the case of an unattainable "total determination" (ibid., 157). Furthermore, self-citation signals the coherence of the Court's own jurisprudence and thus serves to strengthen constitutional adjudication (ibid.).

5.3.2 The Citation Practice of the Supreme Court of Canada

The judicial reasoning culture of the SCC is, to a remarkable extent, based on other decisions (see also the binding effect of precedent in Sect. 5.1.2). In their judgments, the justices not only state the outcome of their decision, but also explain how they arrived at it. To this end, citations are used: "Judges do not simply declare outcomes but also give reasons; in Canada, these reasons are typically

[6]The Federal Constitutional Court itself is frequently cited by other courts—even constitutional jurisprudence in Asia occasionally refers to its decisions. Schlaich/Korioth (2018: 4) interpret this as evidence of the growing importance of comparative legal argumentation and, more generally, of increased consideration of the constitutional law of other nations. The Federal Constitutional Court, by contrast, "is notably restrained in its use of comparative legal arguments" (ibid.).

organized around citations of judicial authority" (McCormick 1995: 453). In order to signal credibility and thus achieve persuasion, the court uses citation as a 'weapon': "As in the case with other courts in the Anglo-American world, the Supreme Court's weapon of choice in the persuasive arsenal is citations to judicial authority. These citations are drawn from a range of sources [...]" (McCormick 1996: 890). As a result, many studies have addressed various questions regarding the SCC's citation practice, including which courts it cites, how citation practices have developed over time, and whether citation practices depend on the personalities of individual judges.

A study worth highlighting in this context is by Rado (2020), who provides a comprehensive statistical analysis of the SCC's citation practice. The study focuses primarily on references to foreign decisions (in Nußberger's terminology, 'system-external' 2006; see also Chap. 2.3.3) and legally non-binding legal sources. As the basis for his study, Rado (2020: 57) cites the general openness of the SCC:

> Observed from the perspective of citation of foreign judgments, the Supreme Court of Canada (SCC) is often considered one of the world's most cosmopolitan and proactive actors in transnational judicial conversation. However, there are also other forms of non-domestic legal sources that Courts engage with, such as: foreign law, international case law, and international treaties.

The SCC not only draws on foreign decisions, but—remarkably, especially when compared to the preference for supreme court decisions at the German Federal Constitutional Court—often also cites foreign lower courts, particularly from England, the USA, and Australia. The proportion of citations from supreme court decisions and those from lower courts is almost balanced: 54.7% of citations in Canadian judgments were taken from supreme courts, while the remaining 45.3% were from lower courts (Rado 2020: 65). In particular, the SCC's constitutional decisions regularly refer to *foreign case law;* by contrast, such citations are comparatively rare, for example, in labor law cases (ibid., 69).

The frequency of 'foreign' citations depends not only on the area of law. As Rado (ibid., 79) notes, it also correlates with the individual preferences of the justices. For example, former *Justice Binnie,* when the number of citations is normalized to a monthly average for better comparability, cited non-domestic legal sources 3.5 times per month[7]. At the lower end of the range, with a maximum of 3.5 and a minimum of 0.58 foreign law citations per month, is *Justice Wagner.* Rado therefore proposes dividing the spectrum of individual judges into "globalist" and "localist," but also refers to an interview with an SCC justice who points to various influences on the preference for domestic or foreign legal sources (ibid., 81; interview transcript 82):

[7] In the study, the number of citations was correlated only with the justices themselves, not with other variables such as the length of the judgments.

> There are many reasons for the engagement or non-engagement with non-Canadian legal sources. First, we have to realize that … until last year, it was the Chief Justice who decided which judge was going to write each decision. The nature of the case is key, because, obviously, you cannot involve non-domestic legal sources, foreign or international, in every case. There are only specific cases that have that potential. And if you are not called to write on those decisions, of course you will not appear in the list of judges who referred to such sources. Second, it depends on whether you are with the majority or minority. Third, it depends whether it [the case] comes from Quebec, or another province. That can certainly have an impact on how much a judge is contributing. Fourth, the number of years that judges have served in the Court also plays a role. The longer a judge serves, the more confident is the judge with non-domestic legal sources. Fifth, many references to international or foreign legal sources will be found by the clerks. So, clerks play an important role in presenting these sources to the judge. To sum up, there are many factors that influence whether and to what extent a judge engages with non-domestic legal sources.

Given the multitude of possible reasons, it is not possible to clearly analyze the purpose a judge pursues by citing foreign legal sources. Nevertheless, it is clear that the SCC stands out for its pronounced dialogic approach in its jurisprudence. Even though the court can still be described as having a "global consciousness," Rado (ibid., 83) notes from a diachronic perspective (in the study period from 2000–2016) a decline in references to foreign legal sources and a "slowbalization." Since foreign legal sources are not binding for the SCC in any case, a judge can also rely on other means in their reasoning and consult previous decisions of the SCC (and, if applicable, other SCC justices). Self-citation (in English also *follow-up citation*) makes it possible, among other things, to empirically reveal the influence of individual decisions and individual justices. In addition to the notable fact that some justices are cited significantly more often than others, McCormick (1996) also points out the transience of their influence. The frequency with which certain justices are cited is not constant: there are "high drop-off rates for citation frequencies over time for individual cases, and individual members of the Court" and the "products sold in the Supreme Court 'supermarket' have a short shelf-life; individual items become stale-dated more than twice as fast as it seems to be the case for the California State Supreme Court in the 1970" (McCormick 1996: 484). Whether this comparison between the SCC and the *California State Supreme Court* still holds true for today's decisions is unclear; McCormick's analysis refers to decisions from 1989 to 1993. However, in interpreting his data, he makes two observations about citation that can be considered timeless.

First, types of citation cannot be treated equally in (even quantitative) analyses:

> To be sure, a simple count oversimplifies the process of citation by assuming what is clearly not the case: that citation is a citation and all deserve to be counted equally. On the contrary; some cases are briefly indicated in passing, as single examples of a general point or as one of a string of cases illustrating a trend, while others are considered at length. Some cases are cited approvingly, others criticised or rejected or distinguished, although in practice the citation ratio is heavily in favour of the former. (McCormick 1996: 875).

Second, the selection of a citation should be understood as a creative process that is only seemingly objective:

> Judges often suggest that there is little choice involved in choosing citations—that they cite only what they need to cite, and they cite it because they need to. Such self-deprecation cannot be taken at face value, at least not for all cases and least of all for the important cases that make law. Kerans J. refers to this as the 'flat rock theory' of precedent: reading cases is like turning over rocks, and if you just turn over enough rocks you will eventually find the exact piece of law you need. But this denies the creativity whereby a judge persuasively weaves together strands of precedent to shape a just outcome for the particular case that will also serve as a guide to future cases, a process which partakes as much of art as it does of science. (McCormick 1995: 457)

5.4 Interim Conclusion IV

The aim of this chapter was to establish the (primarily) legal foundations for an analysis of citation practices in continental European and Anglo-American law. To this end, first, the fundamental characteristics of the two legal systems were presented; second, the Federal Constitutional Court and the Supreme Court of Canada were introduced as their respective representatives; and third, the (few) studies on the citation practices of these two courts were discussed.

Sect. 5.1 first introduced the descriptive framework of comparative law. Legal systems can, among other things, be characterized by their methods of interpretation and the sources of law used in decision-making. These two criteria also proved useful in the comparison of the continental European and Anglo-American legal systems in Sects. 5.1.1 and 5.1.2. While continental European law, also referred to as statutory law, relies on codifications, i.e., systematized legal rules, Anglo-American law bases its decision-making on precedents. Conversely, this does not mean that *civil law* in practice does not take precedents into account, nor that there are no statutes in *common law.* The central difference lies in the distinction between *must* and *may:* German courts *may* consider decisions from other cases or their own previous decisions, but they are not *required* to do so. In contrast, courts in *common law* jurisdictions are bound by precedent—they must engage with relevant previous cases.

Another fundamental difference lies in the method of decision-making. In *civil law,* cases are decided—at least ideally—by subsumption, that is, by subsuming the facts under legal norms; syllogisms are formed deductively. Legal reasoning and the development of law in *common law* proceed inductively, as analogies are drawn from the specific case to other, previously decided cases. These two very different approaches reflect fundamentally different conceptions of law. In Germany, the systematically 'discoverable' law is identical to the codified law, whereas in Canada, law is by no means equated with the *statutes.* The consistent drive for systematization in continental European law can be interpreted as both a cause and a consequence of its proximity to legal scholarship. A manifestation of this scholarly approach (and, not least, of the ideal of subsumption as an ostensibly impersonal method) in German law is the overall depersonalized style of writing. In terms of (de)personalization, the two legal systems differ markedly.

The theoretical differences identified in the comparison were also found in practice, that is, in the presentation of two concrete 'actors' from each legal system. The introduction of the Federal Constitutional Court and the Supreme Court of Canada in Sects. 5.2.1 and 5.2.2 also documented some discrepancies between theoretical ideals and practical implementation. This applies, for example, to subsumption. Due to the indeterminacy and abstractness of fundamental rights provisions, the Federal Constitutional Court is sometimes left with no option but to base its decisions on external content that is not legally binding in theory. In addition to differences attributable to the respective legal systems, there are also differences in the scope of the supreme courts' responsibilities: The jurisdiction of the Federal Constitutional Court is limited to constitutional matters, and it acts only upon external impetus, such as a constitutional complaint; it is therefore not *per se* part of the regular appeals process or a super-revision instance. The Supreme Court of Canada, by contrast, has a much broader jurisdiction. It deals with constitutional matters as well as all areas of law of public interest. These differences are particularly noteworthy, as they are central to the compilation of the corpus, which faces the challenge of establishing comparability (see also the explanations on the compilation of the corpus in Sect. 6.3).

The citation practices of the two courts were described in Sects. 5.3.1 and 5.3.2. It was first noted that there is neither *a single* citation practice for an entire legal system nor *the one* citation practice for a particular court. Who is cited, what is cited, and how often citations occur are subject to a variety of influences (such as the writing socialization of the judge or the subject matter of the case). Despite these influences, tendencies in the citation behavior of the two courts could be identified, particularly regarding the choice of legal sources. The Supreme Court of Canada is very open to a wide range of legal sources; it receives and cites foreign law as well as the law of lower courts. The Federal Constitutional Court, in this respect, shows less diversity; it most frequently cites itself. This practice is especially criticized because these self-citations are often drawn from the standards sections formulated by the court itself.

The state of research on both courts cannot be considered equally advanced. While comprehensive quantitative data are available for the Supreme Court of Canada thanks to the study by Rado (2020), the existing analyses of the Federal Constitutional Court are more essayistic in nature. The focus of all legal studies has been on who or what is cited. Other characteristics besides the source of the citation (such as the type, i.e., direct vs. indirect, for example) or the manner of integration have so far not been addressed.

Chapter 6
How and Why Do Courts Cite? An Empirical Study Using the Example of the Federal Constitutional Court and the Supreme Court of Canada

The investigation in this study—guided by the question 'How and why do courts cite?'—pursues two objectives. The first objective is to provide a descriptive characterization of the citation practices of the two exemplary courts under both comparative and diachronic perspectives. The second objective is to attempt a reconstruction of citation functions based on the citation features identified in the characterization.

The description of citation practice includes a broad frequency analysis of citation features in a large corpus consisting of 495 decisions from the years 1985 to 2020. By quantifying citation properties, the study aims to determine whether, and if so which, prototypical uses of citations emerge in the decisions. The citation features to be quantified consist of six deductively defined analytical categories, developed in the theoretical part of this study as particularly insightful with regard to their functions: 1. the number and category of sources, 2. the frequency and distribution of citation types, 3. the textual integration of the cited sources, 4. citation-related modalization procedures and evaluative attributions, 5. evidentiality markers, and 6. source labeling. The quantitative survey of the citation characteristics of the two courts can be found, following a recapitulation of the theoretical findings (Sect. 6.1), in Sects. 6.2 to 6.5.6. Based on the empirical results obtained therein, Sect. 6.6.1 identifies prototypical citation features, while Sect. 6.6.2 discusses potential citation functions in court decisions, shifting the perspective from quantitative to qualitative. As discussed in Chap. 3, the analysis of citation properties provides a basis for attempting to reconstruct citation functions; however, clear assignments are not possible, since the intention of the citer cannot be unequivocally inferred from either the citation itself or its embedding context. The analysis of citation functions must therefore always remain at the level of interpretation and should be understood not as a functional assignment, but rather as a delimitation of possible functions.

© The Author(s), under exclusive license to Springer-Verlag GmbH, DE, part of Springer Nature 2025
J. Steigler-Herms, *How and Why Do Courts Cite?*,
https://doi.org/10.1007/978-3-662-71934-3_6

6.1 Recapitulation of Theoretical Findings

The act of citing can be realized in different ways and for different purposes. Both aspects—the how and the why of citation—are the subject of the empirical investigation. In particular, the analysis of the 'why' is a challenging endeavor, as the identification of citation functions is always linked to the reconstruction of intentionality, and intentions cannot be directly inferred from a text. To prepare for the analysis, the theoretical part of this study has therefore sought to combine descriptive approaches to the how of citation practice with interpretive approaches to the why, in order to model possibilities for empirical evaluation. Before presenting the research design and the variables to be examined, the following section recapitulates the essential findings of the theoretical discussion on citation practices and citation functions.

Chap. 2 introduced definitions and typologies. It was shown that the term 'citation' is an umbrella term whose reference and definition vary depending on the discipline. From a philological perspective, it is essential to distinguish between a literary studies understanding of the term, which encompasses various forms of intertextual reference, and linguistic typologies, which, in addition to intertextual citation types, also include quotations without pretext reference under the concept of citation. When both typologies are combined, five citation types emerge.

- *The direct quotation:* In a direct quotation, the material from a pretext is transferred unchanged into a new context; it is characterized by verbatim reproduction and graphematic markers (e.g., The first sentence of the Basic Law states: "Human dignity shall be inviolable").
- *The indirect quotation:* In an indirectquotation, the material from the pretext is partially adopted but not reproduced verbatim. The citing instance makes minor transformations and does not use graphematic markers (e.g., The first sentence of the Basic Law states that human dignity is inviolable).
- *The mixed quotation:* A mixed quotation is a hybrid form combining direct and indirect elements; verbatim passages are embedded within indirect contexts (e.g., The first sentence of the Basic Law states that human dignity is "inviolable").
- *The pure quotation:* A pure quotation is a quotation that refers to language itself. This allows for the discussion of properties of the cited term (e.g., 'Dignity' is a term that is difficult to define).
- *The modalizing quotation:* In a modalizing citation, quotation marks are used for pragmatic purposes. The use of quotation marks is intended to guide the recipient's understanding of the term; the quotation marks signal that the communicator's intended meaning of the term deviates from the usual usage, for example, from the actual denotation or from stylistic conventions (e.g., The Federal Constitutional Court 'guards' the constitution).

In addition, reference and paraphrase should be mentioned. Although reference and paraphrase are often neglected in existing typologies and not classified as citations, as forms of intertextual reference they are essential types to be considered in the present study.

- *The reference:* In a reference, a pretext is neither quoted verbatim nor reformulated in the referring text. References are to be understood as search instructions, i.e., the reader is provided only with the bibliographic information. Indicators of a reference, especially to distinguish it from a paraphrase, can be source labels such as "see *for further information* Mustermann (2010)". These labels are not a necessary component of references. They can provide information about the relationship between the reference and the proposition (e.g., the label "a.A." for "alternative view" in German court decisions).
- *The paraphrase:* A paraphrase is the conveyance of the meaning of pretext content using reformulation strategies. There are various reformulation strategies, such as shortening and reducing the pretext, using synonyms, as well as the—largely irrelevant in court decisions—techniques of metaphrasing and periphrasing. In metaphrasing, connotative content is neutralized (for example, when transposing a poem into prose, "lion" in the referring text and "king of the jungle" in the pretext). Conversely, periphrasing involves enriching the signified through the use of connotations and associations (i.e., "king of the jungle" in the referring text and "lion" in the pretext).

With the addition of reference and paraphrase to the typology, there are a total of seven types, which can in turn be divided into three categories: material citation types (direct and mixed citation), immaterial citation types (indirect citation, reference, paraphrase), and quotations without pretext (modalizing and pure citation). The problem is that, without comparison to the pretext, it is generally not possible to determine whether a passage is a paraphrase, an indirect citation, or original content accompanied by a further reference. For this reason, the following empirical analysis employs the aforementioned, comparatively coarse distinction between material, immaterial, and non-intertextual citation types (see also Sect. 6.4 for further details).

Legal scholarship approaches to the description of citations do not operate with such differentiations. In legal studies, all forms of intertextual references are understood as citations. Thus, the legal concept ofcitation is fundamentally based on the literary studies understanding and presupposes reference to a pretext as its defining criterion. Quotation types that are not based on a pretext (such as the modalizing and the pure quotation) are therefore not included. Unlike literary studies, legal perspectives on citations do not concern themselves with how a quoting text integrates the quoted pretext material (e.g., verbatim or indirect), but rather focus on the typology of sources rather than on the citations themselves. An example of such a typology can be found in Nußberger (2006), who distinguishes between system-internal, system-external, and system-foreign citations (more precisely: sources). The primacy of analyzing sources over analyzing manifestations of pretexts is also evident in the concept of the 'chain citation.' A chain citation is an intertextual proposition accompanied by several source references, so that the 'chain' is formed by the sources (not by the quotations). Thus, legal scholarship is primarily interested in the type and number of sources, and less in the different forms of pretext transmission.

The different conceptions of citations demonstrate the diversity with which citations can be described. For a comprehensive characterization of citation practices—according to the findings of Chap. 2—it is necessary to examine how the material of a pretext is transferred into a quoting text (e.g., directly or indirectly), who is being cited (e.g., supranational law or legal scholarship sources), and how many sources are cited (e.g., chain citations). In cases where there is no reproduction of a pretext but quotation marks are still used, it is important to ask what purpose the quotation marks serve (e.g., signaling a shift in register in modalizing quotations or highlighting conceptual properties in pure quotations).

Chap. 3 has shown that citations can fulfill numerous functions: they serve as evidence, confer authority, embellish texts and their authors, enable economical text production, and ensure coherence. A comprehensive enumeration of all potential functions is not possible. The reason for this is the variable functional orientation of citations, coupled with the intertwining of functional levels. For example, a quotation may be used to support a statement at the textual-functional level by providing an example; the act of providing evidence can, in turn, serve an authorial function by strengthening the validity and authority of the citer. The specific function(s) a citation is intended to fulfill in a given context cannot be readily inferred from the citation itself. Against this background, Chap. 3 has emphasized that it is not possible to provide an integrative account of all possible citation functions and has focused on four functions identified by the relevant research canon for utilitarian text types.

- *Ornamentation:* When used ornamentally, a quotation contributes to stylistic variation. Shifts in register can be instrumentalized and legitimized through quoting or through the use of quotation marks—whether quotation marks are used to indicate material quotations or in the case of modalizing quotations.
- *Authority:* A citer can strengthen their authority through citations and quotations, for example by demonstrating erudition; in this respect, the quotation serves self-representational purposes. Additionally, when affirmatively adopting a pretext, it serves as evidence that one is not alone in one's view and can refer to other persons or texts, possibly even to authoritative persons or texts. The citation can also be used as a means of projecting authority, either by the citer appropriating the authority of the source, or by projecting their own authority onto the quoted material. Even in cases of rejection or distancing from the quoted pretext, the authority of the citer can be enhanced, as by rejecting, the citer assigns themselves a position that allows them to decide on validity.
- *Coherence:* In its function of coherence, the citation serves, first, to position oneself within textual networks and, second, to signal the consideration of such networks. The function of coherence differs from the other functions in that it is obligatory in many discourses. While a citer *may* use ornamental quotations, the creation and demonstration of coherence—such as in science and law—is mandatory.

- *Economy:* Closely related to the function of coherence is the function of economy. Drawing on existing content from textual networks can save both substantive work and effort at the level of formulation.

While it is theoretically undisputed that citations can fulfill the aforementioned functions, there is a lack of empirical approaches to functional analysis. Empirical approaches must address at least two issues: the problem of distinguishing between functions and the necessity of reconstructing intentionality. Whether a citation serves, for example, to signal coherence, is used for economic purposes, or fulfills both roles simultaneously, is encoded within the citation itself. Chap. 3 has therefore, also drawing on Chap. 2, addressed the development of possible research questions regarding citation features that may allow inferences about potential functions.

- *What type of citation is used (direct quotation, indirect quotation, mixed quotation, paraphrase, reference)?* A clear assignment between citation types and citation functions cannot be made; however, citation types do vary in their suitability for realizing different functions. For ornamental-stylistic effects through deviations in style, for example, material quotations are particularly suitable.
- *Who or what is being cited, and what is the status of the cited source?* This question arises, among other things, from the focus on source categorization in law. The consideration of sources is always the result of a selection process, where a distinction can be made between legally binding sources (such as the Basic Law in the Federal Constitutional Court) and optional sources (such as academic texts). For the latter, the question of citation motivation is even more pressing, since they are not legally binding and can therefore be interpreted as intentionally functionalized as a result of a selection process.
- *How often is each source cited?* This question is closely related to the question of source category and supplements it with quantitative aspects. In general, courts refer to many sources in their decisions. The quantity of sources consulted can provide insight into the weighting and influence of other texts (see Pfister 1985); for example, the proximity to scholarship often attributed to German law can be substantiated by a quantitative analysis of references to academic sources.
- *How is the author or source mentioned? (e.g., in parentheses or in the running text):* The analysis of how the source is integrated refers to the local textual positioning of the source reference. The mere fact that a source or the author of a cited content is named does not in itself provide insights into potential citation motivations, since providing this information is mandatory under copyright law; unmarked citations can be prosecuted as a violation of the right to authorship recognition (§ 13 UrhG). However, analyzing the positioning of the mention can be informative. A cited author can be indicated either in parentheses and footnotes or—beyond the obligatory marking—integrated into the running text and thus placed prominently. The specific form of the former (parentheses and, among other things, punctuation before page numbers) depends primarily on disciplinary conventions. The latter, in turn, can serve as an indicator of

potential functionalization. A prominent placement in the running text may suggest particular emphasis on the author or the cited text. If an author's name is mentioned for persuasive purposes, this is known as *name dropping,* where the citer seeks to project the authority of the cited author onto themselves.
- *How is the citation embedded? (e.g., evaluation of the citation through adjectives):* In Chap. 3, it was argued in this context that it is less the content of a cited pretext that determines possible functionalizations, and more the way in which the citing text engages with the pretext—specifically, whether the citing text accepts or rejects the cited content. The adoption of a pretext occurs within a tension between affirmation and deconstruction, and depending on whether a citation is accepted, rejected, or, for example, discussed, the citation assumes a function that is highly dependent on the manner of its embedding.

The last analytical criterion, concerning citation embedding, has in turn raised the question of measurable indicators that would allow such positioning to be demonstrated. Chap. *4* therefore addresses considerations regarding the measurement of (subtle) positioning. For this purpose, the theoretical framework of *stancetaking* was employed, and the two subcategories of epistemic modality and evidentiality were discussed. Epistemic modality refers to the writer's assessment of the factuality of a proposition; the writer assigns a degree of factuality to a proposition and can either reinforce or limit it. Markers of epistemic modality, i.e., modalization procedures such as hedges and boosters, manifest the relationship of the citer to the cited content and can provide insight into whether the citer attributes factuality to the external content or wishes to qualify it. Qualifications can be made, for example, using hedges, and reinforcements using boosters.

- *Hedges:* Hedges are modalization procedures that create distance from the factuality of a proposition. Examples include adverbs that limit validity, such as "possibly," or modal verb constructions like "could be understood as." Hedges are attributed various functions, including self-protection of the 'hedging' instance, which signals that it does not claim validity, or a politeness function, where criticism can be softened to protect the person being criticized.
- *Boosters:* Boosters are reinforcing modalization procedures. They indicate the incontestability of a proposition. Examples of boosters include modalization procedures with "definitely" or constructions with the epistemically used modal verb "must."

Closely related to the concept of epistemic modality is the concept of evidentiality. Evidentiality refers to the linguistic marking of information that has contributed to a statement. Thus, a citation is per se an evidential. Evidentiality markers, such as citation-accompanying phrases or the subjunctive, are suitable for measuring positioning insofar as they can contain an epistemic-modalizing element. Examples of evidentiality markers include citation-accompanying phrases and the subjunctive, which can also be used as a marker of distance.

- *Citation-accompanying phrases:* Prominent examples of citation-accompanying phrases are the so-called *verba dicendi,* which can introduce or conclude a citation (e.g., "say," "claim"). The function is not limited to verbs; prepositions (e.g., "according to") or entire prepositional phrases ("according to prevailing opinion") can also be used to mark citations.

- *Subjunctive of reporting:* Citations can be rendered in either the indicative or the subjunctive (I or II). The latter can be helpful for analyzing positioning, as pragmatic approaches to the use of the subjunctive assume that it creates distance between the citing instance and the cited content, and thus can imply questioning or doubt.

The analysis of modality and evidentiality in law is a relatively underexplored field. However, the few existing studies demonstrate the potential of this approach. For example, it has been shown that legal scholarship articles use more positioning markers than court decisions, and the frequency of positioning markers in the latter varies with the structure of the decision (e.g., more stance markers in dissenting opinions than in majority opinions, see Vass 2015 and Szcyrbak 2014).

The content of *Chap. 5* is the presentation of the Federal Constitutional Court and the Supreme Court of Canada, their differences—arising, among other things, from their respective legal systems—and, crucially, their citation practices. While the decisions of the Federal Constitutional Court (BVerfG) are considered objective and depersonalized, decisions shaped by judge-made law (and thus those of the SCC) are characterized by a subjective element. For the Federal Constitutional Court, it is assumed—due to system-specific requirements and the high status of the court—that intertextual references primarily serve a legitimizing and authoritative function, and frequent self-citation is observed. However, empirical analyses of the BVerfG's citation practices remain a desideratum. In contrast, empirical studies are available for the Supreme Court of Canada. In a quantitative study, Rado (2020) attests to the SCC's great openness to *other* sources, such as foreign legal sources. Based on this, Rado (ibid.: 57) describes the SCC as "one of the world's most cosmopolitan and proactive actors in transnational judicial conversation."

6.2 Research Questions & Hypotheses

Based on the results summarized in Sect. 6.1 and with two objectives—first, a systematic description of the citation practices of the BVerfG and the SCC, and second, an analysis of citation functions—the study addresses two research questions.

> Research Question 1: How do the Federal Constitutional Court and the Supreme Court of Canada cite?
> Research Question 2: Why do the Federal Constitutional Court and the Supreme Court cite?

To capture citation practices in a multidimensional way, the question of 'how' encompasses the analysis of several citation features. It is operationalized as follows:

F 1.1: How often do the Federal Constitutional Court and the Supreme Court of Canada cite which sources?
F 1.2: What types of citations do the Federal Constitutional Court and the Supreme Court of Canada use?
F 1.3: At what position do the Federal Constitutional Court and the Supreme Court of Canada incorporate the cited sources?
F 1.4: Which and how many citation-related modalization procedures do the Federal Constitutional Court and the Supreme Court of Canada use?
F 1.5: Which and how many attributions and reference labels do the Federal Constitutional Court and the Supreme Court of Canada use?
F 1.6: Which and how many evidentiality markers do the Federal Constitutional Court and the Supreme Court of Canada use?
F 1.7: To what extent do the citation practices of the Federal Constitutional Court and the Supreme Court of Canada differ, and how have the citation practices of both courts developed over time with regard to the analytical criteria formulated in Research Questions 1.1 to 1.6?

The extent to which the features addressed in the research questions can be used to describe citation practices, and the extent to which they provide insight into citation functions, has already been discussed in the theoretical recap. Such questions have not yet been comprehensively posed with regard to the citation practices of the Federal Constitutional Court and the Supreme Court of Canada; nor have comparative perspectives on the citation practices of the two courts been adopted.

Differences between the citation practices of the BVerfG and the SCC can be expected for the following reasons: There are fundamental differences in binding sources—civil law is primarily bound by codified law, while common law is primarily bound by precedent—and in methodology. In civil law, legal reasoning is conducted deductively by subsuming facts under norms, whereas in common law, legal reasoning proceeds inductively by seeking analogies to previously decided cases. Beyond these binding sources, further fundamental differences emerge: The civil law tradition is considered closely aligned with academia and draws on scholarly knowledge in decision-making. The SCC, in turn, is noted for its openness to foreign and international jurisprudence. In addition to these differences in source binding (codification vs. precedent) and in the preference for non-binding sources (scholarly sources vs. international case law), further distinctions can be observed regarding the role of judges and the style of judgments. At the BVerfG, judges generally act as a collective; decisions are rendered in the name of the judiciary, with individual decision-makers being scarcely visible. This is also reflected in the BVerfG's style of reasoning, which is described as objective, depersonalized, factual, impersonal, and scholarly (see also Sect. 5.1.1). In the decisions of the SCC, judges are much more present. In earlier decisions, the court issued *seriatim* opinions, in which each judge would state their position on the case in turn. Although the *seriatim* method has in more recent times been replaced by *per curiam* decisions authored collectively, the role of the individual judge remains prominent; the personal pronoun "I" is used, explicitly linking the reasoning to a specific person. The common law style of reasoning is sometimes (critically) attributed with subjective elements. For example, the *attitudinal model* assumes that judicial decision-making ultimately involves the rationalization and justification of personal values (see Sect. 5.2.2).

The differences outlined above suggest that the citation practices of the two courts also differ, though the extent of these differences remains unclear. It is plausible that the objectifying tendency in the BVerfG's decisions and the subjective tendency in the SCC's decisions are reflected in their citation practices. For example, it is conceivable that the SCC exhibits more subjective filtering of cited content and therefore makes more frequent use of epistemic modalization procedures. To prevent the empirical investigation from being overly guided by speculation, Hypothesis H1 is formulated openly:

> H1: There are differences between the citation practices of the Federal Constitutional Court and those of the Supreme Court of Canada.

To test this hypothesis, a frequency analysis of occurrences in all described analytical categories will be conducted, and the frequencies for both courts will be compared and tested for significant differences using a t-test. Unlike Research Question 1, Research Question 2—'Why do courts cite?'—cannot be answered directly on the basis of the quantitative analysis results. Therefore, the discussion of possible citation functions will be based not only on the identified frequencies, but also on selected examples from a qualitative perspective. Whether citations serve different functions in the decisions of the BVerfG and the SCC will be explored in an exploratory manner.

6.3 Corpus

The study corpus n_{total} consists of 495 decisions issued between 1985 and 2020, including 270 decisions of the Federal Constitutional Court (subcorpus n_{BVerfG}) and 225 decisions of the Supreme Court of Canada (subcorpus n_{SCC}). The corpus was compiled as part of subproject B02 of the Collaborative Research Center 1385 'Law and Literature'. Only those decisions published in the official collections were included· No distinction was made between orders and judgments resulting from oral hearings. The overall length of the decisions and the relationship between citation and decision structure were not taken into account; for the present study, it is therefore irrelevant in which part of the decisions the citations appear (e.g., in the reasoning section or in a dissenting opinion). In principle, inclusion in the overall corpus was also independent of the specific type of constitutional proceedings (for the Federal Constitutional Court, this includes, for example, constitutional complaints and concrete judicial review). However, since the SCC deals not only with constitutional matters but also, for example, with criminal cases, only decisions relating to *constitutional law* were included in the corpus n_{SCC} to ensure comparability. For reasons of resource availability, data collection was carried out in five-year intervals; the year 2019 was also included. Based on these fundamental criteria, the distribution by year is shown in Table 6.1.

Table 6.1 Number of decisions analyzed by court and year

	1985	1990	1995	2000	2005	2010	2015	2019	2020
BVerfG	67	40	33	20	11	26	26	17	30
SCC	24	68	30	11	22	26	25	10	9

The numbers given in the table refer to the number of decisions reviewed. However, not every one of these decisions contains a citation—at least not with regard to the types of citations considered relevant in this study, namely, citations of sources that are not legally binding. The following were fundamentally *not* included in the corpus:

- Precedents or self-citations
- Citations of case law from lower courts of the same country (i.e., for the BVerfG, no citations of other German courts, and for the SCC, no citations of other Canadian courts)
- Citations of statutes, ordinances, and regulations
- Procedural citations, such as references to expert opinions, statements by the parties involved, decisions of lower courts, and procedural materials.

For example, when the Federal Constitutional Court cites the Basic Law, this provides little insight into intended functions, since the Basic Law must be considered and thus cited by the Court in its decision-making and reasoning. The same applies to references to decisions of lower courts; if the BVerfG, for instance, decides to overturn or invalidate a BGH decision, the content of the latter must be presented. The use of other sources, such as references to foreign legal systems, is, however, discretionary, left to the judges, and thus offers insight into the motivations for citation.

Example 1 cites academic literature and shows a citation included in the corpus; Example 2 cites the Basic Law and was therefore not included in the corpus:

(1) The binding effect of fundamental rights on German state authority does not, even abroad, amount merely to an objective legal obligation (correctly **Hölscheidt,** Jura 2017, p. 148<150 f.>; different view **Löffelmann,** in: Dietrich/Gärditz/Graulich/Gusy/Warg [eds.], Reform der Nachrichtendienste zwischen Vergesetzlichung und Internationalisierung, 2019, p. 33<38>). (BVerfGE 154, 152–312 1st Senate—19.05.2020, para. 92)

(2) A withdrawal of the fundamental rights protection guaranteed to every individual is not required, in particular, in order to avoid undermining **Art. 19(3) GG.** (BVerfGE 154, 152–312 1st Senate—19.05.2020, para. 69)

According to these criteria, the corpus consists of citations whose sources can be classified as legal scholarship (e.g., academic textbooks, including commentaries on statutes), foreign legal sources (e.g., French case law), and non-legal texts (e.g., dictionaries) (see also Sect. 6.4 on the categorization criteria). In line with the broad understanding of the concept of citation adopted in this study, both modalizing and verbatim citations were included, provided they appeared in combination with intertextual elements, i.e., together with a source reference:

(3) This "patchwork" of national protection systems limited to the respective territory is, as a result of international agreements, subject to the need for harmonization (see v. Gamm, Urheberrechtsgesetz, 1968, § 121 para. 4). (BVerfGE 81, 208–228 1st Senate—23.01.1990, para. 54)

As the example shows, and as will be discussed in more detail in Sect. 6.4, several difficulties arose in identifying citation types. Without knowledge of the pretext being cited, it was not possible to determine, for example, whether a citation was substantive or modalizing. To verify such unclear cases, a sample of 56 pretexts was compiled and compared with the cited elements.

In the presentation of results below, whenever a citation from the BVerfG or SCC is provided, the "citation of the citation" is always indented and presented without quotation marks for clarity, regardless of length. Quotation marks are only used if the court itself used them. Punctuation, including the different quotation marks used in German and English, is reproduced exactly as in the original. Longer quotations from the courts are indicated by a smaller font size. Emphases made by the courts, such as italics, are retained; any emphases added by the author are indicated by bold type. The bibliographic reference for the cited court decision is given at the end of the citation in parentheses. The sources cited by the courts are also provided for each example.

6.4 Methodology and Categories of Analysis

To answer Research Question 1, 'How do courts cite?', citation characteristics are quantified, i.e., a frequency analysis is conducted. Frequency analysis is part of the standard repertoire of quantitative approaches in both empirical legal studies and empirical literary studies (see also Bernhart 2018 for quantitative literary studies). The study examines six deductively defined categories of analysis. In line with the previously presented operationalization of 'how', these are

a) the number of sources and a source categorization
b) the choice of citation types
c) the textual integration of the cited source
d) modalization procedures: hedges & boosters
e) attributions & reference labeling
f) evidentiality markers: subjunctive & citation-accompanying phrases

The analysis of each category includes both a diachronic and a comparative perspective. Coding of the analysis categories and subsequent quantification were carried out using the software MAXQDA (Release 22.2.1). To test for statistically significant quantitative differences between the two courts, a two-tailed t-test was performed. For a consistent, transparent, and reproducible analysis process, a coding manual was created for each of the six analysis categories. The coding manual contains the following specifications.

a) *Number and category of cited sources*

This category involves recording the number of sources for the citations in the corpus and assigning these sources to the categories ‘legal scholarship’, ‘foreign case law’, and ‘non-legal texts’ (based on the typology by Nußberger 2006). As defined in the presentation of the corpus, sources from domestic law, statutes, self-citations, and procedural citations were not considered, i.e., sources of this kind are not represented in the frequencies determined for this analysis category. In the following example, in accordance with this definition, one indirect citation and *one* source were counted. The reference to the Basic Law and the direct quotation from it were *not* included:

(4) That under Art. 80 para. 1 sentence 4 of the Basic Law the “authorization” is further delegated, is permitted on the one hand by the assumption that the original formal statutory authorization has been incorporated by the subdelegating regulation and is henceforth contained only therein (cf. **Frowein,** DÖV 1969, p. 621<621>). (BVerfGE 151, 173–191 1st Senate—18.06.2019, para. 20)

The source “Frowein, DÖV 1969, p. 621< 621>” falls into the first category of legal scholarly texts. This includes all legal scholarly texts regardless of their national context (e.g., legal monographs as well as articles in professional journals or contributions in edited volumes). The second category, ‘foreign case law’, includes all references to statutes and judgments whenever they do not pertain to national law. If the Federal Constitutional Court (BVerfG) cites, for example, the Federal Court of Justice (BGH) or itself, this is an unrecorded reference to domestic law; however, if the BVerfG cites, for instance, the SCC, this constitutes a foreign legal source. References to the Court of Justice of the European Union (CJEU & General Court) and the European Court of Human Rights (ECtHR) occupy a special position in this category. From the SCC’s perspective, references to these two courts constitute foreign law; for the BVerfG, however (even though the BVerfG itself assesses the status of EU law differently), they are recorded in the separate category of ‘supranational law’.

The third category, non-legal texts, is broadly defined. It includes texts from other academic disciplines (e.g., sociology, psychology), dictionaries, encyclopedias, and literary sources.

b) *Citation types*

Based on established theoretical typologies, five citation types can be distinguished: direct citation, mixed citation, indirect citation, pure citation, and modalizing citation. In addition, reference and paraphrase must be considered, which, although not recognized as citation types in typologies, are nevertheless included below as forms of intertextuality. The following analysis does not distinguish between all seven forms named, but rather between materially-present citation types, immaterial citation types, and pure and modalizing attributions. Materially-present citation types include direct and mixed citations; immaterial citation types include indirect citation, paraphrase, and reference. The following reasons underlie this grouping.

Capturing pretext-based types is problematic to the extent that, without knowledge of the cited pretext, it is not possible to reconstruct whether, for example, a passage is an indirect citation or a paraphrase. According to theory, the distinguishing criterion between indirect citation and paraphrase is the degree of transformation or reformulation. In an indirect citation, the wording of the pretext is retained; only syntactic transformations are made (e.g., the main clause of the pretext is embedded as a subordinate clause in the citing text, so that the verb position is adjusted). In this respect, the substance of the pretext is indeed present in indirect citations, but this presence is not explicitly (graphematically) marked as such. In contrast, a paraphrase involves substitutions, e.g., through lexical reformulations. Which of these operations have been performed in the act of citation cannot be determined from the citation itself without comparison with the pretext. Identification of paraphrases is further complicated when more than one source is cited, as it is not readily apparent which content is taken from which source and to what extent. The following passage, therefore, is counted as an immaterial form of citation—regardless of the number of sources recorded in the analysis category:

(5) The French Conseil constitutionnel also examines the proportionality of a sovereign measure in the three steps mentioned (cf. Nußberger, NVwZ-Beilage 2013, p. 36< 38, 40>; Jouanjan, in: v. Bogdandy/Grabenwarter/Huber, IPE VI, 2016, § 99 para. 72), […]. (BVerfGE 154, 17–152, 2nd Senate—05.05.2020, para. 125)

A similar problem arises with the group of materially-present quotations. Although they can be distinguished from immaterial citations by the mandatory use of quotation marks, it is not possible to clearly differentiate between direct and mixed quotations within this group. There are no established definitions that would allow for a precise distinction between direct and mixed quotations. Cumming (2003: 77) defines the indirect quotation as a literal "portion" in a context of indirectness; the 'portion size' or the length of the literally quoted content remains unspecified. Therefore, in the quantitative survey, any content from the opening to the closing quotation mark, regardless of its length, is considered *one* materially-present quotation type. Thus, the following two examples are each counted as one materially-present quotation, regardless of their length:

(6) Formalist approaches to equality rights involve a **"decontextualized application of objectified rules and definitions"** that fails to account for, among others, […] (S. McIntyre, "Answering the Siren Call of Abstract Formalism with the Subjects and Verbs of Domination", in F. Faraday, M. Denike and M. K. Stephenson, eds., Making Equality Rights Real: Securing Substantive Equality under the Charter (2nd ed. 2009), 99, […]). (Ontario (Attorney General) v. G 2020 SCC 38–20.11.2020, para. 44)

(7) Prof. Sonia Lawrence makes the critical point that choices are themselves shaped by systemic inequality:
. . . a contextual account of choice produces a sadly impoverished narrative, in which choices more theoretical than real serve to eliminate the possibility of a finding of discrimination . . . . The result is a jurisprudence which almost mocks a more nuanced version of the what and how of discrimination, through frequent recourse to the idea that any harm to the claimant was actually the result of her choice, or her unwise exercise of her own judicially protected liberty. (Fraser v. Canada (Attorney General) 2020 SCC 28—16.10.2020, para. 90)

As a result of the identification issues mentioned above, further differentiation within the two categories 'materially-present' and 'immaterially-present' had to be omitted for the purposes of empirical analysis.

Another identification or delimitation problem sometimes arises between material quotations, especially short material quotations, and pure as well as modalizing quotations. Pure and modalizing quotations were only coded if they appeared in an intertextual context, i.e., in connection with a source reference. For quotations such as the following, the problem arose that it could not be determined whether the cited term represented a material adoption from the indicated source or a typographically highlighted modalization of the statement:

(8) This **"patchwork"** of systems of national protection rights limited to the respective territory is, as a result of international agreements, subject to the pressure to harmonize (see v. Gamm, Urheberrechtsgesetz, 1968, § 121 para. 4). (BVerfGE 81, 208–228 1st Senate—23.01.1990, para. 54)

Since cases of this kind are not exceptional, a pretext sample was created. In this process, 'suspicious' cases—i.e., terms that were singularly cited and deviated from the usual style—were compared with the indicated source. In total, 56 pretexts were checked. It should be noted here that the comparison with the cited pretext was carried out exclusively in these 56 cases.

Regardless of the type, all citations were only coded if they originated from a source that, according to the specifications of the corpus compilation, was to be considered.

c) *Text-local integration of the citation source*

The variable 'text-local integration of the citation source' has two possible manifestations: first, placement of the citation source *within* the running text, and second, integration of the citation source *outside* the running text, limited to the obligatory mention (e.g., in parentheses or, as is sometimes the case with the SCC, without parentheses but after the end of the sentence). These two categories are hereinafter referred to as 'integration within the running text' and 'integration outside the running text'. For both categories, the same rule applies: they were recorded according to the specifications for compiling the corpus. For the following example, this means that the positions of the sources 'Manssen' and 'Jarass' were coded, as these are legal literature; the integration of the Basic Law was not recorded, as it does not constitute a source to be considered:

(9) Although completing a vocational (initial) training is protected by Art. 12 para. 1 GG (see **Manssen,** in: v. Mangoldt/Klein/Starck, GG, 7th ed. 2018, Art. 12 para. 61; **Jarass,** in: Jarass/Pieroth, GG, 15th ed. 2018, Art. 12 paras. 93 ff.). (BVerfGE 152, 274–331 2nd Senate—19.11.2019, para. 120)

The preceding example represents an 'integration outside the running text'. This category is assigned to all sources that are not mentioned in the running text. At the Federal Constitutional Court, this means a reference in parentheses.

(10) While the Basic Law previously contained no provisions on the revenue authority of municipalities, so that although the federal government could not, the states could change the revenue authority of municipalities for trade tax (see in detail **Zitzelsberger,** Grundlagen der Gewerbesteuer, 1990, p. 222) [...]. (BVerfGE 125, 141–174 2nd Senate—27.10.2010, para. 68)

By contrast, at the Supreme Court of Canada, the citation of sources is inconsistent; there are references in parentheses as well as mentions after the end of a sentence (after a period or a colon). All of these variants of source citation are classified without further differentiation as 'integration outside the running text'.

(11) The first, "most direct and authoritative evidence" of the legislative purpose of a provision is found in statements of purpose in the legislation itself—whether at the beginning of a statute, in the section in which a provision is found, or in sections providing interpretive guidelines: **Sullivan, at pp. 274–76.** (R. v. Appulonappa 2015 SCC 59–27.11.2015, para. 49)

A citation source is classified as 'integration within the running text' if either the author's name, the title of the publication, or both (see Example 12) are mentioned in the running text.

(12) For example, **Shetreet, in Judges on Trial: A Study of the Appointment and Accountability of the English Judiciary (1976),** emphasizes in the following passage at pp. 1718 the importance of freedom from the influence of certain powerful nongovernmental interests: [...]

If a citation source is mentioned by name several times in the running text of a decision—because, for example, there is more than one reference to their work—the name was coded multiple times. This does not apply to pronominal references, for which only the antecedent was recorded (Example 13 = *one* integration in the running text). If a publication has several authors and all are mentioned, they are coded as *one* citation source (Example 14).

(13) As **Professor Hogg** writes, Johannesson is "[t]he most extreme example" of a finding of encroachment. He points out that, "[w]hen one considers that the control of land use is ordinarily within property and civil rights in the province, and is always a question of vital local concern, it would surely have been wiser for the Court to treat the by-law as valid under the double-aspect doctrine" (Hogg, at p. 22–25). (Quebec (Attorney General) v. Lacombe 2010 SCC 38–15.10.20, para. 154)

(14) As **Professor Beaulac and Dr. Bérard** explain: […]. (Quebec (Attorney General) v. 9147–0732 Québec inc. 2020 SCC, para. 22)

For references to the case law of other countries, it was established that either the case title and/or the deciding court (e.g., 15) must be mentioned in the running text in order to be considered as embedded in the text. Such a case is *not* present if only the country of the referenced case law is named. The same applies to generic references to authors (i.e., without names, using phrases such as "in the literature"), which *do not* constitute embedding of the cited source in the running text (see examples 16 & 17).

(15) **The United Kingdom Supreme Court** reached a similar conclusion in Essop v. Home Office (U.K. Border Agency), [2017] UKSC 27, [2017] 3 All E.R. 551. (Fraser v. Canada (Attorney General) 2020 SCC 28–16.10.2020, para. 64)

(16) The vast majority of **constitutional and supreme courts** of the other member states share, within their respective jurisdictions, the view of the Federal Constitutional Court that the (application) primacy of Union law is not unlimited, but is subject to restrictions imposed by national (constitutional) law (see, for the **Kingdom of Denmark**: Højesteret, judgment of 6 April 1998—I 361/1997 –, sec. 9.8; for the **Republic of Estonia**: Riigikohus, judgment of 12 July 2012–3–4–1–6–12 –, para. 128, 223; for the **French Republic**: Conseil Constitutionnel, decision no. 2006–540 DC of 27 July 2006, recital 19; decision no. 2011–631 DC of 9 June 2011, para. 45 […]). (BVerfGE 140, 317–376 2nd Senate, 15.12.2015, para. 43)

(17) The provision in question is also considered constitutional in the **literature** (see in particular Dengler, NJW 1980, p. 163; Baumbach/Lauterbach/Albers/Hartmann, ZPO, 38th ed., note 4 to § 528 with approving commentary by Schwab, NJW 1979, p. 697; without comment Stein/Jonas-Grunsky, ZPO, 20th ed., note IV to § 528 (see also Grunsky, JZ 1977, p. 206)). Only a few authors deny the compatibility of the provision with the principle of equality, essentially for the same reasons as the referring courts (see in particular Lampenscherf, MDR 1978, p. 365; Zöller/Schneider, ZPO, 12th ed., note VI 2 to § 528). (BVerfGE 55, 72 1st Senate—01.10.1980 para. 56)

A special case arises with sentences in parentheses. If the cited sources are embedded in sentence form, they are counted as belonging to the subcategory 'placement in the running text' despite the parentheses. In general, each intertextual reference—even if there are several sources cited, as is often the case with paraphrases—was assigned *one* embedding category. For the following example, this means that the category 'embedding outside the running text' was counted once:

(18) The withdrawal of such a matter requires an objective reason. In addition, it must comply with the principle of proportionality (see BVerfGE 79, 127< 153 ff.>; 138, 1< 19 f. para. 55>; 147, 185< 223 f. para. 80>; Löwer, in: v. Münch/Kunig, GG, vol. 1, 6th ed. 2012, Art. 28 para. 55; Mehde, in: Maunz/Dürig, GG, Art. 28 para. 118 ff. <November 2012>; Dreier, in: idem, GG, vol. 2, 3rd ed. 2015, Art. 28 para. 114, 118; Nierhaus/Engels, in: Sachs, GG, 8th ed. 2018, Art. 28 para. 72 f.; Schwarz, in: v. Mangoldt/ Klein/Starck, GG, vol. 2, 7th ed. 2018, Art. 28 para. 194 ff.; Hellermann, in: Epping/Hillgruber, BeckOK GG, Art. 28 para. 48.1< 15 May 2020>). para. 50. (BVerfGE 155, 310–357 2nd Senate 07.07.2020, para. 50)

For one and the same intertextual reference, both categories could be assigned if, for example, one of the cited sources was named in the running text and additional sources were listed in parentheses:

(19) It is sufficient that this view is widespread among the various branches of Islam and is in particular traced back to two passages in the **Qur'an** (Sura 24, verse 31; Sura 33, verse 59) (see **Asad,** The Message of the Qur'an—Translation and Commentary, 2009, pp. 676 f., 810; see also Heine, Dress Code, in: Handbook of Law and Culture of Islam in German Society, 2000, pp. 184< 186 f.>). (BVerfGE 138, 296–376 1st Senate—27.01.2015, para. 89)

d) *Modalization procedures: Hedges and boosters*

Epistemic modalization procedures negotiate the validity of a statement. To distance oneself from or weaken a proposition, *hedges* can be used; to strengthen it, *boosters.* The coding of modalization procedures includes both hedges and boosters. The ability to weaken or strengthen is not limited to a particular word form. Therefore, all weakening and strengthening linguistic elements referring to the intertextual reference were coded. These include, among others, adverbs, adjectives, and modal verbs in an epistemic function. An example from the corpus of an introduction that strengthens the validity of the citation is the following:

(20) **There is today no doubt that** "[t]he superior courts have the inherent power to review the legality of administrative actions" (D. P. Jones and A. S. de Villars, Principles of Administrative Law (3rd ed. 1999), at p. 6). (Blencoe v. British Columbia (Human Rights Commission) 2000, para. 147)

It was deductively determined that modalization procedures would be analyzed; the identification of specific forms, on the other hand, was carried out inductively, i.e., unlike comparable studies, no pre-established word list of possible hedges and boosters was used prior to the analysis. For this reason, and also due to the focus on modalization procedures related to citations, no concordance software was used. Only those modalization procedures were recorded that refer to *external* content considered relevant according to the corpus compilation guidelines. Hedges and boosters referring to unanalyzed citations (e.g., citations of statutes) as well as to *the court's own* content were not considered. Modalization procedures within the citations themselves were also not coded.

e) *Attributions and reference labeling*

In order to also capture subjectivization procedures that, unlike hedges and boosters, do not relate to the degree of factuality of a proposition but rather evaluate a non-factual property of the citation, the subcode 'evaluative attributions' was used. This category included all characterizations of a citation or a cited author by the citer—usually in the form of adjectives. An example of this is the following attribution:

(21) […], a role based on its willingness to go wide and deep in the global search for the best intellectual resources it can find, as Professor Ran Hirschl **eloquently** explains: […] (Quebec (Attorney General) v. 9147–0732 Québec inc. 2020 SCC, para. 106)

In addition to such commentary, there are also so-called reference labelings, which do not refer to a cited content but to a reference or a source citation. These are additions that can, among other things, show the reader the relationship between a reference and the preceding proposition. An example of this can be found in the following passage:

(22) The term of office of a temporary judge is of considerable importance for the question of whether a tenured civil servant, as required by Arts. 92, 97 GG, can succeed not only in freeing himself from the ties to his original authority, but also in maintaining his inner independence despite the impending return within two years to the position of a subordinate official (**critical, for example**: Ruthig, in: Kopp/Schenke, VwGO, 23rd ed. 2017, § 18 para. 4; […]). (BVerfGE 148, 69 2nd Senate—22.03.2018, para. 25)

f) *Evidentiality Markers: Subjunctive and citation-accompanying expressions*

Evidentiality markers indicate evidence, i.e., they show how a communicator arrived at a statement. Citations themselves are evidentials. Quotative evidentiality markers ensure that intertextual references—beyond the source citation and, if applicable, the graphematic marking—can be recognized as such. For the present study, two evidentiality markers are of particular interest: the subjunctive and citation-accompanying expressions. The analysis of these two markers is promising in that they can provide insight into the positioning (intentions) of the citer. Evidentiality markers—unlike hedges and boosters—do not in themselves have an epistemic-modalizing effect, but they *can* be used in an epistemic-modalizing way.

The question of the epistemic-modalizing function of the quotative subjunctive was already raised in Sect. 4.3.1. All instances of the reportative subjunctive (regardless of whether it is subjunctive I or II) were coded. The category of the subjunctive is a special case, as a comparison between the two courts is not possible. The reportative subjunctive does not exist in English, and indirect quotation in English is marked by shifts in tense. These do not inherently contain subjectivizing elements and are therefore not relevant for the present study. The reportative subjunctive was therefore only coded in the German decisions. Each individual occurrence was counted. The following example thus contains three reportative subjunctives:

(23) Basing a decision on a specific period of separation, which—regardless of the actual breakdown of the marriage—should, at the request of only one spouse and against the declared will of the other, generally lead to the dissolution of the marriage, **is said to be** comparable to the legal concept of termination, which is not compatible with the idea of a marriage intended for life **is said to be** (Bastian/Roth-Stielow/Schmeiduch, 1. EheRG, 1978, paras. 10 et seq. on the introduction to §§ 1564 et seq. BGB). (BVerfGE 53, 224 1st Senate—28.02.1980, para. 98)

Citation-accompanying expressions, most often verbs, are found in both languages, allowing for a comparative perspective. An example of a quotation-accompanying verb in English is the following:

(24) Professor Tetley, in the article excerpted above, **confirms** this understanding of Canadian maritime law: [...]. (Desgagnés Transport Inc. v. Wärtsilä Canada Inc. 2019 SCC 58, para. 13)

Although verbs are a frequent word class in citation-accompanying expressions, the latter are not limited to a single word class. Other examples include prepositions ("according to") or prepositional phrases ("according to prevailing opinion"). All citation-accompanying expressions were recorded, regardless of their word class.

6.5 Results of the Quantitative Analysis

The presentation of the results in this chapter is structured as follows: First, the results for the Federal Constitutional Court are presented, followed by those for the Supreme Court of Canada. Each presentation also includes a diachronic perspective, focusing on the development of each analysis category between the years 1985 and 2020. This is followed, for each analysis category, by a comparative analysis examining the extent to which the values determined for the BVerfG and those for the SCC differ from each other.

6.5.1 Number and Categories of Sources

In the 270 decisions analyzed, the Federal Constitutional Court refers to a total of 3,664 sources ($M = 13.57$, $SD = 30.58$). Of these, the vast majority—3,096 sources—are legal literature. By comparison, the BVerfG rarely refers to foreign legal sources (195 sources) or to other non-legal texts (373 sources). References to supranational law appear 190 times. The overall distribution of all sources used is shown in percentage terms in Fig. 6.1.

Examples of the rare category of non-legal texts include the comparatively frequently cited Federal Statistical Office as well as dictionaries used to define individual terms:

(25) According to data provided by the **Federal Statistical Office** from the 2010 earnings structure survey, 73% of all full-time employees in pay group 1 with a university degree earned less than a civil servant in pay grade R 3 in Rhineland-Palatinate. (BVerfGE 139, 64–148 2nd Senate—05.05.2015, para. 192)

(26) In colloquial usage, "Nachteil" ("disadvantage") means "damage, loss, unfavorable situation" (**Wahrig, Deutsches Wörterbuch,** 8th ed. 2008, p. 1047); "something that has a negative effect on someone compared to another, impairs them, harms them" (**Duden—Deutsches Universalwörterbuch, 5th ed. 2003, p. 1120**); or "an evil appearing as a reduction or deterioration, in general damage, loss, interruption, impairment" (cf. **Jacob and Wilhelm Grimm, Deutsches Wörterbuch, vol. 7, reprint 1984, col. 184 f.**). (BVerfGE 126, 170–233 2nd Senate—23.06.2010, para. 98)

In the least frequently occurring category of references to foreign case law, a decision concerning custody and parental rights violations stands out. In this decision,

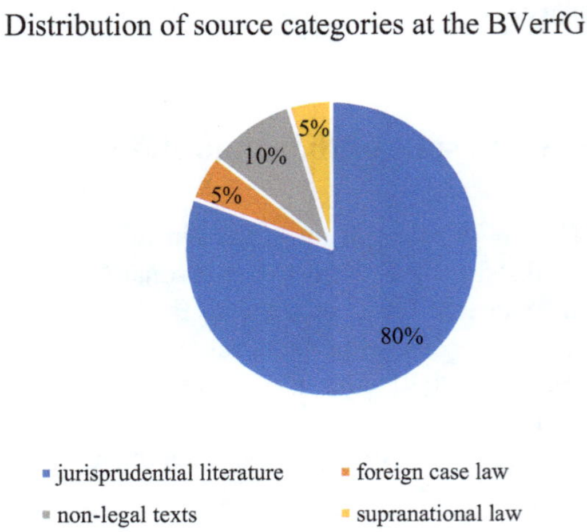

Fig. 6.1 Distribution of source categories at the BVerfG decisions

the Federal Constitutional Court (BVerfG) provides a comprehensive overview of the case law in other countries:

(27) In all 27 countries of the European Union, there is the possibility of joint parental custody for children born out of wedlock, provided that the paternity of the unmarried father is legally established. In terms of the specific arrangements for parental custody, seven EU member states, unlike German law, grant the mother sole custody by law, but allow the father to obtain custody either by parental agreement or by court order (Finland: §§ 9, 10 Finnish Custody Act; Ireland: Sec. 6 A para 1 Guardianship of Infants Act 1964 as amended by Sec. 6 Children Act 1997, Sec. 9 Guardianship of Infants Act 1964; Luxembourg: Art. 380 Lux. CC; Netherlands: Art. 1:253c Dutch Civil Code; Sweden: 6:5 Swedish Parental Code; United Kingdom: Sec. 4 para. 1c Children Act 1989; Cyprus: Sec. 6 Illegitimate Children Law CAP 278). In 18 EU member states, unmarried parents are largely or entirely treated the same as married parents and acquire joint custody by operation of law (Belgium: Art. 373, Art. 374 § 1 Belgian Civil Code; Bulgaria: Art. 68 para. 1, Art. 72 Bulgarian Family Code; Denmark: Chap. 2 § 7 of the Danish Act on Parental Responsibility; Estonia: §§ 49, 50 Estonian Family Law; France: Art. 372 French Civil Code; Greece: Art. 1515 Greek Civil Code; Italy: Art. 317 bis Italian Civil Code; Latvia: Art. 178, 181 Latvian Civil Code; Lithuania: Art. 3.165 Lithuanian Civil Code; Malta: Art. 90 para. 1, Art. 86 Maltese Civil Code; Poland: Art. 93 § 1 Polish Family and Guardianship Code; Portugal: Art. 1911 in conjunction with Art. 1901 Portuguese Civil Code; Romania: Art. 97 Romanian Family Code; Slovakia: § 28 para. 2 Slovak Family Act; Slovenia: Art. 102, Art. 105 para. 1 Slovenian Marriage and Family Relations Act; Spain: Art. 156 Spanish Civil Code; Czech Republic: § 34 para. 1, § 52 para. 1 Czech Family Act; Hungary: § 72 para. 1 Hungarian Family Act). (BVerfGE 127, 132–165 1st Senate—21.07.2010, para. 23)

In this decision, the BVerfG lists 27 countries, which is noteworthy given that references to foreign case law (as the analysis clearly shows) are rare. Only 23 of all decisions refer at least once to foreign case law. The Federal Constitutional Court refers to Canada only once; specifically, to a decision of the Supreme Court of Canada (SCC) and, in this context, to the Canadian *Criminal Code:*

(28) In Canada, in 2016, following the Supreme Court of Canada's decision in Carter v. Canada (see judgment of 6 February 2015,—[2015] 1 S.C.R. 331 -), which declared the absolute criminal prohibition of assisted suicide and euthanasia unconstitutional, a law ("Bill C-14") came into force specifying the conditions under which assisted suicide and euthanasia—still subject to criminal penalties—are exceptionally exempt from punishment. Under this law, a physician or nurse is not to be punished for homicide or assisting suicide if they provide "medical assistance in dying," a term that

> encompasses both active euthanasia and assistance with suicide (see Art. 227 (1) Criminal Code and Art. 241 Criminal Code). (BVerfGE 153, 182–310 2nd Senate—26.02.2020 para. 31)

Although the dominance of legal references applies to all the years of decisions analyzed, some developments can be observed from a diachronic perspective. Regardless of the source category, there has been a significant increase in the number of cited sources. While in 1980 the BVerfG used only a few sources, averaging 6.84 sources per decision, by 2020 the number had risen to 37.33 sources per decision; the number of sources has more than quintupled. With regard to the diachronic development of the average number of sources per text, the year 2005 is particularly striking; with a mean of M = 37.36 sources per decision, the average is conspicuously higher than in earlier decisions (see Table 6.2).

The diachronic development of the composition of source categories is also noteworthy. This is particularly true for the frequency of the category 'foreign case law', which has increased over the years.

The *Supreme Court of Canada* cites a total of 3,198 sources in the 225 decisions analyzed, averaging M = 14.21 sources per decision (SD = 24.71). As with the Federal Constitutional Court of Germany (BVerfG), references to legal scholarship also dominate the composition of source categories at the SCC; however, the differences between the respective source categories are significantly smaller. Without diachronic differentiation, the SCC cites 1,814 legal scholarly sources, 1,096 foreign judicial sources, and 288 non-legal sources. The overall figures for all years analyzed are presented in Table 6.2 and Fig. 6.2.

Within the category of foreign sources, the frequent citation of the U.S. Supreme Court is particularly notable, with 256 references. Reception of German law and German case law is rare, with only four occurrences. One such case involves the citation of a BVerfG justice, another refers to the German Criminal Code (StGB):

Table 6.2 Absolute and relative source frequencies in the BVerfG decisions diachronic

Federal Constitutional Court	1985	1990	1995	2000	2005	2010	2015	2019	2020
Number of decisions	67	40	33	20	11	26	26	16	30
Legal scholarship	206 / 3.07	142 / 3.55	146 / 4.42	134 / 6.7	346 / 31.45	653 / 25.12	255 / 9.81	463 / 28.94	937 / 31.23
Foreign case law	1 / 0.01	2 / 0.05	1 / 0.03	0 / 0	5 / 0.45	27 / 1.04	46 / 1.77	72 / 4.5	45 / 1.5
Non-legal texts	13 / 0.19	28 / 0.7	17 / 0.52	6 / 0.3	60 / 5.45	51 / 1.96	30 / 1.15	75 / 4.69	138 / 4.6
Supranational law	3 / 0.04	8 / 0.2	0 / 0	0 / 0	0 / 0	22 / 0.85	51 / 1.96	89 / 5.56	20 / 0.67
Total	220	172	164	140	411	731	331	610	1120
Average number of sources per decision	4.28	4.3	4.97	7	37.36	28.12	12.73	38.125	37.33

Fig. 6.2 Distribution of source categories in the SCC decisions

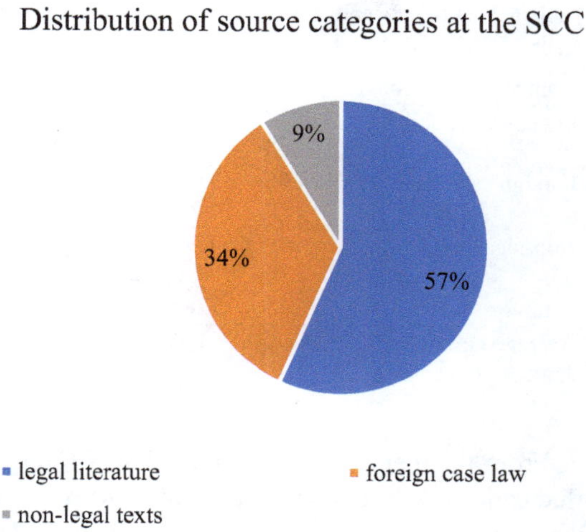

(29) An offence of this type has been in force for many years in s. 323(a) (i) of **the German Criminal Code (Strafgesetzbuch)**: […]. (R. v. Penno 1990 2 SCR 865–04.10.1990, para. n/a)

(30) **Justice Susanne Baer of the German Constitutional Court** has also urged against a narrow focus on constitutional text: […] ("Dignity, liberty, equality: A fundamental rights triangle of constitutionalism" (2009), 59 U.T.L.J. 417, at p. 441). (Quebec (Attorney General) v. 9147–0732 Québec inc. 2020 SCC, para. 77)

In the least frequently cited category of non-legal texts, as with the BVerfG, there are also several references to dictionaries. In addition, this category includes literary texts. The following decision, in which Kafka and Shakespeare are cited, illustrates this:

(31) **Franz Kafka** was not being entirely whimsical when he wrote, "If you have the right eye for these things, you can see that accused men are often attractive" (The Trial (1976), at p. 203). […] Novelists may steer clear of controversial characterizations of ethnic characteristics, such as **Shakespeare's** portrayal of Shylock in The Merchant of Venice. (R. v. Keegstra 1990 3 SCR 697–13.12.1990, para. n/a)

Although the mean values presented indicate an overall low frequency of non-legal sources, this is not consistent across all decision years. In 2020, for example, an average of 3.5 non-legal sources per decision were cited. Differences in the frequency of source categories can be observed diachronically not only for non-legal texts. Particularly noteworthy is that the dominance of legal scholarly texts, as determined by the average source composition, does not hold true for every year. As shown in Table 6.3, in the year 185, more than twice as many foreign legal sources were cited.

Table 6.3 Absolute and relative source frequencies in the SCC decisions diachronic

SCC	1985	1990	1995	2000	2005	2010	2015	2019	2020
Number of decisions	24	68	30	11	22	26	25	10	9
Legal scholarship texts	70 / 2.92	402 / 5.91	301 / 10.03	91 / 8.27	107 / 4.86	127 / 4.88	185 / 7.4	230 / 23.0	301 / 33.44
Foreign case law	166 / 6.92	334 / 4.91	169 / 5.63	37 / 3.36	74 / 3.36	99 / 3.81	55 / 2.2	55 / 5.5	107 / 11.89
Non-legal texts	9 / 0.38	42 / 0.62	67 / 2.23	31 / 2.82	38 / 1.73	15 / 0.58	39 / 1.56	15 / 0.58	32 / 3.56
Total	245	778	537	159	219	241	279	300	440
Average number of sources per decision	10.23	11.44	17.9	14.45	9.95	9.26	11.16	30	48.89

From this perspective, the quantity of foreign legal sources cited shows some fluctuations. While in 1985 an average of 6.9 foreign case law texts were cited per decision, the average drops to approximately 2 to 4 foreign sources per decision between 1990 and 2014. Only from 2019 does this figure rise again to 5.5; the highest value is reached in 2020, with an average of 11.89 foreign legal sources per decision. The year 2020 stands out overall, as it marks the highest value for all sources cited; on average, 48.89 sources were cited per decision in that year. By comparison, the value in 1985 was much lower, at just 10.2 sources per decision. Thus, the number of sources cited has nearly quintupled between 1985 and 2020. It should be emphasized, however, that this is a sudden increase in frequency from 2019 onwards, rather than a continuous rise.[1]

From a *comparative perspective* on the frequency of source usage by the BVerfG and the SCC, the following values should be noted: The two courts do not differ significantly in terms of the frequency with which they use legal scholarship and non-legal texts (legal scholarship: $t(447.75) = 1.66$, $p = 0.098$, 95% confidence interval [0.64, 7.32]; non-legal texts: $t(491) = 0.26$, $p = 0.798$, 95% confidence interval [0.75, 0.97]). However, there is a significant difference in the citation frequency of foreign case law, with $t(288.46) = 5.68$, $p = <0.001$, 95% confidence interval [5.58, 2.69].

6.5.2 *Frequency and Distribution of Citation Types*

The following section first addresses the pre-text-based citation types, followed by the non-pre-text-based citation types. In total, 4,647 pre-text-based citations were coded in the decisions of both courts: 1,093 citations in the decisions of the Federal Constitutional Court and 2,734 citations in the decisions of the SCC. A

[1] In this context, it should be noted that, with the exception of 2019 and 2020, the data was collected in five-year intervals.

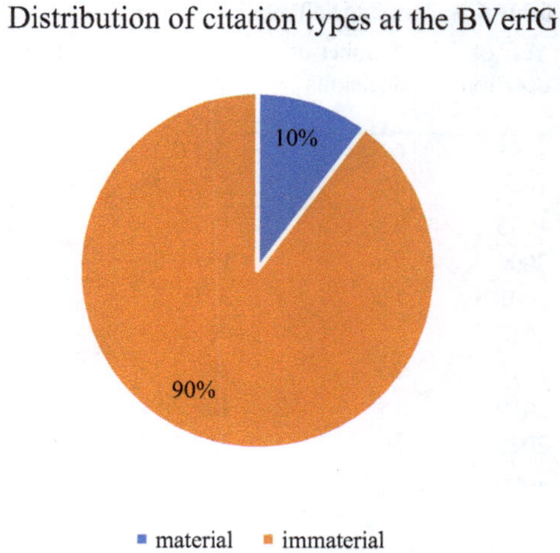

Fig. 6.3 Distribution of pre-text-based citation types in the BVerfG decisions

key finding of the frequency analysis of material and immaterial citation types at the Federal Constitutional Court is that the BVerfG clearly prefers immaterial citation types. In total—taking into account the criteria for inclusion in the corpus presented in Sect. 6.3—1,717 immaterial intertextual elements and 196 material citation types were identified. The distribution is illustrated in Fig. 6.3.

On average, a decision issued between 1985 and 2020 contains only 0.73 *material citation types.* This low value is reflected in the fact that numerous decisions—specifically, 210—do not contain a single direct or mixed quotation. The 196 identified material citations are thus found in 60 of the decisions. A comparatively high value is observed in 2019, when an average of approximately three material elements was used per decision. Apparent higher mean values are found for the immaterial citation types, whose preference has already been shown in the pie chart. The average number here is 6.36 immaterial citation types per decision. For immaterial citations as well, 2019 is the year with the highest mean value. The clear preference for immaterial over material citation types holds for every year analyzed. All absolute and relative frequencies of both citation types are listed in Table 6.4.

As several examples illustrate, the Federal Constitutional Court generally limits the substantive adoption of a pretext to individual words or short phrases; the adoption of entire sentences is an exception:

(32) This promotes investment and consumption, so that inflation can **"approach a level of 2%"** (cf. Recital 2 of Decision <EU> 2015/774 of the European Central Bank of 4 March 2015 on a secondary market public sector asset purchase programme <ECB/2015/10>, OJ EU No. L 121 of 14 May 2015, p. 20; see also Deutsche Bundesbank, Monthly Report June 2016, p. 39). (BVerfGE 154, 17–152, 2nd Senate—05.05.2020, para. 3)

Table 6.4 Absolute and relative frequency of pre-text-based citation types in the BVerfG decisions

Year of decision	Number of decisions	Absolute and relative number of material citation types	Absolute and relative number of immaterial citation types
1985	67	14 / 0.21	116 / 1.73
1990	40	23 / 1.74	108 / 2.7
1995	33	11 / 0.33	76 / 2.3
2000	20	16 / 0.8	74 / 3.7
2005	11	3 / 0.27	107 / 9.73
2010	26	40 / 0.65	347 / 13.37
2015	26	20 / 0.77	189 / 7.27
2019	16	45 / 2.81	254 / 15.88
2020	30	35 / 1.17	446 / 14.86
Total	270	196 / 0.73	1717 / 6.36

(33) The concept of taxes in the Basic Law is linked to the concept of general tax law, although it goes beyond the **"concentration of ordinary statutory norms"** (cf. Lerche, Werbung und Verfassung, 1967, pp. 33 f.). (BVerfGE 55, 274, 2nd Senate—10.12.1980, para. 80)

As will be discussed in the interpretation, the extent of immaterial citation cannot be precisely determined due to the lack of graphematic marking. Furthermore, in the case of immaterial quotations, it is not transparent which content has been taken from which pretext and in what manner:

(34) The core area of sovereign rights is, in any case, violated if it is eliminated or if there is no longer sufficient scope for its exercise (cf. BVerfGE 103, 332< 366>; Pieroth, in: Jarass/Pieroth, GG, 10th ed. 2009, Art. 28 para. 22; Vogelgesang/Lübking/Ulbrich, Kommunale Selbstverwaltung, 3rd ed. 2005, para. 32; Mückl, Finanzverfassungsrechtlicher Schutz der kommunalen Selbstverwaltung, 1998, p. 59; see also Stern, Staatsrecht Vol. I, 2nd ed. 1984, § 12 II 4, p. 416). However, not every individual manifestation of these rights enjoys the absolute protection of the core area guarantee (cf. BVerfGE 103, 332< 366>; Henneke, in: Schmidt-Bleibtreu/Hofmann/Hopfauf, GG, 11th ed. 2008, Art. 28 para. 78). (BVerfGE 125, 141–174 2nd Senate—27.10.2010, para. 93)

From a diachronic perspective, as expected given the result of an increasing frequency of sources (Sect. 6.5.2), there is generally an increase in the frequency of both types of citations in the Federal Constitutional Court. However, for substantive citations, this increase must be described as minor, as a low standard deviation of SD = 2.11 indicates the closeness of the values; there are no major differences between the analyzed decision years for substantive quotations.

In contrast to the Federal Constitutional Court, the distribution of substantive and immaterial types of citations at the Supreme Court of Canada is almost balanced (Fig. 6.4).

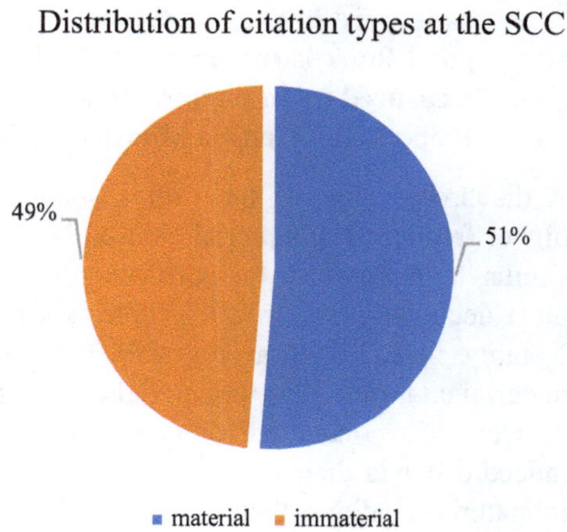

Fig. 6.4 Distribution of pre-text-based types of citations in the SCC decisions

In the 225 decisions of the SCC analyzed, a total of 1,398 substantive and 1,332 immaterial types of citations were coded. The average number of substantive references per decision is 6.21, which is slightly higher than the mean of 5.92 in the category of immaterial citations. For both categories, as the following table shows, the year 2020 stands out as particularly high (Table 6.5).

Especially in comparison to the BVerfG's citations, which often contain only a few words, the extensive use of material citations by the SCC is striking. The SCC adopts entire sentences and passages of text, as illustrated by the following material example:

(35) John Milton recognized the universal value of literature in his Areopagitica; A Speech for the Liberty of Unlicenced Printing, to the Parliament of England (1644): **[A]s good almost kill a Man as kill a good Book; who kills a Man kills a reasonable creature, God's Image; but he who destroys a good Book, kills reason itself, kills the Image of God,**

Table 6.5 Absolute and relative frequency of pre-text-based citation types in the SCC decisions

Year of decision	Number of decisions	Absolute and relative number of material citation types	Absolute number of immaterial citation types
1985	24	95 / 3.96	109 / 4.54
1990	68	351 / 5.16	314 / 4.62
1995	30	216 / 7.2	216 / 7.2
2000	11	64 / 5.81	64 / 5.82
2005	22	88 / 4	90 / 4.09
2010	26	77 / 2.96	105 / 4.04
2015	25	139 / 5.56	168 / 6.72
2019	10	134 / 13.4	126 / 12.6
2020	9	234 / 26.00	140 / 15.55
Total	225	1402 / 6.32	1332 / 5.92

as it were in the eye. Many a man lives a burden to the Earth; but a good Book is the precious life-blood of a master spirit, embalmed and treasured upon purpose to a life beyond life. (Little Sisters Book and Art Emporium v. Canada Minister of, para. 273)

A diachronic view of the values obtained for the SCC shows that a (slightly) higher frequency of material citation types does not occur in every year. Although similar high averages for both categories of citation types can be calculated for most decision years, in 2015 there is a preference for immaterial citation types. Notably, in 2020, the averages for the two categories diverge significantly (63% material citations, 37% immaterial citations).

The t-test conducted for comparative analysis shows that the two courts do indeed differ in their use of citation types. With regard to the frequency of use of immaterial citations, there is no significant difference. A two-tailed t-test for independent samples (assuming equal variances) shows that the difference between the frequency of immaterial citations in the BVerfG and the frequency of immaterial citations in the SCC is not statistically significant, $t(525)=0.14$, $p=0.892$, 95% confidence interval [1.81, 2.07]. In contrast, the differences in the frequency of use of material citation types are significant at $p < 0.001$: A two-tailed t-test for independent samples (not assuming equal variances) shows that the difference between the frequency of material citations in the BVerfG and the frequency of material citations in the SCC is statistically significant, $t(233.8)=6.89$, $p=<0.001$, 95% confidence interval [7.12, 3.94].

Pure and modalizing quotations are found much less frequently than pre-text-based quotation types.[2] The corpus contains a total of 64 pure quotations, 33 of which are found in the SCC and 31 in the BVerfG. Pure quotations are used to discuss word meanings and therefore often occur in combination with intertextual references to dictionaries:

(36) In legal terminology, **"besonders"** ("special") is regularly used as the opposite of **"allgemein"** ("general"). In this sense, the Grimm Dictionary describes the term "besondere(r,s)" in its adverbial use with the Latin synonyms "singulatim", "separatim", "specialiter", and "particulariter", or in its adjectival use with the Latin terms "peculiaris" and "singularis", which in German can be explained as "distinct, as something individual opposed to the general, often rare and outstanding, but also strange, peculiar, idiosyncratic" (cf. Jacob and Wilhelm Grimm, Deutsches Wörterbuch, entry "BESONDER", vol. 1, reprint 1984, col. 1630 ff.). (BVerfGE 151, 202–374 2nd Senate—30.07.2019, para. 162)

[2] It should be noted once again that only those pure and modalized quotations were coded that appeared in combination with a source reference. Furthermore, the values determined can only be given with reservations, as it was not possible to compare every coded quotation with the pre-text. Only a sample of pre-texts was checked (see also Sect. 6.4 on the analysis methodology).

Per definitionem, only the first two bolded terms are pure quotations, as they—unlike the subsequent quotations—are not materially taken from the pre-text. As will be discussed in the interpretation, however, material quotations are sometimes used for the very function that theory actually attributes to pure quotations: This is shown by the third citation in Example 15, "besondere(r,s)". This term is quoted directly, but used in the function of a pure quotation to determine its meaning. An example from the SCC further illustrates that pure quotations can also be used to address and, more specifically, as in the following passage, to reject formulations in a cited text:

(37) While the WHO, in the medical context, uses the word "disability" to refer to functional limitation (the second aspect), I prefer to use the expression **"functional limitation"** to emphasize that in legal terms it is all three aspects considered together that constitute the disability). (Granovsky v. Canada (Minister of Employment and Immigration) 2000 SCC 28–18.05.2000, para. 34)

In this quotation, the quoter positions themselves with respect to the terminology of the pre-text and states that, instead of the term "disability" used in the pre-text, they prefer the term "functional limitation".

Modalizing quotations appear 59 times in the corpus, including 47 modalizing quotations in the BVerfG and 12 in the SCC. These include 'clear' cases, i.e., cases in which the cited lexeme does not occur, and ambiguous cases, in which a word related to the cited lexeme appears in the pre-text. An example of the former is the following:

(38) This **"patchwork"** of systems of national intellectual property rights limited to the respective territory is, as a result of international agreements, subject to the obligation of harmonization (cf. v. Gamm, Urheberrechtsgesetz, 1968, § 121 para. 4). (BVerfGE 81, 208–228 1st Senate—23.01.1990, para. 54)

The term "patchwork" is not used at the cited location in the source. The following example is more complex in terms of its classification within the quotation typology, as the word class of the lexeme is changed in the act of quoting (Example 41 shows the SCC passage, Example 42 the text from Hogg):

(39) Courts must be careful not to endorse a **"colourable"** statute, that is, one that in form appears to relate to a matter within the legislative competence of the enacting order of government, but in substance addresses a matter falling outside its competence: see Hogg Constitutional Law of Canada (5th ed. Supp.), at p. 15–19). (Quebec (Attorney General) v. Canada (Attorney General) 2015, para. 31)

(40) The courts are, of course, concerned with the substance of the legislation to be characterized and not merely its form. the **"colourability"** doctrine is invoked when a statute bears the formal trappings of a matter within

> jurisdiction, but in reality is addressed to a matter outside jurisdiction. In the Alberta Bank taxation Reference, for example, the Privy Council held that the legislation, although ostensibly designed as a taxation measure, was in reality directed at banking.

Even though the word "colourable" is very close to the wording of the pre-text, according to standard definitions it does not constitute a material quotation, which generally presupposes verbatim adoption. Examples such as this show that material and modalizing quotations—contrary to what theory suggests—can be closely linked, and that the typologies developed in theory only very imperfectly reflect actual citation practice.

6.5.3 Text-local Integration of the Citation Source

In the analysis category 'text-local integration of the citation source', a total of 4,316 codings were made: 1,782 for the Federal Constitutional Court and 2,534 for the Supreme Court of Canada. For the Federal Constitutional Court, there is a clear preference for the obligatory mention of sources in parentheses, with an absolute value of 1,640. By contrast, the proportion of sources integrated into the running text is low, with an absolute value of 142 embeddings (see Fig. 6.5).

In the majority of cases—specifically, in 222 of the Federal Constitutional Court's decisions—citation sources are not mentioned even once in the running text; only 45 decisions use in-text placement at least once. The mean value for the subcategory 'embedding in running text' is therefore low, at only 0.53 (Md = 0, SD = 1.74). The highest value for sources mentioned in the running text is found in decision BVerfGE 141, 317–376 2nd Senate—15.12.2015. With

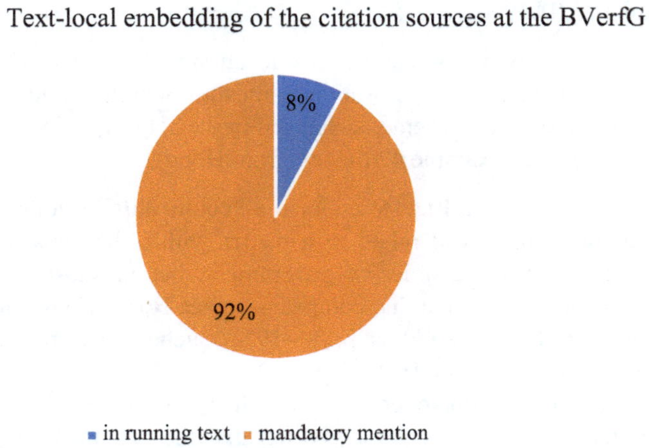

Fig. 6.5 Text-local integration of the citation source in the BVerfG decisions

14 occurrences, this value is far above the calculated mean. In this decision, the BVerfG refers several times, among others, to the European Court of Justice. The embedding of the ECJ in the running text can be considered frequent in this category, as the ECJ accounts for just over 16.9% of the 142 in-text placements (24 out of 142 occurrences). An example of the prominent placement of the ECJ can be found in the following passage:

(41) Thus, the **European Court of Justice** has also recognized that the combination of emergency rescue and patient transport enables the public emergency service, due to the improved revenue situation, to fulfill its tasks in the public interest overall under economically balanced conditions and thus in the required quality and reliably (ECJ, Case C-475/99, Ambulanz Glöckner, ECR 2001, I-8089 para. 61). (BVerfGE 126, 112–158 1st Senate—08.06.2010, para. 114)

What is also striking in the references to the ECJ is the repeated use of the abbreviated form 'the Court', as in the following excerpt:

(42) The **Court** in the Mangold decision concluded that a national provision such as § 14(3) sentence 4 TzBfG was contrary to Community law and must be disregarded (ECJ, judgment of 22 November 2005, Case C-144/04, ECR 2005, p. I-9981 para. 77 f.). This statement was justified with two arguments, the relationship between which remains unclear (see Thüsing, European Law Principle of Equal Treatment as a Binding Obligation for Employers?, ZIP 2005, p. 2149< 2150 f.>). (BVerfGE 126, 286–331 2nd Senate—06.07.2010, para. 69)

The information that this refers to the *European* Court of Justice—and not, as a legal layperson might assume, to the Federal Court of Justice or similar—is only provided in the parenthetical citation. Also relatively frequent in the text are references to studies with empirical results. Approximately 20% of all sources cited in the running text (29 out of 152) are sources providing quantitative data. With 9 occurrences in the running text, the Federal Statistical Office is particularly prominent in this category:

(43) According to **data from the Federal Statistical Office,** in 2008 a maximum of 76.8%—and thus the majority—of all children lived with their married parents, while at least 7.1% of children lived with parents who were in a non-marital partnership. [...] (see Statistical Yearbook 2009, Table 2.17). (BVerfGE 127, 263–292 1st Senate—12.10.2010, para. 42)

References to personal names (e.g., legal scholars) are less common. In total, only 11 individuals are mentioned in the running text:

Table 6.6 Development of average frequencies at the Federal Constitutional Court in the category 'text-local embedding of the cited source'

	1985	1990	1995	2000	2005	2010	2015	2019	2020
Running text	0.14	0.36	0.12	0.11	0.09	1	1.08	1.69	1.07
Parentheses	1.85	2.67	2.33	3.79	6.18	12.96	6.61	15.69	14.47

(44) Wilms and Jäger (JuS 1988, p. 268< 273>) are of the opinion that the court could at most have established its own inability to function, since there was no statutory ground for disqualification; it should not have regulated succession in place of the electoral body. **Doehring** takes the view that filling such a gap is not permissible, as this would result in a composition of the court that no longer reflects the will of parliament (NJW 1987, p. 3234). This view cannot be followed. (BVerfGE 82, 286–305 1st Senate—10.07.1990, para. 87)

From a diachronic perspective, the decisions of the Federal Constitutional Court show no quantitative peculiarity regarding placement in the running text; in all years, the mean value remains consistently low, between 0.09 and 1.69. The clear preference for placement in parentheses applies to each of the years analyzed (Table 6.6).

The citation practices of the Supreme Court of Canada differ fundamentally from those of the Federal Constitutional Court with regard to the text-local embedding of cited sources. For the SCC, there is no clear preference for the placement of sources; with 1,289 placements in the running text and 1,245 placements in parentheses or similar, there is an almost 50/50 distribution, with a quantitatively minimal preference for sources embedded in the running text (Fig. 6.6).

In qualitative terms, it is striking that, when sources are integrated into the running text, the cited source is mentioned in full—when referring to individuals, this often includes (academic) titles and appositions introducing the person:

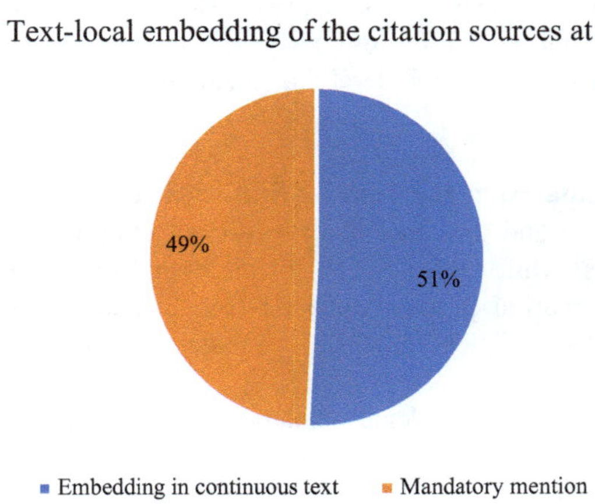

Fig. 6.6 Text-local embedding of cited sources in the SCC decisions

(45) **Justice Susanne Baer of the German Constitutional Court** has also urged against a narrow focus on constitutional text: ...constitutional text matters, but...constitutionalism should not be reduced to mere textualism. ("Dignity, liberty, equality: A fundamental rights triangle of constitutionalism" (2009), 59 U.T.L.J. 417, at p. 441). (Quebec (Attorney General) v. 9147–0732 Québec inc. 2020 SCC, para. 77)

(46) **As Professor (now Mr. Justice) Tarnopolsky** has noted in a passage quoted by the Court of Appeal (at pp. 21–22), these judicial intrusions, devised to meet a problem particular to the United States, should not be imported here; see "The Equality Rights in the Canadian Charter of Rights and Freedoms" supra, at p. 256. (Mckinney v. University of Guelph 1990 3 SCR 229–06.12.199, para. n/a)

(47) There can be no disputing the indispensable nature of interjurisdictional co-operation among securities regulators today. **Paul Bourque, the Executive Director of the Commission,** described this problem as follows: [...]. (Global Securities Corp. v. British Columbia Securities Com, para. n/a)

However, embedding in the running text is not limited to individuals; for example, dictionaries are also frequently mentioned in the text:

(48) **Black's Law Dictionary** defines "cruelty" as "[t]he intentional and malicious infliction of mental or physical suffering on a living creature, esp. a human; abusive treatment; outrage" (11th ed. 2019), at p. 475). (Quebec (Attorney General) v. 9147–0732 Québec inc. 2020 SCC, para. 82)

Unlike the Federal Constitutional Court, a diachronic perspective reveals a change at the SCC. While in 1985, 1990, and 1995, embedding in the running text predominated, after a tie in 2000, a shift occurred; the Court increasingly places cited sources in parentheses (see Table 6.7).

The values in the table demonstrate the establishment of this trend and a decline in sources embedded in the running text (in 2005, the value for parenthetical embedding is 43.65% higher than for embedding in the running text; by 2020, it is already 159.59% higher).

From a comparative perspective, the differences that can be observed may already be apparent from the preceding presentation of the individual values: The Federal Constitutional Court and the SCC do not differ significantly in terms of the frequency of embedding cited sources beyond the obligatory mention. The results of the descriptive statistics show that the Federal Constitutional Court has slightly higher values in the category 'embedding outside the running text'

Table 6.7 Development of average frequencies at the SCC in the category 'text-local embedding of cited sources'

	1985	1990	1995	2000	2005	2010	2015	2019	2020
Running text	5.33	7	9.1	5.46	3.23	2.46	3.56	5.2	9.33
Parentheses	2.46	2.53	4.34	5.46	4.64	4.27	9.2	16.7	24.22

(M = 6.14, SD = 12.44) than the Supreme Court of Canada (M = 5.56, SD = 10.51). A two-tailed t-test for independent samples (assuming equal variances) shows that the difference between the Federal Constitutional Court and the SCC in this category is not statistically significant, t(489) = 0.56, p = 0.58, 95% confidence interval [1.49, 2.66]. However, there is a significant difference in the frequency of sources embedded in the running text. The results of the descriptive statistics show that the Federal Constitutional Court has noticeably lower values for the frequency of sources embedded in the running text (M = 0.53, SD = 1.74) than the SCC (M = 5.75, SD = 11.07). A two-tailed t-test for independent samples (not assuming equal variances) shows that the difference between the Federal Constitutional Court and the SCC with respect to the variable 'embedding in the running text' is statistically significant, t(232.29) = 6.99, p = <0.001, 95% confidence interval [3.74, 6.7].

6.5.4 Modalization Procedures: Boosters and Hedges

In the category of modalization procedures, a total of 257 boosters and hedges were coded, 185 of which were found in SCC decisions and 72 in decisions of the Federal Constitutional Court.

The Federal Constitutional Court uses more boosters than hedges (48 boosters and 24 hedges). Propositions are reinforced, among other things, by emphasizing unanimity or by adding phrases such as "rightly so":

(49) The clause "and thereby causes a disadvantage to the person whose financial interests he is entrusted to protect" is, **according to unanimous opinion in case law and legal literature,** to be applied to both variants of the offense (see already RGSt 69, 58< 59>; cf. Dunkel, GA 1977, p. 328< 331>; Mayer, in: Materialien zur Strafrechtsreform, vol. 1, 1954, p. 333< 353>; Wegenast, Missbrauch und Treubruch, 1994, p. 11). (BVerfGE 126, 170–233 2nd Senate—23.06.2010, para. 19)

(50) The literature, however, **rightly** predominantly supports a limited amendment competence of the federal government on the basis of Art. 125a para. 1 sentence 1 GG (cf. F. Kirchhof, in: Festschrift für Rupert Scholz, 2007, p. 637< 648>; Schoch, DVBl 2007, p. 261 < 264>). (BVerfGE 155, 310–357, 2nd Senate—07.07.2020, para. 80)

An example of a weakening of validity through a hedge can be found in the following passage:

(51) A decisive cause **probably** lies in the right to choose a health insurance fund and the way it is exercised. The right to choose, simply and somewhat exaggeratedly put, is exercised less often by the sick than by the healthy; the sick do not change their fund (cf. Nopper, Der Risikostrukturausgleich aus Sicht einer Allgemeinen Ortskrankenkasse, in: Jabornegg/Resch/Seewald <eds.>, op. cit., p. 137< 148>). (BVerfGE 113, 167–273, 2nd Senate—18.07.2005, para. 187)

Table 6.8 Average number of modalization procedures in the BVerfG decisions diachronic

	1985	1990	1995	2000	2005	2010	2015	2019	2020
Ø MP	0.11	0.23	0.15	0.58	1.09	0.27	0.04	0.5	0.4

As will be discussed in the interpretation, it cannot be determined for every modalization procedure, without knowledge of the pretext, whether the Federal Constitutional Court itself is responsible for the modalization or whether it was adopted from the pretext.

On average, the Federal Constitutional Court uses 0.27 modalization procedures per decision (SD = 0.8). This average remains similarly low across all years analyzed (see Table 6.8).

At the SCC, more boosters than hedges are also used; the decisions contain 109 boosters and 76 hedges. Boosting procedures were used in 58 decisions, whereas hedges appeared in only 38 decisions. Among the boosters, constructions with "clear" or "clearly" are particularly frequent, with 24 occurrences:

(52)\ These submissions were **clearly** supported in the findings of the Report of the Royal Commission on Aboriginal Peoples, vol. 3, supra, at p. 204: [...]. (Lovelace v. Ontario 2000 SCC 37–20.07.2000, para. 70)

Examples of hedges that are also used multiple times include the adverb "perhaps" as well as verbal mitigations with "seem":

(53) Recent research **seems to suggest** that the vast majority of forensic psychiatrists and psychologists, including those who have given evidence with respect to legal insanity in a large number of cases, have no effective understanding of the legal test about which they are expressing an opinion: R. Rogers and R. E. Turner, "Understanding of Insanity: A National Survey of Forensic Psychiatrists and Psychologists" (1987), 7 Health L. Can. 71. See also J. Ziskin and D. Faust, Coping with Psychiatric and Psychological Testimony (4th ed. 1988), vol. I, at pp. 389–408. (R. v. Chaulk 1990 3 SCR 1303–20.12.1990, para. n/a)

There are also instances of boosters and hedges being used in parallel:

(54) Despite the semantic difference between the expressions "cruel and unusual treatment or punishment" (as in the Canadian Charter and the constitution of Trinidad and Tobago) and "cruel and unusual punishments" (as in the eighth amendment to the United States Constitution) and "inhuman or degrading treatment or punishment" (as in the European Convention), **it seems clear** that the essential thrust of these provisions, however expressed, is the same, and their meaning has been assimilated. (Quebec (Attorney General) v. 9147–0732 Québec inc. 2020 SCC, para. 106)

Table 6.9 Average number of modalization procedures in the SCC decisions diachronic

	1985	1990	1995	2000	2005	2010	2015	2019	2020
Ø MP	0.79	0.68	1	1.36	0.14	0.38	3.08	3.5	1.89

On average, an SCC decision contains 0.83 modalization procedures (SD = 1.45). Unlike the Federal Constitutional Court, this value is significantly higher in some years; an increase in the frequency of modalization devices can be observed in more recent decisions (see especially 2015 and 2019) (Table 6.9).

As the following diagram shows, the SCC uses significantly more modalization procedures overall and on average than the BVerfG (Fig. 6.7).

The difference in the frequency of modalization procedures between the two courts is statistically significant. This is confirmed by a two-tailed t-test (for unequal variances) with the following values: $t(333.15) = 4.05$, $p = <0.001$, 95% confidence interval [0.23; 0.66].

6.5.5 *Attributions and Source Labeling*

A total of 551 attributions and labels were coded in the decisions of both courts, including 311 codings for the BVerfG and 240 for the SCC. In the case of the BVerfG, explicit, evaluative attributions of the content of a citation or the cited author are rare (16 occurrences); 295 of the codings represent source labeling. Within this very frequent category, three different types can be distinguished. First, numerous source labels provide information on how a cited source relates to a given proposition. In the following example, for instance, the source 'Hermes', according to the label, shares the interpretation of the Federal Constitutional Court; the source 'Windhorst' appears to advocate a different interpretation:

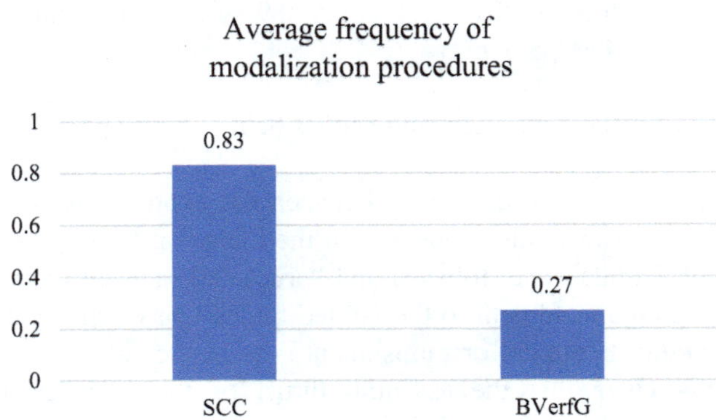

Fig. 6.7 Frequency of modalization procedures in comparison

(55) A requirement for consent does not arise from the provisions in § 16 para. 3 sentences 2 and 3 LuftSiG, according to which the federal government may reclaim responsibilities of the aviation security authorities previously delegated to the states, nor from the repeal of the predecessor regulation effected by Art. 2 no. 10 of the Act to Revise Aviation Security Tasks (§ 31 para. 2 no. 19 sentences 2 to 4 LuftVG, old version), which permitted such a retransfer only at the request of the affected state (**see also Hermes,** in: Dreier, GG, vol. 3, 2nd ed. 2008, Art. 87d para. 33; Hömig, in: Hömig, GG, 8th ed. 2007, Art. 87d para. 5; Pieroth, in: Jarass/Pieroth, GG, 10th ed. 2009, Art. 87d para. 2; Durner, in: Friauf/Höfling, Berliner Kommentar, as of November 2006, Art. 87d para. 27; Heitsch, Die Ausführung der Bundesgesetze durch die Länder, 2001, pp. 284 f.; **contra: Windthorst,** in: Sachs, GG, 5th ed. 2009, Art. 87d para. 40). (BVerfGE 126, 77–112 2nd Senate—04.05.2010, para. 151)

A second type is the reference to further 'sources within the cited source'. For this, the BVerfG often uses the label 'm.w.N.' (with further references) or similar constructions:

(56) Rather, taking into account the particular circumstances of the individual case, it must be determined whether the parties concerned must seriously expect economic disadvantages, i.e., whether the occurrence of damage is likely, so that the asset value is already diminished due to the risk of loss (see BGHSt 24, 386< 387>; 33, 244, NJW 1971, p. 64; **further references in Fischer,** Strafgesetzbuch, 57th ed. 2010, § 266 paras. 150 ff.; Kindhäuser, ibid., § 266 para. 110). (BVerfGE 126, 170–233 2nd Senate—23.06.2010, para. 137)

In addition, as a third type, there are content-related source labels that specify the particular aspect on which a source provides (further) information:

(57) In the case of the element of disadvantage, the interpretation must take into account the legislative intent to establish this element as independent alongside that of breach of duty; it must therefore not conflate this element with the element of breach of duty, that is, subsume it under the latter (**on this risk see Saliger,** ZStW 112< 2000>, p. 563< 610>; idem, HRRS 2006, p. 10< 14>). (BVerfGE 126, 170–233 2nd Senate—23.06.2010, para. 112)

On average, a BVerfG decision contains just over one feature (1.16, SD=2.42) from the category of attributions and labels; as already mentioned, the former are exceptional. The figures in the following table therefore refer mainly to source labeling. From 2005 onwards, the average value (with the exception of 2015) is exceeded and is higher than in the comparatively older decisions (Table 6.10).

Of the 240 codings in this analysis category for the SCC, almost all—quite the opposite of the BVerfG—are attributions; only two reference labelings are found

Table 6.10 Average number of attributions and labelings in the BVerfG decisions diachronic (BVerfG) over time

	1985	1990	1995	2000	2005	2010	2015	2019	2020
Ø Attr. & Ett	0,47	0,75	0,51	0,79	1,82	2,45	0,77	3,19	2,2

Table 6.11 Average number of attributions and comments in the SCC decisions diachronic

	1985	1990	1995	2000	2005	2010	2015	2019	2020
Ø Attr. & Ett	1,33	1	1,55	1,45	0,32	0,77	0,64	1,8	2,0

in the Canadian decisions. On average, 1.07 attributions (SD = 1.99) (or labelings) are used per SCC decision. Particularly characteristic is the evaluation of external content and of the source of the citation. There are numerous, mostly content-independent comments that highlight the quality of a source:

(58) As Martha Minow **elegantly** noted, the ability to be open-minded is enhanced by such knowledge and understanding: [...] (Yukon Francophone School Board, Education Area #23 v. Yukon, para. 34)

From a diachronic perspective, there is no significant development in the frequencies (Table 6.11).

A comparison of the mean values of the total frequencies identified (M = 1.07 for the SCC and M = 1.16 for the BVerfG) initially reveals no notable difference. The same applies to the inferential statistical analysis: a two-tailed t-test for independent samples (assuming equal variances) shows that the difference between the SCC and the BVerfG with regard to the frequency of attributions and labelings is not statistically significant, $t(489) = 0.46, p = 0.645, 95\%$ confidence interval [0.31, 0.49]. From a qualitative perspective, however, a major difference should be noted: while the BVerfG almost exclusively comments on the source and does not make explicit remarks about the content of the quotation or the author of the quotation, the SCC behaves in the opposite manner. The SCC makes almost no source labelings and instead explicitly evaluates the quotation and its author.

6.5.6 *Evidentiality Markers: Subjunctive and Citation-accompanying Expressions*

In the category of evidentiality markers, 1,077 codings were made for the SCC and 366 for the BVerfG (a total of 1,443 codings). As mentioned at the outset that this category only allows for limited comparability, as the reportative subjunctive does not exist in English. Even in the German decisions, however, the use of the reportative subjunctive cannot be considered particularly frequent; it appears in only 44 decisions. Notably, the subjunctive is sometimes used to mark citations even when the act of reporting is evident and the content does not actually allow for any epistemic positioning:

(59) On behalf of the Federal Ministry of Justice and Consumer Protection, the Institute of Criminology at the University of Tübingen, under the direction of Prof. Kinzig, evaluated electronic monitoring within the framework of supervision of conduct. The study covers all 74 individuals who, between January 1, 2011, and August 31, 2013, were issued an order pursuant to § 68b (1) sentence 1 no. 12 StGB. In only 64 cases **was** the electronic ankle bracelet actually applied. Furthermore, a control group comprising 74 individuals **was** formed (see Bräuchle/Kinzig, Die elektronische Aufenthaltsüberwachung im Rahmen der Führungsaufsicht, Kurzbericht über die wesentlichen Befunde einer bundesweiten Studie mit rechtspolitischen Schlussfolgerungen, undated, p. 2; Bräuchle, Die elektronische Aufenthaltsüberwachung gefährlicher Straftäter im Rahmen der Führungsaufsicht, Eine Studie zur Rechtsdogmatik und Rechtswirklichkeit, 2016, pp. 78, 80, 86). (BVerfGE 156, 63–182, 01.12.2020 2nd Senate, para. 174)

With regard to citation-introducing phrases, it is striking that their use is usually accompanied by unspecific generalizations of the source. Instead of explicitly naming the source by embedding an author's name, phrases such as "in the literature" are used:

(60) **The literature overwhelmingly shares this understanding** of inheritance law and the guarantee of inheritance, which are reflected in Art. 14 (1) sentence 1 GG and Art. 6 (1) GG, and thus guide inheritance law and inheritance tax law (see Leisner, Verfassungsrechtliche Grenzen der Erbschaftsbesteuerung, 1970, p. 111; Löhle, Verfassungsrechtliche Gestaltungsspielräume und -grenzen bei der Besteuerung von Erbschaften und Schenkungen, 2001, pp. 25, 102 f.; Papier, in: Maunz/Dürig, GG, Art. 14 GG para. 301 ff. <March 2010>; Reinisch, Erbschaftsteuer und Verfassungsrecht, 1999, pp. 69 ff.). (BVerfGE 126, 400–433 1st Senate—21.07.2010, para. 98)

The mean number of evidentiality markers is M = 1.37 features per BVerfG decision. With the exception of 2015, this mean is exceeded in decisions issued from 2005 onwards (see Table 6.12).

As already suggested by the high number of sources embedded in the running text, the SCC contains numerous citation-introducing phrases (1,077 occurrences).

Table 6.12 Average number of evidentiality markers in the BVerfG decisions diachronic

	1985	1990	1995	2000	2005	2010	2015	2019	2020
Ø Evident	0,47	0,63	0,45	0,5	1,91	2,81	0,73	4,25	2,73

Table 6.13 Average number of evidentiality markers in SCC decisions diachronic

	1985	1990	1995	2000	2005	2010	2015	2019	2020
Ø Evident	3.92	5.71	8.14	2.45	2.54	2.88	3.08	5.09	7.22

These are almost exclusively introductory *verba dicendi.* Examples include the verbs "to state" (89 instances), "to note" (80 instances), "to point out/to make a point" (74 instances), "to observe" (48 instances), "to suggest" (33 instances), "to define" (28 instances), and "to express" (27 instances). The act of citing is also explicitly named through verbs such as 'to cite' and 'to quote' (29 occurrences):

(61) To **refer** again to the passage from Professor Colvin **quoted** above, while an insane person is "formally acquitted", "alternative coercive measures" are imposed—namely, potentially indefinite detention under a Lieutenant-Governor's warrant. (R. v. Chaulk 1990 3 SCR 1303–20.12.1990, para. n/a)

On average, 4.81 citation-introducing phrases are used per decision. This value is undercut in 5 years and exceeded in 4 years (see Table 6.13).

The large difference between the means (M = 1.37 for the BVerfG and M = 4.81 for the SCC) demonstrates that the two courts differ in their frequency of use of evidentiality markers. The comparatively lower frequency at the BVerfG is particularly noteworthy given that two possible forms of evidentiality marking were recorded for the BVerfG (subjunctive and citation-accompanying expressions), whereas for the SCC only citation-accompanying expressions were included (Fig. 6.8).

A two-tailed t-test for independent samples (equal variances not assumed) confirms that the difference between the SCC and the BVerfG with respect to the variable 'frequency of evidentiality markers' is statistically significant, $t(294.44) = 5.3$, $p = <0.001$, 95% confidence interval [4.72, 2.15].

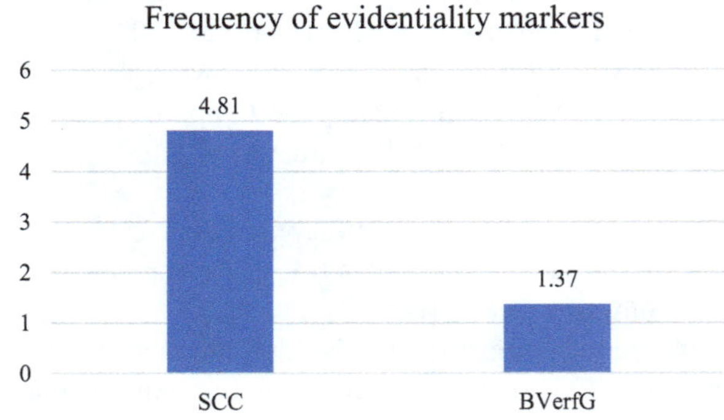

Fig. 6.8 Frequency of evidentiality markers in comparison

6.6 Interpretation

The first aim of the following interpretation, in accordance with research question 1, ‘How do courts cite?’, is to provide a summary characterization of prototypical citation practices based on the frequencies identified. The second aim, in line with research question 2, ‘Why do courts cite?’, is to reconstruct the functionalization of citations on the basis of the identified prototypical citation patterns. This also includes an exploration of the many significant differences between the citation practices of the BVerfG and the SCC, for example by relating the prototypical citation features to the specific requirements of each legal system, reflecting on the possibilities and limitations of reconstructing citation functions, and weighing the advantages and disadvantages associated with the different citation practices.

6.6.1 How Do Courts Cite? Prototypical Tendencies in the Citation Practices of the BVerfG and the SCC

Based on the frequencies presented in the results, the citation practices of the Federal Constitutional Court of Germany and the Supreme Court of Canada can be summarized as follows: The BVerfG is prototypically characterized by immaterial citations of legal scholarship, with obligatory mention of the cited sources in parentheses. The following example can be considered a typical instance of intertextual reference for these analytical categories at the BVerfG:

(62) The requirement of neutrality is not contradicted by the fact that the holder of a government office is regularly perceived in their dual role as federal minister and party politician. From the perspective of citizens, the intertwining of public office and party affiliation may result in only limited expectations of neutrality toward individual government members (see Krüper, JZ 2015, p. 414< 416>; Payandeh, Der Staat 55< 2016>, p. 519< 532 ff.>; Putzer, DÖV 2015, p. 417< 422 f.>; Tanneberger/Nemeczek, NVwZ 2015, p. 215< 216>). (BVerfGE 154, 320–353, 2nd Senate—09.06.2020, para. 55)

The use of parenthetical source references by the BVerfG is accompanied by a very limited use of citation-accompanying phrases. Chain citations, in which multiple sources are assigned to a single intertextual proposition, are characteristic. On average, each intertextual reference is accompanied by 3.35 source citations.[3] Also noteworthy is the high number of source labels, which provide the reader

[3] This value was calculated from a total of 3,664 source citations and 1,093 identified intertextual citation types. The counting of the latter will be discussed in Sect. 6.6.2.

with keywords about the content of a reference or indicate how a further source relates to the cited content (e.g., by the abbreviation "a.A.," meaning "alternative view"). In contrast, procedures of modalization and evidentiality markers are not prototypical features of citations in BVerfG decisions, given the frequencies observed.

From a diachronic perspective, the increase in the number of sources consulted is particularly striking. Over the period studied, the total number of cited sources has increased almost tenfold (for comparison: M=4.28 sources per decision in 1985 and M=4.3 in 1990 vs. M=38.13 in 2019 and M=37.33 in 2020, with a sudden rise beginning in 2005). This increase affects all source categories, meaning the number of references to legal scholarship, non-legal texts, and foreign case law have all risen. Notably, the composition has changed as well. While references to foreign case law accounted for only about 0.5% of all sources in 1985 and non-legal texts for about 6%, these shares are significantly higher in 2020 (4% of all sources are foreign legal sources and 12% are other texts). Correspondingly, the share of references to legal scholarship has dropped from 93.64% in 1985 to 84% in 2020. The overall increase in intertextual references likely explains the rise in the variables 'evidentiality markers' and 'source labeling' as well. The comparatively high frequency of sources in recent years may create a need for labeling; especially in chain citations, these labels help orient the reader in classifying the sources. In contrast, the BVerfG's citation practice has remained consistent in two analytical categories: among other things, the low standard deviations show that the BVerfG has consistently preferred immaterial citation types and has used modalization procedures only rarely throughout the years.

The prototypical citation of the Supreme Court of Canada is a lengthy material reference to legal scholarship, often with prominent placement of the cited author. A 'prototypical' citation practice at the SCC emerges only narrowly, as both analytical categories mentioned show an almost 50/50 distribution. 51% of references are material, 49% immaterial; 51% of all cited authors are embedded in the running text, and 49% are not introduced by obligatory mention. These are thus only very slight preferences. The frequent embedding of the cited author in the running text is accompanied by a high number of citation-accompanying phrases (especially reporting verbs). The following example can be considered typical of SCC citations in this regard:

(63) As Professor Mewett has rightly admonished, "[p]erhaps no phrase is bandied about with more imprecision and with more unawareness of its legal and social significance than the privilege against self-incrimination": "Law Enforcement and the Conflict of Values" (1970), 12 Crim. L.Q. 179, at p. 186. (R. v. S. (R.J.) 1995 1 SCR 451–02.02.1995, para. 488)

At least in comparison to the citation practice of the BVerfG, positioning elements on the part of the citer—whether in the form of modalization procedures or attributions—can be considered characteristic. In decisions from 2020, an average of approximately four modalization procedures and attributions are used per decision.

From a diachronic perspective, two developments are particularly notable: While embedding the cited author in the running text dominated in earlier years, in more recent decisions cited authors are increasingly moved out of the running text. As with the BVerfG, there is also an increase in the number of cited sources. Comparing the decision years 1985 and 2020, the number of sources has increased roughly fivefold (with a sharp rise between 2000 [M = 7.0] and 2005 [M = 37.36]). The development of frequencies in the source categories is also interesting: Comparing the oldest analyzed decision year, 1985, with the most recent, 2020, it is striking that in 1985, references to foreign case law accounted for 68% of all references, making it the most frequent source category; in 2020, this share has dropped to 24%, and legal scholarship now dominates with 69% of all sources.

A diachronic look at the frequency of source categories reveals a divergent development between the two courts. The BVerfG shows increasing openness to considering foreign case law, while the SCC shows a relative decrease in this category in favor of more references to legal scholarship. As a result of these opposing trends, the citation practices of the two courts have converged; in terms of the feature 'frequency of source categories,' their practices are now more 'similar' in recent decisions than in earlier ones. Overall, many differences can be observed between the citation practices of the two courts, confirming the hypothesis 'H1: There are differences between the citation practices of the Federal Constitutional Court of Germany and the Supreme Court of Canada.' Significant differences are evident in the frequency of material citations, the frequency of references to foreign case law, the frequency of cited authors embedded in the running text, the frequency of modalization procedures, and the frequency of evidentiality markers. Furthermore, it has been shown that the SCC prefers explicit attributions of cited content, while the comparatively subtler source labeling is predominant at the BVerfG. The following Sect. 6.6.2 addresses possible backgrounds and implications of these findings.

6.6.2 *Why Do Courts Cite? Citation Functions in the Decisions of the BVerfG and the SCC*

To reconstruct the functions of citations, the following analysis examines the possible intentions behind citation features and the effects associated with them. The structure of this chapter follows the order in which the results of the analytical categories were presented (1. Number and categories of sources, 2. Frequency and distribution of citation types, 3. Local textual embedding of cited authors, 4. Modalization procedures, 5. Attributions and labeling, and 6. Evidentiality markers).

6.6.2.1 Number and Categories of Sources

Two key findings from the *analysis category of source frequencies and source categories* are that both courts—despite their many differences in citation practices—cite roughly the same number of sources per decision on average, and that legal scholarship constitutes the most frequently cited source category for both courts. The BVerfG cites an average of 13.57 sources per decision, while the SCC cites only slightly more, with an average of 14.21 sources per decision. For both courts, the number of sources consulted has increased over the years. This steady rise in source frequency can be interpreted as an indication of the growing importance of citation practices overall—and, as the comparison of the two courts shows, this is independent of the legal system. The increased significance of citation compared to older decisions may have various reasons. On the one hand, it reflects the increasing dialogicity in the courts' decision-making processes. More influences now shape decisions than, for example, in 1985. On the other hand, the growing number of sources also reflects the courts' views on the requirements for coherent jurisprudence and legitimate reasoning. While the BVerfG, for instance, rarely considered supranational case law in its older decisions, more recent decisions more frequently reference the CJEU. The increasing frequency of references to the CJEU may be due to the broader thematic scope of EU law. Alternatively, it could be inferred that the BVerfG previously attributed little or no relevance to supranational case law, whereas today it regards it—whether approvingly or critically—as a factor to be considered. The frequencies identified support Nußberger's thesis (2006) that citation plays a major role in the development of a common European constitutional law. This is also evident in the general increase in references to foreign case law; within the years analyzed, the BVerfG has become increasingly open to decisions from foreign courts. The presentation of results has already referred to a decision on custody and parental rights violations, in which the BVerfG lists the legal situation in all 27 EU countries (Example 27, BVerfGE 127, 132–165 1st Senate—21.07.2010, para. 23). It can be assumed that this also generates a kind of authority through quantity—by citing many sources, a legal provision is 'normalized' and its contestability reduced. Overall, quantity seems to play an important role in the BVerfG's citation practice; it uses so-called chain citations, where multiple sources are assigned to a single intertextual content. While the BVerfG uses 3.35 sources per citation, the SCC uses only 1.17. The citation thus becomes a quantitative strategy of legitimation, a "doubling of the voice" (Gander 2010, see also Sect. 3.2.2). On the one hand, this creates the impression of a high density of information, which in turn can lead the reader to perceive credibility and thus persuasion (cf. *uncertainty reduction theory* on the influence of perceived information density on attributions of credibility, e.g., D'Angelo/Toma 2015). On the other hand, chain citations make it more difficult to reconstruct the reasoning; the reader cannot discern which content is drawn from which source. It is not possible to reconstruct to what extent and in what way the sources in a chain citation contributed to a statement; their contribution to the decision is leveled out. The lack of transparency in the engagement with sources is all the more surprising given that the BVerfG itself, in one of its decisions, criticizes the citation practice of a tax court and points out that merely listing sources is insufficient:

> Insofar as the referring court believes that the solidarity surcharge under the SolZG 1995 no longer constitutes a permissible supplementary levy within the meaning of Art. 105(2), Art. 106(1) no. 6 GG, the referral order lacks engagement with case law and legal literature (aa). […] aa) Although the referral order reproduces various, even divergent, views from case law and literature, it does not engage with them argumentatively. The mere reproduction of references cannot replace the required engagement (cf. BVerfGE 65, 308 < 316>). (BVerfG, 2nd Senate—07.06.2023, para. 60).

Overall, the BVerfG and the SCC use almost the same number of sources. However, there is a significant difference regarding the frequency of references to foreign case law.

Despite the increase in the frequency of foreign decisions in BVerfG rulings, the relevant figures for the Supreme Court of Canada are statistically significantly higher overall. The high frequency of references to foreign case law at the SCC is likely due, not least, to the court's self-conception. In one of its decisions, it characterizes itself as an open-minded court whose consideration of international sources has earned it praise:

(64) Significantly, this Court's use of international and comparative sources in the interpretation of the Charter has been lauded internationally (see, e.g., Ran Hirschl, "Going Global? Canada as Importer and Exporter of Constitutional Thought", in Richard Albert and David R. Cameron, eds., Canada in the World: Comparative Perspectives on the Canadian Constitution (2018), 305). (Quebec (Attorney General) v. 9147–0732 Québec inc. 2020 SCC, para. 100)

This 'praise' provides insight into the quality criteria applied to judicial decisions, both by others and by the SCC itself. A 'praiseworthy' decision is based on the comparison of sources and the comprehensive consideration of textual networks—the larger the relevant textual network identified by the courts, as can be implicitly inferred from the passage in Example 64, the better. It follows that the SCC itself regards intertextual reference as an appropriate means of decision-making; intertextual reference is thus declared a quality criterion for judicial decision-making. Through citation, the court demonstrates the breadth of its reflection; the act of comparison is accompanied by an act of positioning, which in turn establishes coherence.

The fact that creating coherence through references to other legally relevant texts is not the only motivation behind citations in decisions is demonstrated by the presence of non-legal texts. Literary texts, such as the reference to Kafka in the following example, as discussed in the introduction to this work, do not belong to the relevant textual network and therefore do not have the capacity to create or demonstrate coherence in jurisprudence:

(65) Not only does the criminal process confer on the accused publicity for his dubious causes—it may even bring him sympathy. The criminal process is cast as a conflict between the accused and the state, a conflict in which the accused may appear at his most sympathetic. Franz Kafka was not being entirely whimsical when he wrote, "If you have the right eye for these things, you can see that accused men are often attractive" (The Trial (1976), at p. 203). (R. v. Keegstra 1990 3 SCR 697–13.12.1990, para. n/a)

The reflection on publicly conducted criminal trials and the concern that they could bring not only notoriety but even sympathy to a defendant is illustrated here with a literary quotation. The literary quotation is used to support a statement that does not directly relate to a legally relevant aspect, but rather to the societal impact of criminal trials; thus, a non-legal text is consulted in connection with a non-legal aspect. According to DeStefano (2007), literary quotations confer *ethos* on the judge (see also Sect. 3.2.2): the judge can let the authority of the literary text speak for itself and thereby enhance his own profile—demonstrating that a renowned author shares the same view. Moreover, it is noteworthy that, on the content level, the quotation essentially does not add any aspects beyond those already expressed in the judge's own proposition; in terms of content, it could be omitted without any loss of substance. Kafka's formulation differs primarily in its imagery ("to have an eye for these things") and thus serves an illustrative function. If vividness may be considered a rhetorical ornament—since vividness operates at the level of style rather than content—then the quotation can also be ascribed an ornamental function.

From a diachronic perspective, what stands out in the SCC is the changing proportion of source categories over time. While in some years references to foreign case law constitute the most frequent category, in other years references to legal scholarship predominate. Following Rado (2020), this can be interpreted as an indication that citation practices regarding openness to foreign case law are strongly influenced by the individual preferences of the judiciary (see also Sect. 5.3.2). While the shares of foreign case law and the category of 'non-legal texts' fluctuate from year to year, there is a noticeable increase in the category of 'legal scholarship.' For comparison, the proportion of references to legal scholarship was 57% in 1985 and 69% in 2020. The close relationship to academia, often attributed to the civil law tradition, can, based on the values identified in this study, also be ascribed to the SCC as a common law court. References to legal scholarship are, at the SCC as well as at the BVerfG, an integral part of the network of texts considered relevant.

6.6.2.2 Frequency and Distribution of Citation Types

As revealed by the quantitative analysis, the SCC and the BVerfG differ in their preference for specific *types of citation.* While the SCC frequently employs material citations, verbatim quotations are extremely rare in the decisions of the BVerfG.

In particular, the sometimes considerable length of material citations in the SCC suggests that these citations may, among other things, serve an economic function:

(66) The prejudicial idea that those with mental illnesses are inherently and perpetually dangerous, along with other stigmatizing, prejudicial notions, has led to profound disadvantage for individuals living with mental illnesses (Winko, at paras. 3537; Swain, at p. 994; P. W. Corrigan and A. C. Watson, "Understanding the impact of stigma on people with mental illness" (2002), 1 World Psychiatry 16). This disadvantage has deep historical roots (H. Stuart, J. Arboleda Flórez and N. Sartorius, Paradigms Lost: Fighting Stigma and the Lessons Learned (2012), at pp. 103–111):Mental illnesses are not like other illnesses, because they regularly cause people to lose their rights and freedoms in ways that are unimaginable in other health conditions.. ..Historically, the care of the mentally ill has been deplorable. During the great confinement in the early part of the 1800s, hospital officials in Europe had the authority to round up and imprison people who were mentally ill (termed then madmen and idiots), along with beggars, vagabonds, criminals, the unemployed, and other undesirables. The characterization of the mentally ill as wild beasts justified their forcible confinement and social banishment. (Ontario (Attorney General) v. G 2020 SCC 38—20.11.2020, para. 62)

A large amount of textual material is adopted, so that the SCC does not need to formulate its own wording. While excessive material citation in academia is criticized as "copying" (Bänsch/Alewell 2020: 40 f., see also Sect. 3.3.2) without any original contribution, such criticism cannot be directed at citation in judicial decisions. Judicial decisions are not subject to a requirement of originality, and their quality is not defined by a particularly high degree of creative input; their function lies in the utilization of existing material (see also the advantages of material citation in this chapter). Furthermore, the example raises the question of whether there is an ornamental or stylistically motivated intention behind its use. The use of the citation allows the SCC to depart from the usual style of judicial decisions; for example, the citation incorporates a list that breaks with the otherwise typically condensed style of judicial decisions and employs vocabulary that would also be unusual in such decisions (e.g., the strongly connoted "vagabond" instead of the more neutral "homeless"). The ornamental function of material citations in judicial decisions can also be found at the BVerfG. The BVerfG shows a strong preference for immaterial citations. Against this background, verbatim citation can be described as a deviation from its prototypical citation practice. The status as a deviation or special case raises the question of which characteristics of a pretext lead the BVerfG to consider it worthy of verbatim citation. This question can only be approached through a qualitative examination of the materially cited elements:

(67) In state practice after 1949, a **"wildly proliferating system of subsidies"** (Heun, in: Dreier, GG, vol. 3, 2nd ed. 2008, Art. 104b para. 1) developed in the form of fund management and other mixed financing arrangements. (BVerfGE 127, 165–224 2nd Senate—07.09.2010)

Example 67 represents a material citation that, through its figurative content, breaks with the usual, sober and objective style of BVerfG decisions. The stylistic difference is legitimized by the act of citation; the quotation marks function in this sense as a 'ticket' to a change in register. Such a citation can thus be ascribed an ornamental function; as a stylistic device, the phrase "wildly proliferating system of subsidies" enriches the connotative level. The imagery of the cited (alliterative) phrase makes the position on the spread of the subsidy system evident without further commentary. The exploitation of the connotative level—uncontrollability and, if applicable, the need for intervention—also has an economic aspect, as further commentary and positioning become unnecessary. The same applies to Example 68, which can also be described as a break in register:

(68) Furthermore, it is not possible, in determining the responsibilities of the Federal Court of Auditors in terms of their implementation, to proceed **"generously",** because it has no decision-making authority and the exclusivity principle of competence law applies without restriction only to state action with a decision-making character (see Heintzen, in: von Münch/Kunig, GG, vol. 3, 5th ed. 2003, Art. 114 para.). (BVerfGE 127, 165–224 2nd Senate 07.09.2010)

This example is particularly interesting because it raises questions about the criteria for material citation: As a comparison with the cited pretext Heintzen 2003 shows, the BVerfG modifies the wording of the pretext, in which the relevant passage actually reads as follows:

(69) Because the Federal Court of Auditors has no decision-making authority, **generosity** is possible in determining its responsibilities.

The lexeme, which is used as a noun in the pretext, appears in the BVerfG citation as an adjective. The change in word class during the act of citation can, on the one hand, be described as a minor transformation, since the cited word still belongs to the same word family. On the other hand, the example demonstrates that the dichotomy between literalness and transformation, which is used in theoretical typologies of citation as *the* defining criteria for describing citation types, proves untenable in empirical application.

It is also noteworthy that the BVerfG uses quotation marks at all, despite the transformation of the part of speech; it would also be possible to use an indirect quotation in which the word 'generous' is used without any graphematic marking. The use of quotation marks could therefore indicate that a modalizing function is in the foreground, and that a graphematic marking of a material adoption is not, or at least not primarily, intended. For cases of this kind, it would be helpful to differentiate between double and single quotation marks, as is sometimes done in academic texts (single quotation marks for modalizing quotations and double quotation marks for material quotations). However one reconstructs the function of the quotation marks in this example, it is clear that empirical analysis of citation practices shows that the theoretically defined boundaries between types of quotations become blurred in actual citation practice. Strictly speaking, the quotation in this example cannot be clearly assigned to any one type; it could be described, for example, as a modalizing quotation with a material element, as an indirect quotation with additional modalization, or simply as an incorrect material quotation.[4]

The following example also demonstrates that the previous strict typological distinction between modalizing quotations and intertextual quotation types cannot be maintained in practice:

(70) In sentencing, reference is made to the **“actual”** damage, with the fact that **“only”** a risk-based damage occurred being considered as mitigating (cf. Nack, StraFo 2008, p. 277< 280>). (BVerfGE 170–233 2nd Senate 23.06.2010, para. 147)

The use of single quotation marks suggests that both instances are modalizing quotations; however, a comparison with the corresponding pretext shows that both are in fact material quotations. This is problematic insofar as the reader—whether or not this is intended by the BVerfG—inevitably adopts a modalizing reading, which could distort the interpretation of the quoted statement. Only through their world knowledge, namely that ironic formulations are not to be expected in court decisions, does the reader know that modalization is probably not intended. The modalizing reading ‘triggered’ by the use of a single unit in quotation marks is neutralized solely by the reader’s knowledge of the text type of court decisions. In cases such as Example 70, it remains questionable what added value the BVerfG sees in the use of quotation marks.

By contrast, the interpretation of pure quotations, whose function has been clearly described in the relevant research, is comparatively unproblematic. The function of pure quotations, which in the present study were only recorded when accompanied by a source reference, consists, according to research in the philosophy of language, among other things, in directing language at itself and thus enabling the thematization of the quoted content. Pure quotations are a “device for

---

4 The question of when one must speak of incorrect quotation also arises in the following example: “In colloquial usage, ‘Nachteil’ means ‘damage, loss, unfavorable situation’ (Wahrig, Deutsches Wörterbuch, 8th ed. 2008, p. 1047); [...] or ‘an evil appearing as a reduction, deterioration, in general damage, loss, interruption, impairment’ (cf. Jacob and Wilhelm Grimm, Deutsches Wörterbuch, vol. 7, reprint 1984, col. 184 f.).” (BVerfGE 126, 170–233 2nd Senate—23.06.2010, para. 98) A comparison with the cited pretext shows that the BVerfG adapted the spelling without indicating any changes; the Grimms’ dictionary also writes nouns in lowercase.

talking about language" (Lepore/McKeever 2020: n.p., see also Sect. 2.1.2.6). In this function, their use in court decisions was to be expected: court decisions are fundamentally based on the determination of meanings, for example, the meanings of legal terms. In order to negotiate word meanings—especially according to the method of interpretation based on the ordinary meaning of words—the properties of the word to be interpreted must first be made explicit, for which the pure quotation is a suitable means:

(71) By definition, assisted suicide also presupposes a state of suffering. The word component **"assistance"** by definition excludes those (killing) acts that are carried out against the explicit or presumed will of the person concerned (cf. Kämpfer, Die Selbstbestimmung Sterbewilliger, 2005, p. 35). (BVerfGE 153, 182–310 2nd Senate 26.02.2020, para. 23)

In the following example, the pure quotation serves the author's own terminological engagement in contrast to the word choice in an intertextual reference:

(72) While the WHO, in the medical context, uses the word **"disability"** to refer to functional limitation [...] I prefer to use the expression **"functional limitation"** to emphasize that in legal terms all three aspects considered together that constitute the disability. (Granovsky v. Canada (Minister of Employment and Immigration, para. n.a.)

Another important role of the pure quotation arises in those cases where it must be determined whether a word constitutes a violation of the law or a criminal offense: for example, the entire decision of the BVerfG on the relationship between freedom of expression and protection of honor in collective judgments about soldiers (BVerfGE 93, 266–319 1st Senate 10.10.1995) is based on a discussion of the semantic dimension of the word 'murderer'.

As with material and modalizing quotations, the typological boundaries also become blurred with pure quotations:

(73) In legal terminology, **"particular"** is regularly used as the opposite of **"general".** In this sense, the Grimm dictionary describes the term "particular" in its adverbial use with the Latin synonyms "singulatim", "separatim", "specialiter" and "particulariter", or in its adjectival use with the Latin terms "peculiaris" and "singularis", which in German can be explained as "distinct, as something individual opposed to the general, often rare and outstanding, but also strange, peculiar, idiosyncratic" (cf. Jacob and Wilhelm Grimm, Deutsches Wörterbuch, entry "BESONDER", vol. 1, reprint 1984, col. 1630 ff.). (BVerfGE 151, 202–374 2nd Senate—30.07.2019, para. 162)

Example 73 shows that material quotations can also be used in the function of directing language at itself, in order to discuss the properties of a word, that is, in the function of a pure quotation.

Overall, the use of quotation marks—whether material, pure, or modalizing—is rare in the decisions of the BVerfG; immaterial types of quotation predominate. It was already anticipated in the presentation of the analysis categories and methodology that, without comparison with the pretext, it is not possible to determine which immaterial type of quotation is present (indirect quotation, paraphrase, or reference). This also posed a particular challenge for the analysis: it was not possible to determine where the immaterial reference began or ended, nor (exacerbated by the many chain citations) which content was to be assigned to which cited source. All of this leads to a lack of transparency for the reader, who is presented with the intertextual content in the BVerfG's decisions in such a 'processed' form that it is not possible to form an independent opinion on the positions represented in the pretexts. This results in a merging of the voices of the pretexts and that of the BVerfG.

A comparison with the citation practice of the SCC shows that, unlike immaterial citation, material quotations can be directly received in the text. This has the advantage that the reader can immediately form their own impression of the source in order to develop their own opinion. The use of graphically marked material quotations creates a visible separation between the position of the SCC and that of the pretext; as a result, the voices in the text also remain distinct. It can be assumed that the use of material types of quotation offers an advantage not only to the reader but also to the court itself. Through the many material adoptions, the court is relieved of the work of formulation. The court draws on existing content and formulations and can thus benefit from the economic function of citations.

6.6.2.3 Textual Placement of Citation Sources

The integration of citation sources into the running text, beyond the obligatory mention, is a prototypical feature of the SCC's citation practice; as frequency analysis has shown, the BVerfG rarely integrates citation sources into the running text. The result—that cited authors are given little prominence in BVerfG decisions—is hardly surprising in light of the legal tradition's ideals of decision-making. As part of the continental European Civil Law tradition, the BVerfG is committed to the ideals of an impersonal, 'automatic' subsumption. Legal reasoning, in accordance with this ideal, is primarily conducted by recourse to codified law—in the case of the Federal Constitutional Court, theoretically "sola constitutione" (Jestaedt 2010) and as far as possible without any appearance of a subjective element. At this point, it is worth recalling Montesquieu's legal-philosophical ideal of the judge as the "bouche qui prononce les paroles de la loi" (1834: 296; for ideals of the continental European legal tradition, see also Sect. 5.1.1). With only the obligatory mention, the citation source is barely present in the reading flow. If, by contrast, a citation source is given prominent placement, it is not only the "paroles" that come to the fore, but also the connection of the referenced position to a specific person becomes evident; the resulting personal element would conflict with the ideal of the absence of subjective moments in this legal tradition. According to this ideal, the focus should be on *what* is said, not on *who* says it. Such externalization of the citation source can be interpreted as a consistent focus on the content of a referenced source, with little emphasis on the author. The low emphasis on the citation source is accompanied by an 'incorporation' of external content—due to the low prominence of the citation source and the practice of immaterial citation, it is often impossible to reconstruct whether the passage is a paraphrase or indirect rendering of a pretext with subsequent source reference, or the author's own content with a further reference. This impression is reinforced by the use of chain citations—the sheer number of sources listed in parentheses causes the individual authors to fade into the background.

The practice of depersonalization is not only characteristic of the BVerfG's citation style, but, as legal-linguistic studies have found, is also a general feature of German legal language. All means of depersonalization, such as the use of the passive voice—which is considered typical of legal language—shift the focus from the subject (e.g., the author) to the object (e.g., the aspect under discussion). The use of the passive serves the goal of (pseudo-)objectivity in texts and, not least, obscures the fact that legal decisions are always made by people and ultimately represent a "fiction of automatic subsumption" (Busse 1992: 18).

A diachronic analysis of the results also suggests a connection between the handling of citation sources and the ideals of the legal tradition: there are hardly any fluctuations, and the placement of citation sources in parentheses is a constant feature of BVerfG decisions. The fact that citation sources are consistently rarely integrated into the running text can be interpreted as evidence that the choice of textual location for naming the citation source does not depend on individual writing socialization, but rather represents a cross-author or cross-individual characteristic of citation practice in BVerfG decisions.

It should also be emphasized in this context that among the citation sources embedded in the running text, it is particularly rare for individual authors to be named. Far more frequently represented in this category are, for example, the Federal Statistical Office and the European Court of Justice. This further reinforces the impression of depersonalization efforts in BVerfG decisions. Reference to statistics and figures determined by the Federal Statistical Office can be regarded as a particularly suitable and (seemingly) objective argument for justification and legitimation, since numbers, unlike author-bound positions as discussed in legal scholarship, are generally hardly contestable. The BVerfG projects the validity of the figures onto itself, thereby reducing the vulnerability of its argumentation. The embedding of the European Court of Justice in the running text, in turn, points to an ambivalent relationship between the two courts. The ECJ accounts for the majority of citation sources placed in the running text. Occasionally, it is referred to in abbreviated form as "the Court." According to Richter (2015), such abbreviated source references can indicate the recognition of outstanding prominence. A citation source is so well known that there is no need for a full designation. This could give rise to the suspicion that the BVerfG places the ECJ in the text with the aim of projecting authority. However, it should be noted that the BVerfG does not consistently follow the ECJ's case law. The following example demonstrates that the BVerfG (not infrequently) openly adopts a different position from the ECJ:

(74) This is to be assumed if the integration law and/or the international treaty functionally replace or supplement the treaty. Such "substitute Union law" (see Lorz/Sauer, DÖV 2012, p. 573< 573 ff.>) includes, for example, the ESM Treaty and the law on the ESM Treaty, which, although not transferring sovereign rights, nevertheless brought about a fundamental restructuring of the original Economic and Monetary Union (see BVerfGE 135, 317< 407 para. 180> with reference to BVerfGE 129, 124< 181 f.>; 132, 195< 248 para. 128>; **contra ECJ, judgment of 27 November 2012, Pringle, C-370/12, EU:C:2012:756, paras. 73 ff.**), so that the Senate classified it as a matter of the European Union within the meaning of Art. 23(2) GG (see BVerfGE 131, 152< 219>). (BVerfGE 153, 74–182 2nd Senate 13.02.2020, para. 123)

Given the demonstration of dissent—while simultaneously asserting its own authority by referencing its own previous decision—it can largely be ruled out that the BVerfG refers to the ECJ for the purpose of projecting authority. Overall, it is also questionable whether the textual placement of citation sources in BVerfG decisions can be interpreted as a means of authority projection. As the following example illustrates, prominent placement of citation sources does not necessarily entail affirmation of the cited sources:

(75) Wilms and Jäger (JuS 1988, p. 268< 273>) are of the opinion that the court could at most have established its own incapacity to function, since there was no statutory ground for prevention; it should not have regulated succession in place of the electoral body. Doehring, on the other hand, takes the view that filling the gap is not permissible, as this would result in a composition of the court that no longer reflects the will of parliament (NJW 1987, p. 3234). **This view cannot be followed.** (BVerfGE 82, 286–305 1st Senate 10.07.1990, para. 87)

Due to the prominent subject position of the citation sources, the rejection of their content is particularly evident. In this context, it is conceivable that the BVerfG, by explicitly deconstructing the cited content, is demonstrating its own authority—the court is in a position to place its own view above that of the cited authors. However, such passages, in which the BVerfG's departure from cited content is made so salient by the prominent placement of the citation sources, are the exception rather than the rule.

For the SCC, a completely opposite picture emerges, with about half of the citation sources being placed prominently. In SCC decisions, citation sources, accompanied by an introductory reporting verb, usually serve as the subject of a citation-introducing phrase. Thus, the citation source is not only given a prominent position within the text but also constitutes an essential part of the sentence. Unlike the obligatory mention of citation sources in parentheses, the citation source must be processed by the reader through its syntactic integration into the flow of the text. As described in the corresponding results chapter, citation sources are given considerable space in the decision texts through their full mention—not only are names typically provided, but also academic titles and/or professional designations. As a result, both the citation source itself and the association of the cited content with a specific person are highly salient in the reception. This suggests that SCC decisions weigh not only *what* is stated in a pretext, but also *who* made the statement. This feature of Canadian citation practice may be attributable to the subjective, person-centered aspect that characterizes SCC decisions in light of judge-made law and the practice of *seriatim* decisions. In the practice of *seriatim* decisions—which the court has increasingly abandoned over the years in favor of the *per curiam* structure (see also Sect. 5.2.2)—it was (or is) highly relevant which judge reached which decision, and not only which decision was made for which reasons. The emphasis on the connection between content and person, or the person as the source, is also reflected in the handling of external content. This relationship can be interpreted as evidence that characteristics of the decision-making style are also reflected in citation practices, highlighting the close interconnection between judgment style and citation method. A particularly strong indication of this is provided by the diachronic changes observed for the variable 'embedding of the citation source': since 2005, there has been a dominant preference for externalizing the citation source. A relatively high standard deviation ($SD = 11.07$) in the frequency of citation sources placed in the running text also reflects the variability among SCC decisions with respect to this analytical category. This result is consistent with the depersonalization trends identified by legal studies for the court's general decision-making practice. Whereas the content of decisions was previously tied to individual judges through the aforementioned *seriatim* structure, the SCC now appears as a collective in more recent decisions. In short, the relationship between depersonalization trends in decisions and in citation embedding demonstrates how closely judgment style and citation practice are intertwined. From a functional perspective, it can already be established that the embedding of citation sources (whether intentional or not) creates a personal association with the cited content. However, the specific function of this personal association, understood as an intentional feature, cannot be determined unequivocally. On the one hand, there are indications that the SCC engages in *name dropping* (see also Sect. 3.4.2) and seeks to project the authority of the citation source; on the other hand, the prominent placement may also serve as a form of recognition for the citation source. The fact that information provided often goes beyond the obligatory inclusion of standard bibliographic details supports the interpretation that this is an attempt to project authority in the sense of so-called *name dropping* as a persuasive strategy. Noteworthy are the many academic titles such as doctoral degrees:

(76) As **Professor** Beaulac and **Dr.** Bérard explain: [...] (S. Beaulac and F. Bérard, Précis d'interprétation législative (2nd ed. 2014), Chap. 5, at paras. 5 and 36). (Quebec (Attorney General) v. 9147–0732 Québec inc. 2020 SCC, para. 22)

This impression of authority projection is reinforced by the numerous attributions that do not address the content of the source, but instead highlight attributes of the citation and the citation source that are, from an objective perspective, actually irrelevant (see also the function of attributions in Sect. 6.6.2.5). For example, the eloquence of the citation source is emphasized—an attribute that is, in fact, entirely irrelevant to the substantive level that is primarily significant in judicial decisions. In contrast, the interpretation of the prominent placement of citation sources as authority projection is challenged by the possibility that such placement is intended as a special form of recognition. The following example also supports this thesis:

(77) Geatros J. first noted the alternative remedies sought in Primeau's motion, namely, relief under s. 24(1) of the Charter, and relief by way of a writ of prohibition. **Geatros J.** then followed Re Praisoody (1990), 1 O.R. (3d) 606 (Gen. Div.), 61 C.C.C. (3d) 404 (sub nom. R. v. Devasagayam), and stated that the rights protected by s. 7 of the Charter go beyond the rights protected in ss. 11(c) and 13. **He quoted a passage from E. Ratushny,** "The Role of the Accused in the Criminal Process," in G.-A. Beaudoin and E. Ratushny, eds., The Canadian Charter of Rights and Freedoms (2nd ed. 1989), 451, at pp. 483–84, in which it is suggested that "many of the protections provided by the criminal process may be subverted by calling the suspect or accused as a witness at some other proceeding prior to his criminal trial." He indicated that Primeau did not seek relief prematurely, and concluded (at p. 198):

By compelling Primeau to testify at the preliminary inquiry of Lefort, his right to silence has been effectively denied. It is not an answer for the Crown to say that Primeau's testimony at the preliminary inquiry could not be used against him at his trial. He is entitled to say nothing until his trial, and then only if he chooses to testify. If Primeau were required to testify at this time the Crown would acquire an advantage indirectly that it could not obtain directly.

As the explicit 'chain of reception' in the example shows, the SCC places significant emphasis on identifying to whom particular content can be attributed and where or by whom the cited content has also been received: it would have been possible, after all, to refer either to Geatros J.'s reasoning or to Ratushny's argument; the SCC cites both sources. The prominent placement of the citation source (and, moreover, the choice of substantive quotations) serves to distinguish between original and external content. It prevents the appropriation of the cited content, and—unlike with the BVerfG—the reader can reconstruct which citation source is responsible for which idea.

6.6.2.4 Modalization Procedures: Boosters and Hedges

In the overall corpus $n_{total}=495$, a total of 257 citation-related *boosters and hedges* were identified, meaning that, on average, every second court decision contains at least one of these two modalization procedures. Both courts use noticeably more boosters than hedges. This suggests that external content in judicial decisions is more often used for purposes of affirmation than for deconstruction—especially when considering that non-modalized embedded citations, i.e., those not captured in this analytical category, fundamentally involve an identification between the citation source and the citing party. The preference for boosters over hedges in both courts can be interpreted as an indication that courts tend to (though not exclusively, see also Sect. 6.6.2.5) cite content that aligns with their own position. Against this background, it can be concluded that citations in judicial decisions primarily serve to support argumentation rather than to provide a mitigating, counter-position-inclusive reflection. Additionally, it can be inferred that, for intertextual references in decisions, functions that presuppose affirmation (e.g., economy) tend to dominate over those that are based on deconstruction (e.g., demonstrating one's own authority by asserting the validity of one's own proposition while rejecting external content).

In the decisions of the Federal Constitutional Court (BVerfG), the use of boosters generally follows two patterns. First, the BVerfG often 'boosts' by emphasizing the legality of a proposition expressed in cited texts; this clearly constitutes an affirmative embedding of the intertextual reference. Examples of this can be found in the following two passages:

(78) In this case, **the literature rightly demands** that administrative measures must primarily be directed against the disturbers, and that action may only be taken against the assembly as a whole under the special conditions of a police emergency (Hoffmann-Riem, loc. cit., para. 23 and 53 on Art. 8 GG; Dietel/Gintzel, loc. cit., para. 14 on § 15 VersG; see also v. Münch, loc. cit., para. 39 on Art. 8 GG; Drosdzol, Fundamental Issues of Demonstration Law, JuS 1983, p. 409 (414); Frowein, loc. cit. (1084)). (BVerfGE 69, 315–372 1st Senate 14.05.1985, para. 91)

(79) **The literature, however, rightly takes the predominant view** that the federal government's power to amend is limited on the basis of Art. 125a para. 1 sentence 1 GG (see F. Kirchhof, in: Festschrift für Rupert Scholz, 2007, p. 637< 648>; Schoch, DVBl 2007, p. 261< 264>). (BVerfGE 155, 310–357 2nd Senate 07.07.2020, para. 80)

A second boosting pattern is the reinforcement of a proposition in the context of boosting procedures by linking it to a quantitative level. The BVerfG conspicuously often refers to 'unanimity' and 'predominant' positions; a position appears to be considered legitimate if it is frequently represented:

(80) **The literature is almost unanimous in sharing this understanding** of inheritance law and the guarantee of inheritance rights, which are reflected in Art. 14 para. 1 sentence 1 GG as well as in Art. 6 para. 1 GG, and thus guide inheritance law and inheritance tax law (see Leisner, Constitutional Limits of Inheritance Taxation, 1970, p. 111; Löhle, Constitutional Scope and Limits in the Taxation of Inheritances and Gifts, 2001, pp. 25, 102 f.; Papier, in: Maunz/Dürig, GG, Art. 14 GG paras. 301 ff. <March 2010>; Reinisch, Inheritance Tax and Constitutional Law, 1999, pp. 69 ff.). (BVerfGE 126, 400–433 1st Senate 21.07.2010, para. 98)

As already noted in the interpretation of source frequencies (and especially of citation chains), the BVerfG again relies on quantity at this point—it is considered relevant whether a position is held by the majority or is a dissenting view. The reference, common in legal discourse, to the so-called "prevailing opinion" is thus established as a legitimate argumentative strategy, as illustrated in Example 80. This also serves an economic function, since deviating from or questioning the majority position cannot be done without additional reading and justification effort.

While in the boosting procedures (at least in the two exemplary cases cited) it is clear which view is held in the literature and that the BVerfG shares this view, the situation is more problematic in many cases involving hedging procedures. As the following example shows, it is sometimes impossible to reconstruct who the 'hedging' instance is:

(81) A decisive cause **probably** lies in the right to choose a health insurance fund and the way it is exercised. The right to choose, to put it simply and somewhat pointedly, is exercised less often by the sick than by the healthy; the sick do not change their fund (see Nopper, Risk Structure Compensation from the Perspective of a General Local Health Insurance Fund, in: Jabornegg/Resch/Seewald <eds.>, loc. cit., p. 137< 148>). (BVerfGE 113, 167–273, 2nd Senate 18.06.2005, para. 187)

Without consulting the original text by Nopper, it cannot be reconstructed whether Nopper himself qualified the proposition with the hedge "probably," or whether the BVerfG added the hedge to weaken Nopper's statement. Such cases complicate the interpretation of potential functionalizations of intertextual reference. It cannot be determined whether the intertextual reference is fundamentally affirmative or only partially affirmative; the voice of the BVerfG and that of Nopper merge due to the manner of presentation. For cases of this kind, no statements can be made about the function of the hedge.

As already noted in the presentation of the results, reference labels can also, in part, constitute hedges. The analysis of hedges occurring in the context of reference labeling offers the advantage that it can be clearly reconstructed that these are not quoted hedges and that the BVerfG itself has qualified the reference with the hedge. By using hedges in reference labeling, the BVerfG appears, among other things, to signal uncertainties regarding the interpretation of statements made in a cited source:

(82) By contrast, the question of the appropriate expenditure of funds for specific individual projects is of only secondary importance, which cannot justify information gathering by federal authorities such as the one under review here (see Meyer/Freese, NVwZ 2009, p. 609< 613>; **probably also von Arnim,** in: Isensee/Kirchhof, HStR VI, 3rd ed. 2008, § 138 para. 57). (BVerfGE 127, 165–224 2nd Senate 07.09.2010, para. 87)

(83) It is not necessary to decide whether the principle recognized in electoral law matters, that decisions and measures directly relating to the electoral process may only be challenged by the legal remedies provided for in the electoral regulations and in the electoral review procedure (see BVerfGE 3, 39 ff.; 329 f.; established case law; see most recently BVerfGE 74, 96< 101>), also applies to constitutional disputes (**apparently so Schreiber,** Handbook of Electoral Law for the German Bundestag, 4th ed., 1990, § 49 BWahlG, para. 4). (BVerfGE 83, 156–158 2nd Senate—29.11.1990, para. 2)

Cases of this kind are particularly interesting with regard to functional assignments: In the context of hedges, relevant research first identifies the function of "risk minimization" for the writer (Niemann 2018: 49). By qualifying absolute statements, a writer demonstrates potential negotiability, for example in anticipation of criticism (see Sect. 3.2.1). This function can be employed both in relation to one's own statements and to those of others. Second, hedges referring to external content can also serve to maintain politeness. Hedges mitigate potential *face threatening acts* (Fraser 2010, see also Sect. 3.2.1). Such a function may be particularly relevant when, in the act of citation, the writer distances themselves from the pretext and only partially endorses it. In the examples discussed, however, the use of hedges does not appear to serve the function of avoiding direct criticism, since the hedge is accompanied by a reference to a similarity between the statement of the BVerfG and the source; no criticism is implied. Whether the BVerfG seeks to protect itself in line with the 'risk minimization function' by using hedges in the examples to avoid making absolute statements about the interpretation of the cited text cannot be definitively established. Finally, it is also conceivable—contrary to the common hedging functions identified in the literature—that in these two examples, the BVerfG is actually attributing ambiguity or a lack of clarity to the cited sources. Ultimately, this could indeed reflect a form of 'risk minimization'; the BVerfG signals that there are uncertainties in interpreting the source and protects itself in the event of a misinterpretation by attenuating its own statement.

In the decisions of the SCC, there are overall more hedges and boosters than in those of the BVerfG. The SCC decisions also reveal a comparable mechanism for boosting: the authority of quotations is reinforced by attributing legality to them:

(84) As Professor Mewett has **rightly** admonished, "[p]erhaps no phrase is bandied about with more imprecision and with more unawareness of its legal and social significance than the privilege against self-incrimination": "Law

Enforcement and the Conflict of Values" (1970), 12 Crim. L.Q. 179, at p. 186. (R. v. S. (R.J.) 1995 1 SCR 451–02.02.1995, para. 488)

In some instances, the use of boosters in the SCC presents a similar problem for the reader as the hedges in the BVerfG, in that it is not clear which authority has integrated the epistemic qualifier:

(85) Under the common law, courts have gradually developed the power to monitor the processes of administrative bodies and their legality. There is today **no doubt** that "[t]he superior courts have the inherent power to review the legality of administrative actions" (D. P. Jones and A. S. de Villars, Principles of Administrative Law (3rd ed. 1999), at p. 6). (Blencoe v. British Columbia (Human Rights Commission) 2000, para. 147)

One possibility is that the SCC is 'boosting' the statements of Jones and de Villars by indicating that there is no doubt as to the validity of their proposition. However, another interpretation could be that this is a mixed quotation and that the original authors themselves already pointed to the absence of any doubt. Regardless of which authority uses the booster, it is clear that the SCC attributes full validity to the cited statement; the (own or cited) affirmation eliminates the need for further justification. Particularly interesting are cases that illustrate that the use of hedging cannot fundamentally be equated with distancing from or deconstructing the content of the citation. The following intertextual reference, for example, is used affirmatively through the explicit attribution "best," but this attribution is qualified by a "perhaps":

(86) Its inherent complexity is **perhaps best** exposed by the opinions in Branzburg v. Hayes, 408 U.S. 665 (1972). In this landmark decision, the Supreme Court of the United States dealt with journalist-source privilege for the first time, refusing to recognize any constitutional or common law privilege that would allow a reporter to refuse to reveal confidential information to a grand jury. (R. v. National Post 2010 SCC 16–07.05.2010, para. 108)

In the passage cited, the use of "best" suggests that the epistemic qualifier "perhaps" functions as a hedge for self-protection. The SCC indicates that it cannot claim knowledge of all sources. The example also demonstrates that, for each hedge and each booster, it must be assessed on a case-by-case basis whether it is associated with an affirmation or a deconstruction of the citation, and that quantitative analyses can therefore only be interpreted to a limited extent—not every hedge automatically entails a rejection of the cited source.

The significantly higher frequency of epistemic modalization procedures in the SCC compared to the BVerfG can be attributed to two reasons. On the one hand, linguistic and cultural conventions play a major role in the frequency of stance-taking procedures; as discussed in Sect. 4.4, Kranich's contrastive linguistic study (2011) has already pointed out that English generally uses more hedges than

German. On the other hand, the frequent use of modalization procedures was also to be expected in view of the characteristics specific to each legal system: The use of quotations manifests the "other," while the use of modalization procedures manifests the "self" of the text (Fløttum 2005: 32, see also Sect. 4.2.1). It has already been shown that the "self"—that is, in the case of court decisions, the judges—is much more present on the textual surface of common law decisions than in the seemingly objective, depersonalized civil law decisions. Through the comparatively more frequent use of modalization procedures in relation to external content, quotations in the SCC are represented as positions or opinions. The quotations are presented as objects of evaluation, and their factuality is depicted as negotiable. In contrast, epistemic procedures are used less frequently in the BVerfG—no space is left for epistemic processes, and the quotation is presented as fact.

6.6.2.5 Attributions and Reference Labeling

In the analysis category of *attributions and labeling,* it became apparent that the SCC exclusively uses the former, while the BVerfG almost exclusively employs reference labeling. These labels are, first and foremost, an indication that a reference is being made, rather than an indirect quotation. Every reference label signals that the reference lies outside the text and is not present within it (which, conversely, does not mean that every reference must necessarily be accompanied by a label). Furthermore, they indicate that the authors have engaged with the texts they reference and see added value in this engagement for understanding the respective topic. The nature of this added value varies; the labels themselves can provide clues as to the purpose for which a particular source is cited. As already demonstrated with several examples in the results section, the different forms of labeling can be further subcategorized. Some labels give the reader an indication of how the cited source relates to the author's own proposition (e.g., "a.A."), while others provide a keyword-like hint as to which aspect the reader might find information about in the source. These two examples demonstrate that reference labeling encompasses a wide functional spectrum. This functional spectrum cannot be strictly delimited, as even a label such as "a.A." can serve different functions: On the one hand, the addition of "a.A." documents that the authors of the court decisions have also engaged with positions that do not correspond to their own. This, in turn, signals an act of weighing different viewpoints. Even if only subtly, it demonstrates that not only those positions that support the court's own argumentation are considered (see also Sect. 6.6.2.4 on the dominance of affirmative citation). On the other hand, this addition also serves as a kind of reduction of complexity or as a way of dispensing with further work. It is acknowledged that other views on a topic exist, but these are not deemed 'worthy' of closer examination in the decision. In this context, the addition "a.A." appears as a compromise or shortcut, demonstrating comprehensive consideration of textual networks for cohesion purposes without providing further justification. In this respect, reference labeling is not only an offer to the reader to seek further information, but also fulfills an economic function. The economic aspect of (labeled) references is particularly evident in the frequently used abbreviation "m.w.N." (with further references). In this way, the court fulfills its duty of providing evidence without overburdening the already extensive bibliographic information. Regardless of the specific form of labeling—whether indicating alternative views or further references—they provide significant added value for the reader. Reference labels offer the reader an initial orientation, helping them decide whether a source might be worth reading.

In the citation practice of the SCC, reference labeling is absent. Unlike the BVerfG, the SCC usually comments on its sources explicitly. Particularly interesting are the evaluative dimensions to which the many different attributes refer, including eloquence, influence, or the vividness of a quotation (or its source):

(87) […], as Professor Ran Hirschl **eloquently** explains: […]. (Quebec (Attorney General) v. 9147–0732 Québec inc. 2020 SCC, para. 106)

(88) Most significant of all, however, Lamer J. drew upon (at p. 282) Professor Yves-Marie Morissette's **influential article** "The Exclusion of Evidence under the Canadian Charter of Rights and Freedoms: What to Do and What Not to Do" (1984), 29 McGill L.J. 521, to characterize the determination that lies at the heart of s. 24(2): […]. (R. v. Burlingham 1995 2 SCR 206–18.05.1995, para. 71)

As these two examples illustrate, the attributions often refer to non-content-related attributes. Characteristics of the cited text are highlighted that are actually irrelevant to its substantive content. The quality of a source is justified here by prestigious properties. While the reference to the significant influence of an article, as in Example 88, can at least indirectly attest to substantive quality—after all, it can be assumed that influential, frequently cited texts have convinced many readers with relevant expertise—emphasizing eloquence has nothing to do with content-related aspects. Departing from the ideally objective level of content, which should be central in court decisions, and supporting the argumentation with 'prestige criteria' thus creates the impression of persuasion attempts that are illegitimate according to rationalist legal models.

Furthermore, some attributions also highlight the ornamental value of the cited pretext:

(89) The United States Court of Appeals for the Fifth Circuit, in Dunagin v. City of Oxford, Mississippi, 718 F.2d 738 (1983) (en banc), cert. denied, 467 U.S. 1259 (1984), a case involving the constitutionality of a ban on liquor advertising, made the same point, at pp. 748–49, n. 8, **in slightly more colourful terms:**
There are limits to which important constitutional questions should hinge on the views of social scientists who testify as experts at trial. Suppose one trial judge sitting in one state believes a sociologist who has found no link between alcohol abuse and advertising, while another trial judge sitting in another state believes a psychiatrist who has reached the opposite conclusion. A similar situation actually occurred here. Should identical conduct be constitutionally protected in one jurisdiction and illegal in another? (RJR-MacDonald Inc. v. Canada (Attorney General) 1995 3 SCR, para. 80)

This passage demonstrates that the courts themselves are aware of the decorative function of quotations and see the ornamental quality of a citation as an enrichment for their decision. Positive attributions, as in the examples, are primarily realized through adverbs. The rejection of external content, on the other hand, is comparatively more elaborate and realized at the verbal level:

(90) Our colleague's appeal to stare decisis, **we say with respect, therefore misses the point.** (Fraser v. Canada (Attorney General 2020 SCC 28–16.10.2020, para. 221)

With regard to the reconstruction of functionalization, it should be noted—and this is important not only for the interpretation of attributions—that every explicit deconstruction and challenge through a rejecting stance involves effort. While an affirmatively used citation and quotation can stand on its own, an explicit deconstruction of external content cannot remain without further engagement and justification by the citing authority. Ultimately, it is therefore unlikely that explicitly negative embedded quotations can or are intended to serve an economic function. The opposite is true for more subtle markers of rejection, such as the addition "a.A.". By outsourcing the positioning of this addition, the BVerfG apparently sees no need to comment further on the opposing view.

As with the interpretation of modalization procedures, the frequency of explicit attributions in the SCC and their rarity in the BVerfG can be traced back to the ideals specific to each legal system: Through the act of commenting and evaluating, an authority reveals itself as an agent of opinion formation.

6.6.2.6 Evidentiality Markers: Subjunctive and Citation-Accompanying Phrases

In the analysis category of *evidentiality markers,* the subjunctive and citation-accompanying phrases were coded. Overall, as expected from the high frequency of citation sources placed in the running text, the SCC uses significantly more evidentiality markers than the BVerfG.

In German, the subjunctive can be used as a signal of reported speech; however, its use for marking purposes is not obligatory. Especially from a pragmatic perspective, this raises the question of which factors influence the choice between subjunctive and indicative. Steinseifer (2019) proposes the criterion of epistemic distancing—the subjunctive serves not only to mark the act of reference but also entails epistemic modalization. In the decisions analyzed, there are examples that support an epistemic-modalizing function of the subjunctive, as well as passages that suggest the opposite, namely a use of the subjunctive that is neutral with respect to evaluation and positioning. An example of the latter is the following decision, which discusses the advantages and disadvantages of electronic monitoring using ankle bracelets:

(91) On behalf of the Federal Ministry of Justice and Consumer Protection, the Institute of Criminology at the University of Tübingen, under the direction of Prof. Kinzig, evaluated electronic monitoring within the framework of supervision of conduct. The study includes all 74 individuals who, between January 1, 2011, and August 31, 2013, were issued an order pursuant to § 68b para. 1 sentence 1 no. 12 StGB. In only 64 cases **was** the ankle bracelet actually applied. Furthermore, a comparison group comprising 74 individuals **was** formed (see Bräuchle/Kinzig, Electronic Monitoring within the Framework of Supervision of Conduct, Summary of the Main Findings of a Nationwide Study with Legal Policy Conclusions, undated, p. 2; Bräuchle, Electronic Monitoring of Dangerous Offenders within the Framework of Supervision of Conduct, A Study on Legal Doctrine and Legal Reality, 2016, pp. 78, 80, 86). (BVerfGE 156, 63–182, 2nd Senate 01.12.2020, para. 174)

If one assumes that the subjunctive always entails epistemic distancing, this would mean that the Federal Constitutional Court is questioning whether a comparison group of 74 individuals was actually formed in the referenced study; that is, the Court is either distancing itself from the fact that such a group existed at all, or it is questioning the number of individuals in the group. However, this interpretation seems implausible, as the features of the study being reported are highly descriptive and thus leave little room for epistemic modalization. This suggests that in this passage, the subjunctive is not used to express epistemic distancing, but merely to signal reported speech. An example in which the subjunctive does indeed convey distancing is the following passage:

(92) Furthermore, it is **not possible** to proceed "generously" in determining the responsibilities of the Federal Court of Auditors in terms of their implementation, because it **is said** to have no decision-making powers and the exclusivity principle of competence law applies without restriction only to state action with a decision-making character. (see Heintzen, in: von Münch/Kunig, GG, vol. 3, 5th ed. 2003, Art. 114 para. 9). This approach already misses the point and purpose of the separation of administrative spheres between the federal government and the states and the autonomy and independence of their budget management enshrined in Art. 109 para. 1 GG. (BVerfGE 127, 165–224 2nd Senate 07.09.2010, para. 146).

The reading of the passage is not necessarily epistemic-modalizing; in the reporting part of the passage, there are no clear indications of a rejection of Heintzen's position. In one reading, the reader might initially assume that an approach is being discussed whose flaws have already been criticized by Heintzen. In another reading, the passage could be understood as Heintzen advocating an approach that the Federal Constitutional Court considers incorrect. This latter reading is supported by the commentary on the fallibility of the approach. If one consults the relevant text, it becomes clear that the latter is correct and that Heintzen holds a position on the determination of the Federal Court of Auditors' responsibilities that is exactly the opposite of that of the Federal Constitutional Court:

(93) **Because the Federal Court of Auditors has no decision-making powers, it is possible to be generous in determining its responsibilities** and, in relation to other audit organizations, such as the relationship between the Federal Court of Auditors and the state audit offices, but also within the Federal Court of Auditors itself, it is not necessary to strictly avoid overlaps and double responsibilities; in defining audit tasks, this is not even possible, since the outcome of an audit cannot be precisely predicted; the exclusivity principle of competence law applies without restriction only to state action with a decision-making character.

The comparison between the citing text and the cited text reveals the rejection of the latter. However, this negation is not immediately clear to the reader; it must be interpreted whether the introductory phrase "not possible" belongs to Heintzen's statements, i.e., whether Heintzen is being indirectly quoted, or whether "not possible" is a proposition of the Federal Constitutional Court itself. The analysis of the case study shows that, based solely on the use of the subjunctive, no conclusions can be drawn about the intended functions, and that the criterion of analysis proves to be of little use without comparison to the referenced pretext. Without comparison to the pretext, an affirmative reading is possible, in which the reader assumes that the Federal Constitutional Court agrees with Heintzen and projects the validity of the text onto its own argumentation. On this basis, the citation could be ascribed an economic function, for example, in which one's own reasoning is replaced by a quotation. However, comparison with the pretext shows that a distancing reading is correct, so that no quotation functions can be assumed that presuppose affirmation (e.g., economy, projection of authority).

In the SCC, evidentiality markers are provided by the very frequent use of citation-accompanying phrases. A prototypical feature is the many *verba dicendi* in the introduction of quotations. It is striking that the SCC explicitly names the act of quoting itself with verbs such as "to quote." In this way, as well as through the other citation features analyzed, the act of quoting is much more prominent in SCC decisions than on the surface of Federal Constitutional Court decisions.

It is also noticeable that, as a rule, objective verbs are chosen for this purpose (e.g., "to state"), from which it is not immediately apparent how the introduced quotation relates to the court's own content. Even if the citation-accompanying phrases generally do not bring about epistemic modalization, they do in some cases provide information about the textual action being performed. Verba dicendi such as "to define," for example, indicate that the quotation is being used for the purpose of a definition. Verba dicendi of this kind can thus be described as reader-friendly, as their explicit naming signals to the reader the textual function the quotation is intended to fulfill, such as a definition, an explanation, or a discussion. Whether, and if so, what further intention lies behind this cannot be inferred from the citation-accompanying phrases (for the distinction between textual functions and intentions, see Sect. 3.1). Citation-accompanying phrases are less common in the Federal Constitutional Court, but even in German decisions they provide the reader with helpful orientation regarding textual functions:

(94) **It is particularly objected that** the view of the Federal Court of Justice would lead to a rejection of the submission even if the party's failure had no effect whatsoever on the normal course of proceedings, which includes the holding of a main hearing (see Leipold, loc. cit.). (BVerfGE 69, 126–140 1st Senate 30.01.1985, para. 37)

By indicating the objection, the reader knows that Leipold takes a critical position (at least it appears plausible to assume this, as the pretext was not checked for this example). Particularly interesting is that the use of citation-accompanying phrases—as with all other citation features in the Federal Constitutional Court—is characterized by efforts at depersonalization. Instead of the active constructions frequently found in the SCC (e.g., "Leipold objects that…"), the Federal Constitutional Court uses a passive construction. By decoupling from the person, the subjective attachment to the position is once again eliminated; the reported objection is universalized. It is conceivable that such strategies are intended to increase the weight of a position.

6.7 Conclusion of the Empirical Study

The preceding study adopted two perspectives on citations in court decisions: a quantitative perspective, which examined the extent to which prototypical citation characteristics emerge, and a qualitative perspective, in which possible citation functions were discussed using selected case examples.

The prototypical citation of the BVerfG represents an immaterial reference to a legal scholarly source, characterized by the omission of the source author and the rare use of positioning elements, resulting in a depersonalized style. From a diachronic perspective, the citation style of the BVerfG remains largely consistent with respect to the analytical criteria. Only the analytical criterion of 'source category' stands out diachronically, as the BVerfG has increasingly included more supranational and foreign case law in its more recent decisions compared to its relatively older ones.

The prototypical citation of the SCC also refers to a legal scholarly source, but is a material citation, often accompanied by positioning elements. The integration of the source author and the frequent use of citation-related phrases make the act of citing much more visible on the textual surface of Canadian decisions than in those of the BVerfG. From a diachronic perspective, the citation practices of the SCC vary more than those of the BVerfG. Over the years analyzed, not only has the composition of source categories changed at the SCC, but there are also indications of increasing depersonalization in both citation and decision-making style (e.g., outsourcing the source author). As hypothetically assumed due to their differences in legal systems, the two courts differ in several citation features. They prefer different citation types, different placements of the source author, and the SCC exhibits significantly more frequent use of markers of modality and evidentiality than the BVerfG.

Based on the characteristics of citations in the decisions, further considerations regarding citation functions could be made using individual case examples. These considerations revealed that the citation features examined enable a certain functional spectrum while excluding others. For example, in the case of the SCC, it was shown that placing the source author in the running text may be associated with projecting authority or with an appreciation of the source author. The same applies to material citations, which on the producer side can serve an economic function, while on the recipient side they also ensure transparent handling of external content. Clearly dismissive citations, for instance when the degree of factuality is limited by hedges, are associated with justification, so that the economic function can be excluded in such cases. Overall, a clear assignment of function is not possible. For this reason, research question 2, 'Why do courts cite?', can be answered for the BVerfG and the SCC as follows: Citations in court decisions can serve various functions, depending on how the act of citation is structured. In general, examples of all theoretically developed functions—i.e., ornamental citation, authoritative citation, economic citation, and citation for purposes of coherence—were found in the decisions.

Given the identified prototypical citation features, it appears unlikely that the BVerfG uses citations to save effort at the level of textual formulation in the sense of the economic function. There is also little indication of an intent to project authority—the study showed that the act of intertextual reference is scarcely visible on the textual surface of German decisions, apart from the obligatory source reference. Through the manner of citation, in which all traces of intertextual work are largely erased, the voice of the BVerfG always remains in the foreground. Nevertheless, authoritative citation does play a role in the BVerfG's decisions—on the one hand, the court seems to generate authority through quantity, and on the other, it demonstrates its own authority by deciding on the validity and deconstruction of external content when rejecting it. The use of quotation marks—whether for the graphematic marking of a material citation or for purposes of modality—appears to be employed by the BVerfG primarily for ornamental-stylistic purposes.

The ornamental function of citations could also be identified in some case examples from the SCC. Indications of the ornamental function included, among others, stylistic differences between the decision and the cited text, and the use of citations for illustrative purposes. Unlike the BVerfG, there are indeed reasons to assume that the SCC's decisions benefit from the economic dimension of citation at the level of formulation. Furthermore, it can be assumed that the SCC seeks to project the authority of the source author onto itself. One indication of this is that many attributions go beyond content and comment on attributes of the source author (e.g., their fame), which may serve to persuade the reader. Through these attributions, the numerous evidentiality markers, and the many material citations, the intertextual element is constantly present on the textual surface of Canadian decisions. At the same time, the aforementioned citation features ensure a separation of voices. Unlike the BVerfG, it is generally possible in SCC citations to reconstruct when original and when intertextual content is being presented. Without comparison to the cited pretexts, it proved difficult for the BVerfG to distinguish intertextual content from its own, which is why future empirical studies on citation would benefit from greater consideration of pretexts.

Further research desiderata, open questions, and a concluding discussion are addressed in the following overall conclusion.

Chapter 7
Overall Conclusion, Review, Outlook

The present study has addressed, using the example of the Federal Constitutional Court and the Supreme Court of Canada, the question of how and why courts cite. In this context, comparative and diachronic perspectives were also adopted, by asking to what extent judicial citation practices can differ from one another and how they develop. To answer these guiding questions, a theoretical approach was first used to show how broadly the concept of citation should be understood, which problems and criteria must be considered in interpreting its functions, and to what extent the requirements of different legal systems can influence citation practices. In the empirical analysis of the study, a frequency analysis of citation features was conducted. The quantitative approach made it possible to identify prototypical tendencies in the citation practices of the two courts, to statistically test differences between the two courts, and to trace diachronic developments.

From a comparative perspective, the two courts differ significantly in at least one characteristic for each analysis category in the overall evaluation. Whether these significant differences will persist in the future is questionable. As has been shown, citation practices—such as depersonalized citation methods and the consideration of foreign case law—are converging. In this respect, moments of an increasingly globalized jurisprudence are revealed in citation practice. The diachronic differences in citation practices within a court indicate that the production of decisions is subject to changing requirements, which are met by adapting citation methods—this is manifested, for example, in the Federal Constitutional Court's increasing openness to foreign and supranational case law and the growing tendencies toward depersonalization in the citation practice of the Supreme Court of Canada. For both courts, the frequency of sources referenced in decisions increased significantly overall between 1985 and 2020, which can be interpreted as evidence of the growing relevance of intertextual work in court.

© The Author(s), under exclusive license to Springer-Verlag GmbH, DE, part of Springer Nature 2025

J. Steigler-Herms, *How and Why Do Courts Cite?*,
https://doi.org/10.1007/978-3-662-71934-3_7

Furthermore, several examples demonstrated that citation methods can entail different advantages and disadvantages. The identification of advantages and disadvantages of citation practices can also be regarded as a practical implication of the results. For instance, paraphrasing accompanied by a chain citation enables an economically condensed transmission of pretext content, but it is very nontransparent for the recipient—the immaterial citation eludes the recipient's own reading, as the paraphrased content is already filtered by the citing authority. In terms of transparency, therefore, a comprehensive material adoption, as is prototypical for the Supreme Court of Canada, proves to be more suitable. Due to the clear graphematic distinction between what is foreign and what is one's own, there is, unlike paraphrase, no merging of different voices in the text, and it is transparent to whom which position should be attributed.

Compared to the question 'How do courts cite?', the question of why, as theoretically anticipated, could not be answered unequivocally. All assignments of function had to remain at the level of interpretation. The citation features identified in the frequency analysis provided a useful basis for narrowing down potential functions through qualitative analyses of individual case examples. It was shown that citations in court decisions fulfill the requirement of considering the textual network in the sense of establishing and demonstrating coherence; can be used for the purpose of demonstrating authority by deconstructing the validity of external content; or also for ornamental purposes and for reasons of economy. Examples could be found for all citation functions identified by theoretical research.

The limitations of the case example analysis lie in the fact that no statements can be made about which of the citation functions dominate in court decisions. To determine frequent or prototypical citation functions in court decisions, each individual citation would have to be interpreted and the results of the interpretation subsequently quantified. Whether such an approach would be meaningful is questionable, since it was shown thatseveral functions are possible.

In both the analysis of the question 'How do courts cite?' and the question 'Why do courts cite?', the primarily quantitative approach of this study reached its limits in some respects. A central problem was that, without a comparison with the cited pretexts, it was not possible, among other things, to determine which type of citation was present or, for example, whether it was an original or an indirectly adopted positioning element. Without a clear identification of citation properties, no conclusions can be drawn about potential functions. Therefore, qualitative studies that explicitly address the comparison of pretext material and citation would be desirable in order to develop further considerations regarding the implications of intentional transformation measures with respect to functional dimensions, especially in light of the opaque transformation processes at the Federal Constitutional Court. The comparison with a small pretext sample conducted in this study also showed that existing definitions of citation types do not do justice to the practice of citation and suggests a modification of existing citation typologies. Hybrid forms were found that have not yet been considered in previous research. This concerns, for example, the modalization of external content, since modalizing citations have so far—notably refuted by the present study—not been considered intertextual citation types. Both original and external content can be cited in a modalizing way.

Another desideratum for research must be the analysis of the correlation of citation properties. The present study analyzed citation properties, such as their materiality and the category of sources referenced, separately. However, questions such as whether material citation tends to occur more frequently when citing non-legal texts, or which type of sources correlates with a particularly high use of positioning elements, would also be conceivable and, especially with regard to citation functions, particularly insightful.

Regardless of how courts cite and which specific functions the citation fulfills in specific cases, it is clear that citation is an indispensable instrument of jurisprudence. The analysis of citations in court decisions helps—and this is the most relevant practical implication of this work—to capture influences on jurisprudence, to understand the reasoning culture of courts, and to make their legitimation strategies visible.

Appendix: List of Analyzed Decisions

Federal Constitutional Court
BVerfGE 68, 360–361 1st Senate—08.01.1985
BVerfGE 68, 361–375 1st Senate—08.01.1985
BVerfGE 68, 376–384 1st Senate—08.01.1985
BVerfGE 68, 384–391 1st Senate—08.01.1985
BVerfGE 69, 1–92 2nd Senate—24.04.1985
BVerfGE 69, 92–112 2nd Senate—15.01.1985
BVerfGE 69, 112–122 2nd Senate—15.01.1985
BVerfGE 69, 122–126 1st Senate—30.01.1985
BVerfGE 69, 126–140 1st Senate—30.01.1985
BVerfGE 69, 141–145 1st Senate—30.01.1985
BVerfGE 69, 161–174 2nd Senate—26.02.1985
BVerfGE 69, 174–184 2nd Senate—26.02.1985
BVerfGE 69, 185–188 2nd Senate—26.02.1985
BVerfGE 69, 188–209 1st Senate—12.03.1985
BVerfGE 69, 209–220 1st Senate—12.03.1985
BVerfGE 69, 220–232 2nd Senate—21.03.1985
BVerfGE 69, 233–248 1st Senate—28.03.1985
BVerfGE 69, 248–257 2nd Senate—24.04.1985
BVerfGE 69, 257–272 2nd Senate—25. 04.1985
BVerfGE 69, 272–315 1st Senate—16.07.1985
BVerfGE 69, 315–372 1st Senate—14.05.1985
BVerfGE 69, 373–381 1st Senate—14.05.1985
BVerfGE 69, 381–387 1st Senate—14.05.1985
BVerfGE 70, 1–35 1st Senate—14.05.1985
BVerfGE 70, 35–69 1st Senate—14.05.1985
BVerfGE 70, 69–93 2nd Senate—15.05.1985
BVerfGE 70, 93–101 1st Senate—04.06.1985
BVerfGE 70, 101–115 1st Senate—04.06.1985
BVerfGE 70, 115–125 1st Senate—04.06.1985

© The Editor(s) (if applicable) and The Author(s), under exclusive license to Springer-Verlag GmbH, DE, part of Springer Nature 2025

J. Steigler-Herms, *How and Why Do Courts Cite?*,
https://doi.org/10.1007/978-3-662-71934-3

BVerfGE 70, 126–134 1st Senate—04.06.1985
BVerfGE 70, 134–138 1st Senate—04.06.1985
BVerfGE 70, 138–173 2nd Senate—04.06.1985
BVerfGE 70, 173–180 2nd Senate—05.06.1985
BVerfGE 70, 180–190 2nd Senate—18.06.1985
BVerfGE 70, 191–214 1st Senate—19.06.1985
BVerfGE 70, 215–219 1st Senate—19.06.1985
BVerfGE 70, 219–230 1st Senate—03.07.1985
BVerfGE 70, 230–242 1st Senate—03.07.1985
BVerfGE 70, 242–251 1st Senate—03.07.1985
BVerfGE 70, 251–270 1st Senate—03.07.1985
BVerfGE 70, 271–277 1st Senate—03.07.1985
BVerfGE 70, 278–288 1st Senate—08.10.1985
BVerfGE 70, 288–296 1st Senate—08.10.1985
BVerfGE 70, 297–323 2nd Senate—08.10.1985
BVerfGE 71, 1–23 1st Senate—09.10.1985
BVerfGE 71, 23–25 1st Senate—09.10.1985
BVerfGE 71, 25–38 2nd Senate—15.10.1985
BVerfGE 71, 39–64 2nd Senate—15.10.1985
BVerfGE 71, 64–66 2nd Senate—15.10.1985
BVerfGE 71, 66–80 1st Senate—22.10.1985
BVerfGE 71, 81–108 1st Senate—22.10.1985
BVerfGE 71, 108–122 1st Senate—23.10.1985
BVerfGE 71, 122–137 2nd Senate—11/05/1985
BVerfGE 71, 137–146 1st Senate—06.11.1985
BVerfGE 71, 146–158 1st Senate—11/06/1985
BVerfGE 71, 162–183 1st Senate—19.11.1985
BVerfGE 71, 183–202 1st Senate—19.11.1985
BVerfGE 71, 202–205 2nd Senate—26.11.1985
BVerfGE 71, 206–223 1st Senate—03.12.1985
BVerfGE 71, 224–229 1st Senate—03.12.1985
BVerfGE 71, 230–255 1st Senate—12/04/1985
BVerfGE 71, 255–275 2nd Senate—12/10/1985
BVerfGE 71, 276–299 2nd Senate—12/11/1985
BVerfGE 71, 299–305 2nd Senate—17.12.1985
BVerfGE 71, 305–349 2nd Senate—18.12.1985
BVerfGE 69, 145–150 1st Senate—30.01.1985
BVerfGE 81, 156–207 1st Senate—23.01.1990
BVerfGE 81, 208–228 1st Senate—23.01.1990
BVerfGE 81, 228–242 1st Senate—23.01.1990
BVerfGE 81, 242–263 1st Senate—07.02.1990
BVerfGE 81, 264–274 1st Senate—21–02.1990
BVerfGE 81, 275–278 2nd Senate—03/06/1990
BVerfGE 81, 278–298 1st Senate—07.03.1990
BVerfGE 81, 298–309 1st Senate—07.03.1990

BVerfGE 81, 310–347 2nd Senate—22.05.1990
BVerfGE 81, 347–362 2nd Senate—13.03.1990
BVerfGE 81, 363–387 2nd Senate—22.03.1990
BVerfGE 81, 387–391 1st Senate—03.04.1990
BVerfGE 82, 1–6 1st Senate—03.04.1990
BVerfGE 82, 6–18 1st Senate—03.04.1990
BVerfGE 82, 18–29 1st Senate—04.04.1990
BVerfGE 82, 30–42 2nd Senate—05.04.1990
BVerfGE 82, 43–54 1st Senate—19.04.1990
BVerfGE 82, 60–105 1st Senate—29.05.1990
BVerfGE 82, 106–126 2nd Senate—29.05.1990
BVerfGE 82, 126–156 1st Senate—30.05.1990
BVerfGE 82, 156–158 1st Senate—30.05.1990
BVerfGE 82, 159–198 2nd Senate—31.05.1990
BVerfGE 82, 198–208 1st Senate—12.06.1990
BVerfGE 82, 209–236 1st Senate—12.06.1990
BVerfGE 82, 236–271 1st Senate—26.06.1990
BVerfGE 82, 272–285 1st Senate—26.06.1990
BVerfGE 82, 286–305 1st Senate—10.07.1990
BVerfGE 82, 316–321 2nd Senate—18.09.1990
BVerfGE 82, 322–352 2nd Senate—29.09.1990
BVerfGE 83, 1–24 1st Senate—17.10.1990
BVerfGE 83, 24–36 2nd Senate—30.10.1990
BVerfGE 83, 37–59 2nd Senate—31.10.1990
BVerfGE 83, 60–81 2nd Senate—31.10.1990
BVerfGE 83, 82–88 1st Senate—13.11.1990
BVerfGE 83, 89–111 2nd Senate—13.11.1990
BVerfGE 83, 111–118 1st Senate—14.11.1990
BVerfGE 83, 119–129 2nd Senate—14.11.1990
BVerfGE 83, 130–155 1st Senate—27.11.1990
BVerfGE 83, 119–129 2nd Senate—14.11.1990
BVerfGE 83, 130–155 1st Senate—27.11.1990
BVerfGE 83, 156–158 2nd Senate—29.11.1990
BVerfGE 83, 175–181 2nd Senate—12.12.1990
BVerfGE 93, 181–195 1st Senate—07/05/1995
BVerfGE 93, 362–372 1st Senate—05.12.1995
BVerfGE 92, 126–130 1st Senate—07.02.1995
BVerfGE 92, 158–190 1st Senate—07.03.1995
BVerfGE 92, 191–203 1st Senate—07.03.1995
BVerfGE 93, 319–352 2nd Senate—07.11.1995
BVerfGE 92, 130–137 2nd Senate—09.02.1995
BVerfGE 93, 213–248 1st Senate—09.08.1995
BVerfGE 92, 1–20 1st Senate—10.01.1995
BVerfGE 92, 26–53 1st Senate—10.01.1995
BVerfGE 92, 53–74 1st Senate—10.01.1995

BVerfGE 92, 74–80 2nd Senate—10.01.1995
BVerfGE 93, 266–313 1st Senate—10.10.1995
BVerfGE 93, 248–258 2nd Senate—12.05.1995
BVerfGE 93, 352–361 1st Senate—14.11.1995
BVerfGE 92, 277–365 2nd Senate—15.05.1995
BVerfGE 92, 138–139 2nd Senate—16.02.1995
BVerfGE 93, 1–25 1st Senate—16.05.1995
BVerfGE 93, 195–208 2nd Senate—17.07.1995
BVerfGE 93, 208–213 2nd Senate—18.07.1995
BVerfGE 93, 99–117 1st Senate—20.06.1995
BVerfGE 92, 140–157 1st Senate—21.02.1995
BVerfGE 92, 203–245 2nd Senate—22.03.1995
BVerfGE 93, 121–149 2nd Senate—22.06.1995
BVerfGE 93, 165–179 2nd Senate—22.06.1995
BVerfGE 92, 80–91 2nd Senate—23.01.1995
BVerfGE 92, 245–261 2nd Senate—23.03.1995
BVerfGE 92, 91–122 1st Senate—24.01.1995
BVerfGE 92, 122–126 1st Senate—24.01.1995
BVerfGE 93, 37–85 2nd Senate—24.05.1995
BVerfGE 92, 262–277 1st Senate—26.04.1995
BVerfGE 93, 179–181 2nd Senate—29.06.1995
BVerfGE 93, 85–99 1st Senate—31.05.1995
BVerfGE 100, 195–208 1st Senate—02.02.1999
BVerfGE 100, 209–214 2nd Senate—02.02.1999
BVerfGE 99, 367–401 1st Senate—02.03.1999
BVerfGE 100, 226–248 1st Senate—02.03.1999
BVerfGE 100, 249–263 2nd Senate—02.03.1999
BVerfGE 101, 1–45 2nd Senate—07/06/1999
BVerfGE 101, 46–53 2nd Senate—07/06/1999
BVerfGE 101, 275–297 2nd Senate—07.12.1999
BVerfGE 101, 297–312 2nd Senate—07.12.1999
BVerfGE 101, 141–151 2nd Senate—11/09/1999
BVerfGE 101, 151–158 2nd Senate—10.11.1999
BVerfGE 100, 263–265 2nd Senate—11.03.1999
BVerfGE 101, 158–238 2nd Senate—11.11.1999
BVerfGE 100, 313–403 1st Senate—14.07.1999
BVerfGE 101, 54–105 1st Senate—14.07.1999
BVerfGE 101, 312–331 1st Senate—14.12.1999
BVerfGE 101, 331–360 1st Senate—15.12.1999
BVerfGE 101, 361–396 1st Senate—15.12.1999
BVerfGE 99, 341–360 1st Senate—19.01.1999
BVerfGE 99, 361–366 2nd Senate—20.01.1999
BVerfGE 101, 239–274 1st Senate—23.11.1999
BVerfGE 100, 214–225 1st Senate—24.02.1999.
BVerfGE 100, 266–270 2nd Senate—25.03.1999.

BVerfGE 100, 289–313 1st Senate—27.04.1999
BVerfGE 100, 271–288 1st Senate—27.04.1999
BVerfGE 101, 106–132 1st Senate—27.10.1999
BVerfGE 100, 59–104 1st Senate—28.04.1999
BVerfGE 100, 104–137 1st Senate—28.04.1999
BVerfGE 100, 138–195 1st Senate—28.04.1999
BVerfGE 100, 1–59 1st Senate—28.04.1999
BVerfGE 101, 132–141 2nd Senate—29.10.1999
BVerfGE 102, 167–175 2nd Senate—03.07.2000
BVerfGE 102, 176–192 2nd Senate—03.07.2000
BVerfGE 102, 147–166 2nd Senate—07.06.2000
BVerfGE 102, 122–126 1st Senate—10.05.2000
BVerfGE 102, 192–197 2nd Senate—12.07.2000
BVerfGE 102, 347–369 1st Senate—12.12.2000
BVerfGE 103, 1–20 1st Senate—13 December 2000
BVerfGE 102, 41–63 1st Senate—14.03.2000
BVerfGE 103, 21–41 2nd Senate—14.12.2000
BVerfGE 102, 68–99 1st Senate—15.03.2000
BVerfGE 102, 1–25 1st Senate—16.02.2000
BVerfGE 102, 26–40 1st Senate—16.02.2000
BVerfGE 101, 397–410 1st Senate—18.01.2000
BVerfGE 102, 197–224 1st Senate—19.07.2000
BVerfGE 102, 370–400 2nd Senate—19.12.2000
BVerfGE 102, 224–245 2nd Senate—21.07.2000
BVerfGE 102, 245–253 2nd Senate—21.07.2000
BVerfGE 102, 254–346 1st Senate—22.11.2000
BVerfGE 102, 127–146 1st Senate—24.05.2000
BVerfGE 102, 99–122 2nd Senate—29.03.2000
BVerfGE 114, 396–397 2nd Senate—11/09/2005
BVerfGE 112, 368–407 1st Senate—11.05.2005
BVerfGE 114, 316–338 1st Senate—11.11.2005
BVerfGE 112, 304–321 2nd Senate—12.04.2005
BVerfGE 114, 196–250 2nd Senate—13.09.2005
BVerfGE 113, 113–128 2nd Senate—15.06.2005
BVerfGE 113, 167–273 2nd Senate—18.06.2005
BVerfGE 114, 107–121 2nd Senate—23.08.2005
BVerfGE 113, 63–88 1st Senate—24.05.2005
BVerfGE 114, 339–356 1st Senate—25.10.2005
BVerfGE 114, 73–104 1st Senate—26.07.2005
BVerfGE 125, 141–174 2nd Senate—27.10.2010
BVerfGE 125, 175–260 1st Senate—09.02.2010
BVerfGE 125, 260–364 1st Senate—02.03.2010
BVerfGE 126, 1–29 1st Senate—13.04.2010
BVerfGE 126, 29–55 1st Senate—14.04.2010
BVerfGE 126, 55–77 2nd Senate—05/04/2010

BVerfGE 126, 77–112 2nd Senate—05/04/2010
BVerfGE 126, 112–158 1st Senate—08.06.2010
BVerfGE 126, 170–233 2nd Senate—23.06.2010
BVerfGE 126, 233–268 1st Senate—07/06/2010
BVerfGE 126, 268–286 2nd Senate—07/06/2010
BVerfGE 126, 286–331 2nd Senate—07/06/2010
BVerfGE 126, 331–369 1st Senate—21.07.2010
BVerfGE 126, 369–400 1st Senate—21.07.2010
BVerfGE 126, 400–433 1st Senate—21.07.2010
BVerfGE 127, 1–31 2nd Senate—07.07.2010
BVerfGE 127, 31–60 2nd Senate—07.07.2010
BVerfGE 127, 61–87 2nd Senate—07.07.2010
BVerfGE 127, 87–132 1st Senate—20.07.2010
BVerfGE 127, 132–165 1st Senate—21.07.2010
BVerfGE 127, 165–224 2nd Senate—07.09.2010
BVerfGE 127, 224–263 1st Senate—12.10.2010
BVerfGE 127, 263–292 1st Senate—12.10.2010
BVerfGE 127, 293–335 2nd Senate—12.10.2010
BVerfGE 128, 1–90 1st Senate—12.10.2010
BVerfGE 128, 90–108 1st Senate—07.12.2010
BVerfGE 138, 256–261 2nd Senate—13.01.2015
BVerfGE 138, 261–296 1st Senate—14.01.2015
BVerfGE 138, 296–376 1st Senate—27.01.2015
BVerfGE 138, 377–397 1st Senate—24.02.2015
BVerfGE 138, 397–400 2nd Senate—19.03.2015
BVerfGE 139, 1–19 1st Senate—24.03.2015
BVerfGE 139, 19–64 2nd Senate—21.04.2015
BVerfGE 139, 64–148 2nd Senate—05.05.2015
BVerfGE 139, 148–194 1st Senate—12.05.2015
BVerfGE 139, 194–239 2nd Senate—02.06.2015
BVerfGE 139, 239–245 2nd Senate—02.06.2015
BVerfGE 139, 245–285 2nd Senate—16.06.2015
BVerfGE 139, 285–321 1st Senate—23.06.2015
BVerfGE 139, 321–378 2nd Senate—30.06.2015
BVerfGE 139, 378–380 1st Senate—20.07.2015
BVerfGE 140, 1–42 2nd Senate—15.07.2015
BVerfGE 140, 42–65 2nd Senate—15.07.2015
BVerfGE 140, 65–99 1st Senate—21.07.2015
BVerfGE 140, 115–160 2nd Senate—22.09.2015.
BVerfGE 140, 160–211 2nd Senate—23.09.2015
BVerfGE 140, 229–240 1st Senate—11/10/2015
BVerfGE 140, 240–316 2nd Senate—17.11.2015
BVerfGE 140, 316–317 2nd Senate—02.12.2015
BVerfGE 140, 317–376 2nd Senate—15.12.2015
BVerfGE 141, 1–56 2nd Senate—15.12.2015

BVerfGE 141, 56–81 2nd Senate—16.12.2015
BVerfGE 150, 345–378 2nd Senate—15.01.2019
BVerfGE 151, 67–97 2nd Senate—12.03.2019
Senate BVerfGE 152, 345–401
BVerfGE 151, 98–100 2nd Senate—13.03.2019
BVerfGE 151, 101–151 1st Senate—26.03.2019
BVerfGE 151, 173–191 1st Senate—18.06.2019
BVerfGE 151, 191–202 2nd Senate—02.07.2019
BVerfGE 151, 202–374 2nd Senate—30.07.2019
BVerfGE 152, 1–8 2nd Senate—17.09.2019
BVerfGE 152, 8–35 2nd Senate—17.09.2019
BVerfGE 152, 35–53 2nd Senate—17.09.2019
BVerfGE 152, 53–55 2nd Senate—17.09.2019
BVerfGE 152, 68–151 1st Senate—11.05.2019
BVerfGE 152, 152–215 1st Senate—11.06.2019
BVerfGE 152, 216–274 1st Senate—11.06.2019
BVerfGE 152, 274–331 2nd Senate—19.11.2019
BVerfGE 152, 332–345 1st Senate—05.12.2019
BVerfGE 156, 63–182 2nd Senate—01.12.2020
BVerfGE 156, 182–2212. Senate—01.12.2020
BVerfGE 156, 1–10 2nd Senate—03.11.2020
BVerfGE 154, 1–17 2nd Senate—05.04.2020
BVerfGE 155, 1–76 2nd Senate—05.04.2020
BVerfGE 155, 77–118 2nd Senate—05.04.2020
BVerfGE 154, 17–152 2nd Senate—05.05.2020
BVerfGE 155, 310–357 2nd Senate—07.07.2020
BVerfGE 156, 221–224 2nd Senate—08.12.2020
BVerfGE 154, 320–353 2nd Senate—09.06.2020
BVerfGE 154, 354–372 2nd Senate—09.06.2020
BVerfGE 154, 372–384 2nd Senate—09.06.2020
BVerfGE 153, 72–74 2nd Senate—10.02.2020
BVerfGE 156, 11–63 1st Senate—10.11.2020
BVerfGE 153, 310–358 2nd Senate—11.03.2020
BVerfGE 153, 74–182 2nd Senate—13.02.2020
BVerfGE 152, 345–401 2nd Senate—14.01.2020
BVerfGE 153, 1–72 2nd Senate—14.01.2020
BVerfGE 156, 224–269 2nd Senate—15.12.2020
BVerfGE 156, 270–316 2nd Senate—16.12.2020
BVerfGE 154, 152–312 1st Senate—19.05.2020
BVerfGE 154, 312–320 2nd Senate—19.05.2020
BVerfGE 155, 357–378 2nd Senate—22.07.2020
BVerfGE 156, 335–340 1st Senate—22.12.2020
BVerfGE 153, 182–310 2nd Senate—26.02.2020
BVerfGE 153, 358–403 1st Senate—26.05.2020
BVerfGE 155, 119–238 1st Senate—27.05.2020

BVerfGE 155, 378–417 1st Senate—29.09.2020
BVerfGE 155, 418–419 1st Senate—29.09.2020
BVerfGE 155, 238–310 1st Senate—30.06.2020

Supreme Court of Canada
Valente v. The Queen [1985] 2 SCR 673–19.12.1985
Bhinder v. CN [1985] 2 SCR 561–17.12.1985
Ont. Human Rights Comm. v. Simpsons-Sears [1985] 2 SCR 536–17.12.1985
Re B.C. Motor Vehicle Act [1985] 2 SCR 486–17.12.1985
Dubois v. The Queen [1985] 2 SCR 350–21.11.1985
Order—Manitoba Language Rights [1985] 2 SCR 347–11/04/1985
Dick v. The Queen [1985] 2 SCR 309–31.10.1985
Jack and Charlie v. The Queen [1985] 2 SCR 332–31.10.1985
Krug v. The Queen [1985] 2 SCR 255–10.10.1985
Spencer v. The Queen [1985] 2 SCR 278–10.10.1985
Winnipeg School Division No. 1 v. Craton [1985] 2 SCR 150–19.09.1985
Lamb v. Lamb [1985] 1 SCR 851–27.06.1985
Deloitte Haskins & Sells v. Workers' Comp. Board [1985] 1 SCR 785–13.06.1985
Re Manitoba Language Rights [1985] 1 SCR 721–13.06.1985
R. v. Therens [1985] 1 SCR 613–23.05.1985
Trask v. The Queen [1985] 1 SCR 655–23.05.1985
Rahn v. The Queen [1985] 1 SCR 659–23.05.1985
Operation Dismantle v. The Queen [1985] 1 SCR 441–09.05.1985
Staranchuk v. The Queen [1985] 1 SCR 439–03.05.1985
R. v. Big M Drug Mart Ltd. [1985] 1 SCR 295–24.04.1985
Plantation Indoor Plants Ltd. v. A.G. (Alta.) [1985] 1 SCR 366–24.04.1985
Montréal v. Arcade Amusements Inc. [1985] 1 SCR 368–24.04.1985
Singh v. Minister of Employment and Immigration [1985] 1 SCR 177–04.04.1985
Skoke-Graham v. The Queen [1985] 1 SCR 106–14.03.1985
R. v. Chaulk 1990 3 SCR 1303–20.12.1990
United Transportation Union v. Central Western Railway Corp. 1990 3 SCR 1112–20.12.1990
Whitbread v. Walley 1990 3 SCR 1273–20.12.1990
Canada (Human Rights Commission) v. Taylor 1990 3 SCR 892–13.12.1990
R. v. Andrews 1990 3 SCR 870–13.12.1990
R. v. Keegstra 1990 3 SCR 697–13.12.1990
R. v. Scott 1990 3 SCR 979–13.12.1990
R. v. Kuldip—1990 3 SCR 618–07.12.1990
Re Manitoba Language Rights Order 1990 3 SCR 1417–12/07/1990
Douglas/Kwantlen Faculty Assn. v. Douglas College 1990 3 SCR 570–12/06/1990
Harrison v. University of British Columbia 1990 3 SCR 451–12/06/1990
Mckinney v. University of Guelph 1990 3 SCR 229–12/06/1990
Stoffman v. Vancouver General Hospital 1990 3 SCR 483-06.12.1990
R. v. Lippé 1991 2 SCR 114–05.12.1990
R. v. Garofoli 1990 2 SCR 1421–22.11.1990

R. v. Kokesch 1990 3 SCR 3–22.11.1990
R. v. Lachance 1990 2 SCR 1490–22.11.1990
R. v. Wong 1990 3 SCR 36–22.11.1990
Steele v. Mountain Institution 1990 2 SCR 1385–11/08/1990
R. v. Askov 1990 2 SCR 1199–18.10.1990
R. v. Thompson 1990 2 SCR 1111-18.10.1990
Commission de Transport de la Communauté Urbaine de Québec v. Canada (National Battlefields Commission) 1990 2 SCR 838–10/04/1990
Danson v. Ontario (Attorney General) 1990 2 SCR 1086–10/04/1990
R. v. Hess; R. v. Nguyen 1990 2 SCR 906–10.04.1990
R. v. Penno 1990 2 SCR 865–10/04/1990
R. v. Paquette 1990 2 SCR 1103–02.10.1990
Central Alberta Dairy Pool v. Alberta (Human Rights Commission) 1990 2 SCR 489–13.09.199
R. v. Arkell 1990 2 SCR 695–13.09.1990
R. v. J.(J.T.) 1990 2 SCR 755–13.09.1990
R. v. Logan 1990 2 SCR 731-13.09.1990
R. v. Luxton 1990 2 SCR 711–13.09.1990
R. v. Martineau 1990 2 SCR 633–13.09.1990
Knox Contracting Ltd. v. Canada 1990 2 SCR 338–16.08.1990
Professional Institute of the Public Service of Canada v. Northwest Territories (Commissioner) 1990 2 SCR 367–16.08.1990
R. v. B. (J.) 1990 2 SCR 307–28.06.1990
R. v. P. (J.) 1990 2 SCR 300–28.06.1990
R. v. S. (G.) 1990 2 SCR 294–28.06.1990
R. v. S. (S.) 1990 2 SCR 254–28.06.1990
R. v. T. (A.) 1990 2 SCR 304–28.06.1990
R. v. Hebert 1990 2 SCR 151–21.06.1990
Rocket v. Royal College of Dental Surgeons of Ontario 1990 2 SCR 232–21.06.1990
R. v. F. (J.T.) 1991 1 SCR 285–31.05.1990
R. v. Ladouceur 1990 1 SCR 1257–31.05.1990
R. v. Skinner 1990 1 SCR 1235–31.05.1990
R. v. Sparrow 1990 1 SCR 1075–31.05.1990
R. v. Stagnitta 1990 1 SCR 1226–31.05.1990
R. v. W. (D.A.) 1991 1 SCR 291–31.05.1990
R. v. Wilson 1990 1 SCR 1291–31.05.1990
Reference re ss. 193 and 195.1(1)(C) of the Criminal Code (Man.) 1990 1 SCR 1123–31.05.1990
R. v. Greffe 1990 1 SCR 755–12.04.1990
Starr v. Houlden 1990 1 SCR 1366–05.04.1990
Dywidag Systems International, Canada Ltd. v. Zutphen Brothers Construction Ltd. 1990 1 SCR 705–29.03.1990
R. v. McKinlay Transport Ltd. 1990 1 SCR 627–29.03.1990
Rudolph Wolff & Co. v. Canada 1990 1 SCR 695–29.03.1990

Stelco Inc. v. Canada (Attorney General) 1990 1 SCR 617–29.03.1990
Thomson Newspapers Ltd. v. Canada (Director of Investigation and Research, Restrictive Trade Practices Commission) 1990 1 SCR 425–29.03.1990
Mahe v. Alberta 1990 1 SCR 342–15.03.1990
R. v. Schmautz 1990 1 SCR 398–15.03.1990
Quebec (Attorney General) v. Brunet; Quebec (Attorney General) v. Albert; Quebec (Attorney General) v. Collier 1990 1 SCR 260–28.02.1990
R. v. A 1990 1 SCR 995–15.02.1990
R. v. Storrey 1990 1 SCR 241–15.02.1990
R. v. Van Rassel 1990 1 SCR 225–15.02.1990
Bank of Montreal v. Hall 1990 1 SCR 121–01.02.1990
R. v. Brydges 1990 1 SCR 190–01.02.1990
R. v. Hicks 1990 1 SCR 120–31.01.1990
R. v. Duarte 1990 1 SCR 30–25.01.1990
R. v. Wiggins 1990 1 SCR 62–25.01.1990
R. v. Shubley 1990 1 SCR 3–18.01.1990
MacMillan Bloedel Ltd. v. Simpson 1995 4 SCR 725–14.12.1995
Ruffo v. Conseil de la magistrature 1995 4 SCR 267–14.12.1995
R. v. Fitzpatrick 1995 4 SCR 154–16.11.1995
R. v. Rogalsky 1995 4 SCR 48–11/07/1995
R. v. Patriquen 1995 4 SCR 42–30.10.1995
Husky Oil Operations Ltd. v. Minister of National Revenue 1995 3 SCR 453–19.10.1995
Large v. Stratford (City) 1995 3 SCR 733–19.10.1995
R. v. Harrer 1995 3 SCR 562–19.10.1995
R. v. Pontes 1995 3 SCR 44–21.09.1995
R. v. Wijesinha 1995 3 SCR 422–21.09.1995
RJR-MacDonald Inc. v. Canada (Attorney General) 1995 3 SCR 199–21.09.1995
Hill v. Church of Scientology of Toronto 1995 2 SCR 1130–20.07.1995
Ontario v. Canadian Pacific Ltd. 1995 2 SCR 1031–20.07.1995
R. v. Collins; R. v. Pelfrey 1995 2 SCR 1104–20.07.1995
R. v. Montour 1995 2 SCR 416–30.05.1995
Egan v. Canada 1995 2 SCR 513–25.05.1995
Miron v. Trudel 1995 2 SCR 418–25.05.1995
Thibaudeau v. Canada 1995 2 SCR 627–25.05.1995
Walker v. Prince Edward Island 1995 2 SCR 407–23.05.1995
R. v. Burlingham 1995 2 SCR 206–18.05.1995
R. v. Silveira 1995 2 SCR 297–18.05.1995
Phillips v. Nova Scotia (Commission of Inquiry into the Westray Mine Tragedy) 1995 2 SCR 97–05.04.1995
British Columbia Securities Commission v. Branch 1995 2 SCR 3–13.04.1995
R. v. Jobin 1995 2 SCR 78–13.04.1995
R. v. Primeau 1995 2 SCR 60–13.04.1995
R. v. Crawford 1995 1 SCR 858–30.03.1995
R. v. Simpson 1995 1 SCR 449–03.02.1995

R. v. S. (R.J.) 1995 1 SCR 451–02.02.1995
B. (R.) v. Children's Aid Society of Metropolitan Toronto 1995 1 SCR 315–27.01.1995
Ontario v. Canadian Pacific Ltd. 1995 2 SCR 1028–24.01.1995
British Columbia (Superintendent of Motor Vehicles) v. British Columbia (Council of Human Rights) 1999 3 SCR 868–12/6/1999
R. v. Mills 1999 3 SCR 668–25.11.1999
R. v. Timm 1999 3 SCR 666–11/12/1999
R. v. Liew 1999 3 SCR 227–16.09.1999
New Brunswick (Minister of Health and Community Services) v. G. (J.) 1999 3 SCR 46–09/10/1999
Westbank First Nation v. British Columbia Hydro and Power Authority 1999 3 SCR 134–09/10/1999
British Columbia (Public Service Employee Relations Commission) v. BCGSEU 1999 3 SCR 3–09.09.1999
U.F.C.W., Local 1518, v. KMart Canada Ltd. 1999 2 SCR 1083–09.09.1999
Delisle v. Canada (Deputy Attorney General) 1999 2 SCR 989–02.09.1999
M & D Farm Ltd. v. Manitoba Agricultural Credit Corp. 1999 2 SCR 961–02.09.1999
Bese v. British Columbia (Forensic Psychiatric Institute) 1999 2 SCR 722–17.06.1999
Orlowski v. British Columbia (Forensic Psychiatric Institute) 1999 2 SCR 733–17.06.1999
R. v. LePage 1999 2 SCR 744–17.06.1999
Winko v. British Columbia (Forensic Psychiatric Institute) 1999 2 SCR 625–17.06.1999
R. v. White 1999 2 SCR 417–10.06.1999
Corbiere v. Canada (Minister of Indian and Northern Affairs) 1999 2 SCR 203–20.05.1999
M. v. H. 1999 2 SCR 3–20.05.1999
R. v. Monney 1999 1 SCR 652–23.04.1999
Law v. Canada (Minister of Employment and Immigration) 1999 1 SCR 497–25.03.1999
Vancouver Society of Immigrant and Visible Minority Women v. M.N.R. 1999 1 SCR 10–28.01.1999
Del Zotto v. Canada 1999 1 SCR 3–21.01.1999
Little Sisters Book and Art Emporium v. Canada (Minister of Justice) 2000 SCC 69–15.12.2000
Winnipeg Child and Family Services v. K.L.W. 2000 SCC 48–13.10.2000
R. v. Darrach 2000 SCC 46–12.10.2000
Public School Boards' Assn. of Alberta v. Alberta (Attorney General) 2000 SCC 45–10.06.2000
Blencoe v. British Columbia (Human Rights Commission) 2000 SCC 44–05.10.2000
R. v. Morrisey 2000 SCC 39–29.09.2000

Lovelace v. Ontario 2000 SCC 37–20.07.2000
Reference re Firearms Act (Can.) 15.06.2000–2000 SCC 31
Granovsky v. Canada (Minister of Employment and Immigration) 2000 SCC 28–18.05.2000
Global Securities Corp. v. British Columbia (Securities Commission) 2000 SCC 21–13.04.2000
Arsenault-Cameron v. Prince Edward Island 2000 SCC 1–13.01.2000
R. v. Wiles 2005 SCC 84–22.12.2005
Castillo v. Castillo 2005 SCC 83–22.12.2005
R. v. Henry 2005 SCC 76–15.12.2005
R. v. Pires; R. v. Lising 2005 SCC 66–17.11.2005
Kirkbi AG v. Ritvik Holdings Inc. 2005 SCC 65–17.11.2005
Montréal (City) v. 2952–1366 Québec Inc. 2005 SCC 62–03.11.2005
Reference re Employment Insurance Act (Can.), ss. 22 and 23 2005 SCC 56–20.10.2005
D.I.M.S. Construction inc. (Trustee of) v. Quebec (Attorney General) 2005 SCC 52–10/06/2005
Medovarski v. Canada (Minister of Citizenship and Immigration); Esteban v. Canada (Minister of Citizenship and Immigration) 2005 SCC 51–30.09.2005
British Columbia v. Imperial Tobacco Canada Ltd. 2005 SCC 49–29.09.2005
Minc v. Quebec (Attorney General) 2005 SCC 44–22.07.2005
Toronto Star Newspapers Ltd. v. Ontario 2005 SCC 41–29.06.2005
R. v. Orbanski; R. v. Elias 2005 SCC 37–16.06.2005
Chaoulli v. Quebec (Attorney General) 2005 SCC 35–09.06.2005
Canada (House of Commons) v. Vaid 2005 SCC 30–20.05.2005
R. v. Chow 2005 SCC 24–27.04.2005
Fédération des producteurs de volailles du Québec v. Pelland 2005 SCC 20–21.04.2005
Gosselin (Tutor of) v. Quebec (Attorney General) 2005 SCC 15–31.03.2005
Solski (Tutor of) v. Quebec (Attorney General) 2005 SCC 14–31.03.2005
Rothmans, Benson & Hedges Inc. v. Saskatchewan 2005 SCC 13–18.03.2005
UL Canada Inc. v. Quebec (Attorney General) 2005 SCC 10–17.03.2005
R. v. Decorte 2005 SCC 9–25.02.2005
Reference re Assisted Human Reproduction Act 2010 SCC 61–22.12.2010
R. v. Gomboc 2010 SCC 55–24.11.2010
Beckman v. Little Salmon_Carmacks First Nation 2010 SCC 53–19.11.2010
de Montigny v. Brossard (Estate) 2010 SCC 51–11.10.2010
Communications, Energy and Paperworkers Union of Canada v. Native Child and Family Services of Toronto 2010 SCC 46–11/04/2010
NIL TU, O Child and Family Services Society v. B.C. Government and Service Employees' Union—2010 SCC 45–04.11.2010
Rio Tinto Alcan Inc. v. Carrier Sekani Tribal Council 2010 SCC 43–28.10.2010
Globe and Mail v. Canada (Attorney General) 2010 SCC 41–22.10.2010
Quebec (Attorney General) v. Canadian Owners and Pilots Association 2010 SCC 39–15.10.2010

Quebec (Attorney General) v. Lacombe 2010 SCC 38–15.10.2010
R. v. McCrimmon 2010 SCC 36–08.10.2010
R. v. Sinclair 2010 SCC 35–08.10.2010
R. v. Willier 2010 SCC 37–08.10.2010
R. v. Cornell 2010 SCC 31–30.07.2010
Vancouver (City) v. Ward 2010 SCC 27–23.07.2010
R. v. Nolet 2010 SCC 24–25.06.2010
Ontario (Public Safety and Security) v. Criminal Lawyers' Association 2010 SCC 23–17.06.2010
R. v. Conway 2010 SCC 22–11.06.2010
Toronto Star Newspapers Ltd. v. Canada 2010 SCC 21–10.06.2010
Quebec (Attorney General) v. Moses 2010 SCC 17–14.05.2010
R. v. National Post 2010 SCC 16–07.05.2010
R. v. Morelli 2010 SCC 8–19.03.2010
R. v. Beaulieu 2010 SCC 7–25.02.2010
R. v. Nasogaluak 2010 SCC 6–19.02.2010
Canada (Prime Minister) v. Khadr 2010 SCC 3–29.01.2010
R. v. J.Z.S. 2010 SCC 1–19.01.2010
R. v. Appulonappa 2015 SCC 59–27.11.2015
Caron v. Alberta 2015 SCC 56–20.11.2015
R. v. Moriarity 2015 SCC 55–19.11.2015
Saskatchewan (Attorney General) v. Lemare Lake Logging Ltd. 2015 SCC 53–13.11.2015
407 ETR Concession Co. v. Canada (Superintendent of Bankruptcy) 2015 SCC 52–13.11.2015
Alberta (Attorney General) v. Moloney 2015 SCC 51–13.11.2015
Goodwin v. British Columbia (Superintendent of Motor Vehicles) 2015 SCC 46–16.10.2015
Guindon v. Canada 2015 SCC 41–31.07.2015
Quebec (Commission des droits de la personne et des droits de la jeunesse) v. Bombardier Inc. (Bombardier Aerospace Training Center) 2015 SCC 39–23.07.2015
R. v. Smith 2015 SCC 34–11.06.2015
Kahkewistahaw First Nation v. Taypotat 2015 SCC 30–28.05.2015
R. v. Kokopenace 2015 SCC 28–21.05.2015
Yukon Francophone School Board, Education Area #23 v. Yukon (Attorney General) 2015 SCC 25–14.05.2015
Henry v. British Columbia (Attorney General) 2015 SCC 24–01.05.2015
Quebec (Attorney General) v. Canada (Attorney General) 2015 SCC 22–24.04.2020
Association des parents de l'école Rose-des-vents v. British Columbia (Education) 2015 SCC 21–24.04.2020
R. v. Nur 2015 SCC 15–14.04.2015
Quebec (Attorney General) v. Canada (Attorney General) 2015 SCC 14–27.03.2015

R. v. Sanghera 2015 SCC 13–23.03.2015
Loyola High School v. Quebec (Attorney General) 2015 SCC 12–19.03.2015
Canada (Attorney General) v. Federation of Law Societies of Canada 2015 SCC 7–13.02.2015
Carter v. Canada (Attorney General) 2015 SCC 5–02.06.2015#
Saskatchewan Federation of Labour v. Saskatchewan 2015 SCC 4–30.01.2015
Meredith v. Canada (Attorney General) 2015 SCC 2–16.01.2015
Mounted Police Association of Ontario v. Canada (Attorney General) 2015 SCC 1–16.01.2015
Canada (Attorney General) v. British Columbia Investment Management Corp. 2019 SCC 63–13.12.2019
Desgagnés Transport Inc. v. Wärtsilä Canada Inc. 2019 SCC 58–28.11.2019
R. v. K.J.M. 2019 SCC 55–15.11.2019
R. v. Poulin 2019 SCC 47–11.10.2019
R. v. Stillman 2019 SCC 40–26.07.2019
R. v. Le 2019 SCC 34–31.05.2019
R. v. Mills 2019 SCC 22–18.04.2019
R. v. Morrison 2019 SCC 15–15.03.2019
Orphan Well Association v. Grant Thornton Ltd. 2019 SCC 5–31.01.2019
Frank v. Canada (Attorney General) 2019 SCC 1–01/11/2019
Ontario (Attorney General) v. G 2020 SCC 38–20.11.2020
Quebec (Attorney General) v. 9147–0732 Québec inc. 2020 SCC 32–05.11.2020
Fraser v. Canada (Attorney General) 2020 SCC 28–16.10.2020
British Columbia (Attorney General) v. Provincial Court Judges' Association of British Columbia 2020 SCC 20–31.07.2020
Nova Scotia (Attorney General) v. Judges of the Provincial Court and Family Court of Nova Scotia 2020 SCC 21–31.07.2020
R. v. Thanabalasingham 2020 SCC 18–17.07.2020
Reference re Genetic Non-Discrimination Act 2020 SCC 17–10.07.2020
Conseil scolaire francophone de la Colombie Britannique v. British Columbia 2020 SCC 13–12.06.2020
R. v. K.G.K. 2020 SCC 7–20.03.2020

Literature

Abbott, Barbara (2004): Some Notes on Quotation. Belgian Journal of Linguistics (17), 13–26.

Abraham, Werner (2013): Modalitätsformen und -funktionen: Eine Zusammenschau. Zur grammatischen Grundlegung von Modalität—semantisch-syntaktische Affinitäten zu nominaler Referenz, Aspekt und Quantifikation. In: Abraham, Werner/ Leiss, Elisabeth (Hrsg.): Funktionen von Modalität. Berlin/ Boston: De Gruyter, 25–76.

Aikhenvald, Alexandra (2004): Evidentiality. Oxford: Oxford University Press.

Angenot, Marc (1983): L'Intertextualité. Enquête sur l'Émergence et la Diffusion d'un Champ Nationnel. Revue des Sciences Humaines 60(189), 121–135.

Ayres, Ian/ Vars, Frederick (2000): Determinants of Citations to Articles in Elite Reviews Interpreting Legal Citation. Legal Stud. 427(29), 427–451.

Bachtin, Michail (1934/ 1981): The Dialogic Imagination. Four Essays by M.M. Bakhtin. Austin: University of Texas Press.

Bachtin, Michail (1979): Die Ästhetik des Wortes. Hrsg. und übersetzt. von Grübel, Rainer/ Reese, Sabine. Berlin: Suhrkamp.

Bär, Jochen/ Vollmann, Konrad/ Kraus, Manfred (2003): Pathos. In: Ueding, Gert (Hrsg.): Historisches Wörterbuch der Rhetorik Online: Must–Pop, Berlin, Boston: De Gruyter, https://www.degruyter.com/database/HWRO/entry/hwro.6.pathos/html, letzter Zugriff: 31.12.2021.

Bänsch, Axel/ Alewell, Dorothea (2020): Wissenschaftliches Arbeiten. Oldenbourg: De Gruyter.

Bashir, Ibrahim/ Yunus, Kamariah/ Al-Jarrah, Tamer (2018): Modal Verbs Hedging. The Uses and Functions of "Will" and "Shall" in Nigerian Legal discourse. International Journal of English Linguistics 8(7), 59–72.

Baumann, Carolin (2017): Bedeutung und Gebrauch der Modalverben. Lexikalische Einheiten als Basis kontextueller Vielfalt. Berlin/ Boston: De Gruyter.

Bazzoni, André (2016): Pure Quotation, Metalanguage and Metasemantics. Linguist and Philos (39), 119–149.

Beck, Susanne (2021): Rechtsvergleich. In: Hilgendorf, Eric/ Joerden, Jan (Hrsg.): Handbuch Rechtsphilosophie 2. überarbeite und erweitere Auflage. Stuttgart: J.B. Metzler, 76–78.

Bell, Allan (1991): The Language of News and Media. Oxford: Blackwell.

Benninghoff-Lühl, Sybille (2009): Zitat. In: Ueding, Gert (Hrsg.): Historisches Wörterbuch der Rhetorik Online, Bd. 9: St–Z, Berlin, Boston: De Gruyter, https://db.degruyter.com/view/HWRO/zitat, letzter Zugriff: 31.12.2021.

Berkenkotter, Carol/ Huckin, Thomas (1995): Genre Knowledge in Disciplinary Communication. Hillsdale, NJ: Lawrence Erlbaum.

© The Editor(s) (if applicable) and The Author(s), under exclusive license to Springer-Verlag GmbH, DE, part of Springer Nature 2025

J. Steigler-Herms, *How and Why Do Courts Cite?*,
https://doi.org/10.1007/978-3-662-71934-3

Bernhart, Toni (2018): Quantitative Literaturwissenschaft. Ein Fach mit langer Tradition? In: Bernhart, Toni/ Willand, Marcus/ Richter, Sandra/ Albrecht, Andrea (Hrsg.): Quantitative Ansätze in den Literatur- und Geisteswissenschaften. Systematische und historische Perspektiven. Berlin/ Boston: De Gruyter, 207–220.

Bhagat, Rahul/ Hovy, Eduard (2013): What Is a Paraphrase? Computational Linguistics 39, 463–472.

Bhatia, Vijay Kumar (2004): Worlds of Written Discourse. A Genre-Based View. London: Bloomsbury.

Biber, Douglas/ Johansson, Stig/ Leech, Geoffrey/ Conrad, Susan/ Finegan, Edward (1999): Longman Grammar of Spoken and Written English. London: Pearson Education Limited.

Bloch, Joel (2012): Plagiarism, Intellectual Property and the Teaching of L2 Writing. Bristol: Multilingual Matters.

Brendel, Elke/ Meibauer, Jörg/ Steinbach, Markus (2007): Aspekte einer Theorie des Zitierens. In: Brendel, Elke/ Meibauer, Jörg/ Steinbach, Markus (Hrsg.): Zitat und Bedeutung. Hamburg: Helmut Buske-Verlag, 5–26.

Brinker, Klaus (1983): Textfunktionen. Ansätze zu ihrer Beschreibung. Zeitschrift für Germanistische Linguistik 11(2), 127–148.

Broich, Ulrich (1985): Bezugsfelder der Intertextualität. Zur Einzeltextreferenz. In: Broich, Ulrich/ Pfister, Manfred (Hrsg.): Intertextualität. Formen, Funktionen, anglistische Fallstudien. Tübingen: Max Niemeyer Verlag, 48–51.

Bucalic, Tomislav (2007): Ein typologischer Beitrag zu Formen der Redewiedergabe. In: Brendel, Elke/ Meibauer, Jörg/ Steinbach, Markus (Hrsg.): Zitat und Bedeutung. Hamburg: Helmut Buske-Verlag, 45–66.

Bunia, Remigius/ Dembeck, Till (2010): Freunde zitieren. Das Problem wissenschaftlicher Verbindlichkeit. In: Binczek, Natalie/ Stanitzek, Georg (Hrsg.): Strong Ties/ Weak Ties. Freundschaftssemantiken und Netzwerktheorien. Heidelberg: Winter, 161–195.

Busse, Dietrich (1992): Recht als Text. Linguistische Untersuchungen zur Arbeit mit Sprache in einer gesellschaftlichen Institution. Tübingen: Niemeyer.

Busse, Dietrich (2000): Textsorten des Bereichs Rechtswesen und Justiz. In: Antos, Gerd/ Brinker, Klaus/ Heinemann, Wolfgang/ Sager, Sven (Hrsg.): Text- und Gesprächslinguistik. Ein internationales Handbuch zeitgenössischer Forschung. (Handbücher zur Sprach- und Kommunikationswissenschaft) Berlin, New York: De Gruyter, 658–675.

Bußmann, Hadumod (1990): Heckenausdruck. In: Bußmann, Hadumod (Hrsg.): Lexikon der Sprachwissenschaft. Stuttgart: Kröner 304–305.

Bühler, Karl (1965): Sprachtheorie. Die Darstellungsfunktion der Sprache. Stuttgart: Gustav Fischer Verlag.

Bybee, Joan/ Perkins, Revere/ Pagliuca, William (1994): The Evolution of Grammar. Tense, Aspect, and Modality in the Languages of the World. Chicago/ London: University of Chicago Press.

Byrd, Sharon/ Laby, Arthur/ Lehmann, Matthias (2021): Einführung in die angloamerikanische Rechtssprache. Introduction to Anglo-American Law and Language. München: C.H. Beck.

Canaris, Claus-Wilhelm/ Larenz, Karl (1995): Methodenlehre der Rechtswissenschaft. Berlin/ Heidelberg: Springer.

Cappelen, Herman/ Lepore, Ernest/ McKeever, Matthew (2020): Quotation. In: Zalta, Edward (Hrsg.): The Stanford Encyclopedia of Philosophy, https://plato.stanford.edu/archives/sum2020/entries/quotation/, letzter Zugriff: 21.09.2021.

Celle, Agnès (2018): Epistemic Evaluation in Factual Contexts in English. In: Guentchéva, Zlatka (Hrsg.): Epistemic Modalities and Evidentiality in Cross-Linguistic Perspective, 22–51.

Cheng, Le/ Sin, King Sui (2011): A Sociosemiotic Interpretation of Linguistic Modality in Legal Settings. Semiotica 185 1(4), 123–146.

Cheng, Le/ Wang, Xin (2017): Modals and Modality in Legal Discourse. A Corpus-Based Sociosemiotic Interpretation. International Journal of Semiotics and Visual Rhetoric 1, 19–29.

Christensen, Ralph/ Jeand'Heur, Bernd (1989): Themen einer problembezogenen Zusammenarbeit zwischen Rechtstheorie und Linguistik. In: Müller, Friedrich (Hrsg.): Untersuchungen zur Rechtslinguistik. Interdisziplinäre Studien zu praktischer Semantik und Strukturierender Rechtslehre in Grundfragen der juristischen Methodik. Berlin: Duncker & Humblot, 9–12.

Chubin, Dary/ Moitra, Soumyo (1975): Content Analysis of References. Adjunct or Alternative to Citation Counting? Social Studies of Science 5(4), 423–441.

Cornillie, Bert (2009): Evidentiality and Epistemic Modality. Functions of Language 16(1), 44–62.

Coulthard, Malcom (2004): Author Identification, Idiolect, and Linguistic Uniqueness. Applied Linguistics 24(4), 431–447.

Cronin, Blaise (1984): The Citation Process. The Role and Significance of Citations in Scientific Communication. London: Taylor Graham.

Cumming, Samuel (2003): Two Accounts of Indexicals in Mixed Quotation. Belgian Journal of Linguistics (17), 77–88.

Czermak, Gerhard (2021): Siebzig Jahre Bundesverfassungsgericht in weltanschaulicher Schieflage. Fälle, Strukturen, Korrekturmöglichkeiten. Baden-Baden: Nomos.

Dainow, Joseph (1966): The Civil Law and the Common Law. Some Points of Comparison. The American Journal of Comparative Law 15(3), 419–435.

D'Angelo, Jonathan/ Toma, Catalina (2015): Tell-tale Words. Cues Used to Infer the Expertise of Online Medical Advice. Journal of Language and Social Psychology 32(1), 25–45.

Dalbergenova, Ljasat/ Zharkynbekova, Sholpan (2020): Evidentialität als argumentative Funktion am Beispiel des Deutschen, Russischen und Kasachischen. Zeitschrift für Slawistik 65(1), 134–144.

David, René/ Jauffret-Spinosi, Camille (1992): Les Grands Systems de Droit Contemporains. Paris: Dalloz.

Davidson, Donald (1979): Quotations. Theory and Decision. In: Davidson, Donald (Hrsg.): Essays on truth and interpretation. Oxford: Clarendon, 79–92.

De Beaugrand, Robert-Alain/ Dressler, Wolfgang Ulrich: Introduction to Text Linguistics. New York: Longman Verlag.

De Brabanter, Philippe (2019): The Interpretation of Indexicals in Hybrid Quotation: A Pragmatic Account. Anglophonia. 28, https://journals.openedition.org/anglophonia/2646, letzter Zugriff: 02.06.2022.

Dern, Christa (2003): Sprachwissenschaft und Kriminalistik. Zur Praxis der Autorenerkennung. Sprachwissenschaft und Kriminalistik 31(1), 44–77.

DeStefano, John M. (2007): On Literature as Legal Authority. Arizona Law Review (49), 521–552.

Diewald, Gabriele (1999): Die Modalverben im Deutschen. Grammatikalisierung und Polyfunktionalität. Tübingen: Max Niemeyer Verlag.

Diewald, Gabriele (2013): Modus und Modalverben—Kategorisierungsoptionen im grammatischen Kernbereich der Modalität. In: Abraham, Werner/ Leiss, Elisabeth (Hrsg.): Funktionen von Modalität. Berlin: De Gruyter, 77–112.

Diewald, Gabriele/ Smirnova, Elena (2010): Evidentiality in German. Linguistic Realization and Regularities in Grammaticalization. Berlin: De Gruyter.

Discherl, Fabian/ Pafel, Jürgen (2015): Die vier Arten der Rede- und Gedankendarstellung. Zwischen Zitieren und Referieren. In: Grewendorf, Günther/ von Stechow, Arnim/ Steinbach, Markus (Hrsg.): Linguistische Berichte 241. Hamburg: Helmut Buske Verlag, 3–47.

Du Bois, John (2007): The Stance Triangle. In: Englrebretson, R. (Hrsg.): Stancetaking in Discourse: Subjectivity, Evaluation, Interaction. Amsterdam, Philadelphia: 139–182.

Dudenredaktion (Hrsg.) (2005): Duden. Die Grammatik, Band 4. 7. Auflage. Mannheim u.a.: Dudenverlag.

Ehrlich, Eugene/ Murphy, Daniel (1991): The Harper Collins Concise Dictionary of English Usage. New York: Harper Collins Publishers.

Eichenberger, Kurt (1983): Die Verfassungsgerichtsbarkeit in den Gliedstaaten der Schweiz. In: Starck, Christina/ Stern, Klaus (Hrsg.): Landesverfassungsgerichtsbarkeit. Teilband 1: Geschichte, Organisation, Rechtsvergleichung. Baden-Baden: Nomos 435–460.

Eisenberg, Peter (1999): Grundriß der deutschen Grammatik. Bd. 2. Der Satz. Stuttgart: Metzler.

Fabricius-Hansen, Cathrine (2001): Wessen Redehintergrund? Reportive Modalität aus text-orientierter kontrastiver Sicht (Deutsch—Norwegisch—Englisch). Reports of the Project Languages in Contrast (Språk in kontrast), 14, 1–27.

Fabricius-Hansen, Cathrine (2002): Nicht-direktes Referat im Deutschen—Typologie und Abgrenzungsprobleme. In: Fabricius-Hansen, Cathrine/ Leirbukt, Oddleif/Letnes, Ole (Hrsg.): Modus, Modalverben, Modalpartikeln, Linguistisch-philologische Studien Bd. 25, Trier: Wissenschaftlicher Verlag, 6–29.

Fabricus-Hansen, Cathrine (2019): Redewiedergabe reloaded? Zeitschrift für Germanistische Linguistik (47), 1–27.

Fabricus-Hansen, Cathrine/ Solfjeld, Kare/ Pitz, Anneliese (2019): Der Konjunktiv. Formen und Spielräume. Tübingen: Stauffenburg.

Fløttum, Kjersti (2005): The Self and the Others. Polyphonic Visibility in Research Articles. International Journal of Applied Linguistics 15(1), 29–44.

Fløttum, Kjersti/ Dahl, Trine/ Kinn, Torodd (2006): Academic Voices. Across Languages and Disciplines. Amsterdam: John Benjamins Publishing Company.

Forkel, Hans (1994): Das Bundesverfassungsgericht, das Zitieren und die Meinungsfreiheit. Überlegungen aus Anlaß des Maastricht-Urteils. Juristenzeitung JZ 49(13), 637–688.

Furmaniak, Grégory/ Pic, Elsa (2012): A Study of Epistemic Modality in Academic and Popularised Discourse: The Case of Possibility Adverbs Perhaps, Maybe and Possibly. Revista de Lenguas para Fines Específicos 18.

Gander, Hans-Helmuth (2010): Verdoppelung der Stimme. Zur Funktion des Zitats als Autoritätsgewinn. In: Jacob, Joachim/ Mayer, Matthias (Hrsg.): Im Namen des anderen. Berlin, Boston: De Gruyter, 19–31.

Gansel, Christina (2002): Verba Dicendi. In: Cruse, Alan/ Hundsnurscher, Franz/ Job, Michael/ Lutzeier, Peter (Hrsg.): Lexikologie. 2. Halbband. Berlin/ New York: De Gruyter, 1562–1569.

Garzone, Giuliana (2013): Variation in the Use of Modality in Legislative Texts. Focus on Shall. Journal of Pragmatics 57, 68–81.

Gather, Andreas (1994): Formen referierter Rede. Eine Beschreibung kognitiver, grammatischer, pragmatischer und äußerungslinguistischer Aspekte. Frankfurt a.M.: Peter Lang.

Genette, Gérard (1982): Palimpsestes. La Littérature au Seconde Degré. Paris: Seuil.

Genette, Gérard (1993) : Palimpseste. Die Literatur auf zweiter Stufe (übersetzt von Wolfram Bayer und Dieter Hornig). Berlin: Suhrkamp.

Gippert, Jost (1993): Heckenausdrücke. In: Glück, Helmut (Hrsg.): Lexikon Sprache. Stuttgart/ Weimar: Metzler.

Glendon, Mary Ann (1991): Rights Talk. The Impoverishment of Political Discourse. New York: The Free Press.

Glenn, Partrick (1987): Persuasive Authority. Revue de droit de McGill 32(2), 261–298.

Glenn, Patrick (2006): Aims of Comparative Law. In: Smits, Jan (Hrsg.): Elgar Encyclopedia of Comparative Law. Massachusetts: Edward Elgar Publishing, 57–65.

Goga–Vigaru, Roxana (2012): A Corpus-Based Analysis of Deontic and Epistemic Values of the Modal Shall in Legal Texts. Contemporary Readings in Law and Social Justice 4, 752–763.

Gribanova, Tatiana/ Gaidukova, Tamara (2019): Hedging in Different Types of Discourse. Training, Language and Culture 3(2), 85–99.

Grice, Paul (1975): Logic and Conversation. In: Cole, Peter/ Morgan, Jerry (Hrsg.): Speech acts (= Syntax and Semantics. Bd. 3). New York: Academic Press, 41–58.

Griffig, Thomas (2006): Intertextualität in linguistischen Fachaufsätzen des Englischen und Deutschen. Frankfurt a.M: Peter Lang.

Grimm, Jacob/ Grimm, Wilhelm: Deutsches Wörterbuch Bd. 1. Leipzig: Samuel Hirzel Verlag.

Grimm, Jacob/ Grimm, Wilhelm (1956): Deutsches Wörterbuch Bd. 31. (Nachdr., bearbeitet von Moritz Heyne, Henry Seedorf, Hermann Teuchert). München: Deutscher Taschenbuch Verlag.

Große, Ernst Ulrich (1976): Text und Kommunikation. Eine linguistische Einführung in die Funktion der Texte. Stuttgart: Kohlhammer.

Gröschner, Rolf (2014): Subsumtion—Technik oder Theorie? Baden-Baden: Nomos.

Günthner, Susanne (2000): Zwischen direkter und indirekter Rede. Zeitschrift für germanistische Linguistik 28(1), 1–22.

Hamann, Hanjo (2014): Die Fußnote, das unbekannte Wesen. Potential und Grenzen juristischer Zitationsanalyse. Rechtswissenschaft 5(4), 501–534.

Hart, Christopher (2011): Legitimizing Assertation and the Logico-Rhetorical Module. Evidence and Epistemic Vigilance in Media Discourse on Immigration. Discourse Studies 13(6), 751–769.

Häberle, Peter (1989): Grundrechtsgeltung und Grundrechtsinterpretation im Verfassungsstaat. Zugleich zur Rechtsvergleichung als „fünfter" Auslegungsmethode. Juristenzeitung 44(20), 913–919.

Handschug, Stephan (2003): Eine Einführung in das kanadische Recht. München: C.H. Beck.

Haßler, Gerda (2015): Evidentiality and the Expression of Speaker's Stance in Romance Languages and German. Discourse Studies 17(2), 182–209.

Helbig, Gerhard/ Buscha, Joachim (1986): Deutsche Grammatik. Ein Handbuch für den Ausländerunterricht. Leipzig: Enzyklopädie.

Helbig, Jörg (1996): Intertextualität und Markierung. Untersuchungen zur Systematik und Funktion der Signalisierung von Intertextualität. Heidelberg: Winter.

Helmstetter, Rudolf (2002): Zitat. In: Weimar, Klaus (Hrsg.): Reallexikon der deutschen Literaturwissenschaft: Neubearbeitung des Reallexikons der deutschen Literaturgeschichte, Bd. 3: P–Z, Berlin/ Boston: De Gruyter, 896–899.

Hilgendorf, Eric (2017): Kontinental-europäisches Recht (Civil Law). In: Hilgendorf, Eric/ Joerden, Jan (Hrsg.): Handbuch Rechtsphilosophie. Stuttgart: J.B. Metzler, 30–32.

Holthuis, Susanne (1993): Intertextualität. Aspekte einer rezeptionsorientierten Konzeption. Tübingen: Stauffenburg Verlag.

Holzleithner, Elisabeth/ Mayer-Schönberger, Viktor (2000): Das Zitat als grundloser Grund rechtlicher Legitimität. In: Feldner, Birgit/ Forgó, Nikolaus (Hrsg.): Norm und Entscheidung. Wien, New York: Springer, 318–351.

Hovárth, Katalin (2013): Sind reportative Modalverben epistemisch? In: Abraham, Werner/ Leiss, Elisabeth (Hrsg.): Funktionen von Modalität. Berlin/ Boston: De Gruyter, 131–156.

Höfler, Stefan (2015): Die Redaktion von Verweisen unter dem Aspekt der Verständlichkeit. LeGes Gesetzgebung Evaluation 26(2), 325–349.

Huddleston, Rodney/ Pullum, Geoffrey (2002): The Cambridge Grammar of the English Language. Cambridge: Cambridge University Press.

Hyland, Ken (1998): Boosting, hedging and the negotiation of academic knowledge'. Text-Interdisciplinary Journal for the Study of Discourse 18(3), 349–82.

Hyland, Ken (1999): Academic Attribution: Citation and the construction of disciplinary knowledge. Applied Linguistics 20, 341–367.

Hyland, Ken (2002): Activity and Evaluation: Reporting Practices in Academic Writing. In: Flowerdew, J. (Hrsg.): Academic Discourse. London: Longman, 115–130.

Hyland, Ken (2005): Metadiscourse. Exploring Interaction in Wiriting. London: Continuum.

Hyland, Ken/ Jiang, Feng (2015): ‚The Fact that': Stance Nouns in Disciplinary Writing. Discourse Studies 17(5), 529–550.

Hyland, Ken/ Jiang, Feng (2016): Change of Attitude? A Diachronic Study of Stance. Written Communication 33(3), 251–274.

IDS-Grammatik = Zifonun, Gisela/ Strecker, Bruno/ Hoffmann, Ludger (1997): Grammatik der deutschen Sprache. 3 Bd. Berlin, New York: De Gruyter (Schriften des Instituts für Deutsche Sprache 7).

Jakobs, Eva-Maria (1997): Plagiate im Kontext elektronischer Medien. In: Antos, Gerd/ Tietz, Heike (Hrsg.): Die Zukunft der Textlinguistik. Traditionen, Transformationen, Trends. Berlin/ New York: Niemeyer Verlag, 147–172.

Jakobs, Eva-Maria (1999): Textvernetzung in den Wissenschaften. Zitat und Verweis als Ergebnis rezeptiver, reproduktiver und produktiver Prozesse. Tübingen: Niemeyer.

Jaskot, Maciej/ Wiltos, Agnieszka (2017): An Approach to the Translation of Deontic Modality in Legal Texts. The Case of the Polish and English Versions of the Charter of Fundamental Rights of the European Union. Cognitive Studies/ Études cognitives 17, 1–13.

Jestaedt, Matthias (2010): Autorität und Zitat. Anmerkungen zur Zitierpraxis des Bundesverfassungsgerichts, in: Jacob, Joachim/ Mayer, Matthias (Hrsg.): Im Namen des anderen. Die Ethik des Zitierens. Leiden, Niederlande: Wilhelm Fink, 141–160.

Kalivoda, Gregor/ Montefusco, Lucia (2013): Auctoritas (übers. von Stephan Zimmermann). In: Ueding, Gert (Hrsg.): Historisches Wörterbuch der Rhetorik Online: Berlin, Boston: De Gruyter, abrufbar unter: https://doi.org/10.1515/hwro.1.auctoritas, letzter Zugriff: 30.10.2023.

Kästner, Jürgen (1985): Die Titelangabe zwischen Titelaufnahme und Minimalangabe. Bibliothek Forschung und Praxis 9(2), 188–193.

Kaufmann, Gerhard (1976): Die indirekte Rede und mit ihr konkurrierende Formen der Redeerwähnung. Heutiges Deutsch, Reihe 3, Bd. 1, München: Max Hueber.

Katelhön, Peggy/ Moroni, Manuela (2018): Inszenierung direkter Rede in mündlichen Interaktionen. In: Catalano, Gabriella/ La Manna, Federica (Hrsg.): Verità e menzogna. Quaderni dell'AiG 1. Studi germanici, 179–208.

Kischel, Uwe (2019): Rechtsvergleichung. München: C.H. Beck.

Klatt, Matthias (2020): Autoritative und diskursive Instrumente des Bundesverfassungsgerichts. Jahrbuch des öffentlichen Rechts der Gegenwart (JöR) 68(1), 63–87.

Klatt, Matthias (2023): Das Sondervotum beim Bundesverfassungsgericht. Tübingen: Mohr Siebeck.

Klockow, Reinhard (1980): Linguistik der Gänsefüßchen. Untersuchungen zum Gebrauch der Anführungszeichen im gegenwärtigen Deutsch. Frankfurt a.M.: Haag und Herchen.

Knape, Joachim (2013) Persuasion. In: Ueding, Gert (Hrsg.): Historisches Wörterbuch der Rhetorik Online: Must–Pop. Berlin, Boston: De Gruyter. https://www.degruyter.com/database/HWRO/entry/hwro.6.persuasion/html, letzter Zugriff: 31.12.2021.

Kötz, Hein (2009): Rechtskreislehre. In: Basedow, Jürgen/ Hopt, Klaus/ Zimmermann, Reinhard (Hrsg.): Handwörterbuch des Europäischen Privatrechts. Tübingen: Mohr Siebeck, 1253–1255.

Kranich, Svenja (2011): To Hedge or not to Hedge. The Use of Epistemic Modal Expressions in Popular Science in English Texts, English–German translations, and German Original Texts. Text & Talk 31(1), 77–99.

Krifka, Manfred (2020): Zur Negierbarkeit von epistemischen Modalen. In: Neuhaus, Laura (Hrsg.): Grammatik und Pragmatik der Negation im Deutschen. Berlin: De Gruyter, 1–26.

Kristeva, Julia (1969): Narration et Transformation. Semeiotica 1(4), 422–448.

Kristeva, Julia (1970): Le texte du roman. Approche sémiologuque d'une structure discursive transformationnelle Den Haag.

Kroppenberg, Inge (2004): Kodifikation. In: Cordes, Albrecht et. al (Hrsg.): Handbuch zur deutschen Rechtsgeschichte, abrufbar unter: https://www.hrgdigital.de/HRG.kodifikation, letzter Zugriff: 04.12.2022.

Kutschera, Franz (1975): Sprachphilosophie. München: Fink.

Lakoff, George (1972): Hedges. A Study of Meaning Criteria and the Logic of Fuzzy Concepts. In: Binnick, Robert (Hrsg.): Papers from the Eight Regional Meeting of Chicago Linguistic Society. Chicago: Chicago University Press, 183–228.

Landert, Daniela (2015): Reportable Facts and a Personal Touch. The Functions of Direct Quotes in Online News. In: Arendholz, Jenny/ Bublitz, Wolfram/ Kirner-Ludwig, Monika (Hrsg.): The Pragmatics of Quoting now and then. Berlin/ Boston: Walter de Gruyter, 29–52.

Law, David/ Chang, Wen-Chen (2011): The Limits of Global Judicial Dialogue. Wash. L. Rev 86, 523–577.

Lefèvre, Michel (2002): Redewiedergabe und Modalverben. In: Baudot, Daniel (Hrsg.): Redewiedergabe, Redeerwähnung. Formen und Funktionen des Zitierens und Reformulierens im Text. Tübingen: Stauffenburg 111–122.

Lepsius, Oliver (2006): Entscheiden durch Maßstabsbildung. In: van Ooyen, Robert/ Möllers, Martin (Hrsg.): Handbuch Bundesverfassungsgericht im politischen System. Wiesbaden: Springer VS.

Lepsius, Oliver (2011): Die maßstabsetzende Gewalt. In: Jestaedt, Matthias/ Lepsius, Oliver/ Möllers, Christoph/ Schönberger, Chrstoph (Hrsg.): Das entgrenzte Gericht. Eine kritische Bilanz nach sechzig Jahren Bundesverfassungsgericht. Berlin: Suhrkamp. 161–267.

Leistner, Annika (2014): Syntaktische Integration der Redewiedergabe. Eine Untersuchung der direkten und nicht-direkten Redewiedergabeformen in literarischen Texten. Kassel: University Press.

Lenk, Hartmut (2008): „...moniert die Neue Presse". Verben und Wendungen der Zitateinbettung in Presseschauen. Beiträge zur Fremdsprachenvermittlung 47, 93–114.

Levin, Benjamin (2019): Verbally Identical and Infinitely Richer. Quotation in US Supreme Court Opinions. Law, Culture and the Humanities 15(3), 764–784.

Lipetz, Ben-Ami (1965): Improvement of the Selectivity of Citation Indexes to Scientific Literature through the Inclusion of Citation Relationship Indicators. American Documentation 16(2), 81–90.

Lübbe-Wolff, Gertrud (2022): Beratungskulturen. Wie Verfassungsgerichte arbeiten, und wovon es abhängt, ob sie integrieren oder polarisieren. Berlin: Konrad-Adenauer-Stiftung.

MacCormick, Neil/ Summers, Robert (1997) (Hrsg.): Interpreting Precedents. A Comparative Study. Farnham: Ashgate Publishing.

Maier, Emar (2014): Mixed Quotation. The Grammar of Apparently Transparent Opacity. Semantics & Pragmatics 7, Article 7, 1–67.

Maxwell, Peter Benson (1946): The Interpretation of Statutes. London: Sweet & Maxwell.

McCormick, Peter (1995): Supreme Court Cites the Supreme Court. Follow-Up Citation on the Supreme Court of Canada, 1989–993. Osgoode Law Journal 33(3), 453–486.

McCormick, Peter (1996): What Supreme Court Cases Does the Supreme Court Cite? Follow-Up Citations on the Supreme Court of Canada. Supreme Court Law Review 7, 451–476.

McCormick, Peter/ Zanoni, Marc (2019): By the Court. Anonymous Judgments at the Supreme Court of Canada. Vancouver/ Toronto: UBC Press.

McCormick, Peter (2009): Structures of Judgments. How the Modern Supreme Court of Canada Organizes its reasons. Dalhousie Law Journal 32(1), 35–67.

McCormick, Peter (2016): ‚By the Court': The Untold Story of a Canadian Judicial Innovation. Osgoode Hall Law Journal 53(3), 1048–1082.

Meibauer, Jörg (2007): Syngrapheme als pragmatische Indikatoren: Anführung und Auslassung. In: Döring, Sandra/ Geilfuß, Wolfgang (Hrsg.): Von der Pragmatik zur Grammatik. Leipzig: Universitätsverlag, 21–37.

Meyer, Herman (1967): Das Zitat in der Erzählkunst. Zur Geschichte und Poetik des europäischen Romans. Stuttgart: Metzler.

Michel, Georg (1966): Sprachliche Bedingungen der Wortwahl. Eine Untersuchung an Verben der Redeeinführung. STUF—Language Typology and Universals 19, 339–364.

Montaigne, Michel de [1992]: Essais, nebst des Verfassers Leben (nach der Ausgabe von Pierre Coste, ins Deutsche übersetzt von Johann Daniel Tietz). Zürich: Diogenes.

Montesquieu, Charles-Louis (1834): De l'Ésprit des Lois. Paris: Didot.

Moravcsik, Michael / Murugesan, Poovanalingam (1975): Some Results on the Function and Quality of Citations. Social Studies of Science 5(1), 86–92.

Morawski, Stefan (1970): The Basic Functions of Quotation. In: Algirdas, Julien Greimas (Hrsg.): Sign, Language, Culture. Den Haag: Mouton, 690–705.

Mori, Yoshiki/ Okano, Shinya (2013): Evidentialität als Inferentialität. In: Abraham, Werner/ Leiss, Elisabeth (Hrsg.): Funktionen von Modalität. Berlin/ Boston: De Gruyter, 189–218.

Morlok, Martin (2015): Intertextualität und Hypertextualität im Recht. In: Vogel, Friedemann (Hrsg.): Zugänge zur Rechtssemantik. Interdisziplinäre Ansätze im Zeitalter der Mediatisierung. Berlin/ Boston: De Gruyter, 69–90.

Mortelsmans, Tanja/ Vanderbiesen, Jeroen (2013): Komparative Modalkonstruktionen im Deutschen und Englischen oder deontische Modalität revisited. Abraham, Werner/ Leiss, Elisabeth (Hrsg.): Funktionen von Modalität. Berlin/ Boston: De Gruyter, 279–302.

Mouchel, Christian/ Fortenbaugh, William/ Robling, Franz-Hubert (2013): Ethos. In: Ueding, Gert (Hrsg.): Historisches Wörterbuch der Rhetorik Online: Bie–Eul. Berlin, Boston: De Gruyter. https://www.degruyter.com/database/HWRO/entry/hwro.2.ethos/html, letzter Zugriff 31.12.2021

Narrog, Heiko (2005): Modality, Mood, and Change of Modal Meanings: A New Perspective. Cognitive Linguistics 16(4), 677–731.

Neumeyer, Margarethe (2018): Zum Problem der intertextuellen Auslegung von Menschenrechtsverträgen. MenschenRechtsMagazin 23(2), 103–119.

Niemann, Robert (2018): Wissenschaftssprache praxistheoretisch. Handlungstheoretische Überlegungen zu wissenschaftlicher Textproduktion. Berlin/ Boston: De Gruyter.

Nußberger, Angelika (2006): Wer zitiert wen? Zur Funktion von Zitaten bei der Herausbildung gemeineuropäischen Verfassungsrechts. Juristenzeitung 61, 763–770.

Olsson, John (2009): Word crime. Solving Crime through Forensic Lingustics. London: continuum.

Ostberg, Cynthia/ Wetstein, Matthew (2007): Attitudinal Decision Making in the Supreme Court of Canada. Vancouver/ British Columbia: UBC Press.

Pafel, Jürgen (2011): Two Dogmas on Quotation. In: Brendel, Elke/ Meibauer, Jörg/ Steinbach, Jörg (Hrsg.): Understanding Quotation. Berlin: De Gruyter, 249–276.

Palmer, Frank (1986): Mood and Modality. Cambridge: Cambridge University Press.

Palmer, Henrik/ Christensen, Martin Lolle (2021): The Weight of Precedents. From Abstract Theorizing to Concrete Application. The Case of the ECtHR. In: Frese, Amalie/ Schumann, Julius (Hrsg.): Precendents as Rules of Practice. New Approaches and Methodologies in Studies of Legal Precedents. Baden-Baden: Nomos, 17–40.

Pfister, Manfred (1985): Konzepte der Intertextualität. In: Broich, Ulrich/ Pfister, Manfred (Hrsg.): Intertextualität. Formen, Funktionen, anglistische Fallstudien. Tübingen: Max Niemeyer Verlag, 1–30.

Pic, Elsa/ Furmaniak, Grégory (2012): A Study of Epistemic Modality in Academic and Popularised Discourse. The Case of Possibility Adverbs Perhaps, Maybe and Possibly. Reviste de Lenguas Para Fines Especificos 18, 13–44.

Plank, Frans (1986): Über den Personenwechsel und den anderer deiktischer Kategorien in der wiedergegebenen Rede. In: Zeitschrift für germanistische Linguistik 14(3), 284–308.

Plett, Heinrich (1991): Intertextualities. In: Plett, Heinrich (Hrsg.): Intertextuality. Berlin, New York: Walter de Gruyter, 3–29.

Predelli, Stefano (2003): Scare Quotes and their Relation to other Semantic Issues. Linguistics and Philosophy (26), 1–28.

Rado, Klodian (2020): The Use of Non-Domestic Legal Sources in Supreme Court of Canada Judgments. Is this the Judicial Slowbalization of the Court? Utrecht Law Review 16(1), 57–85.

Rehbinder, Manfred/ Peukert, Alexander (2018): Urheberrecht. München: C.H. Beck.

Reichmann, Gerhard (2013): Textplagiate in der Wissenschaft und deren Verhinderung/ Text plagiarism in science and its prevention. Theoretical considerations and empirical findings / Le plagiat de texte dans le domaine des sciences et saprévention: Considérations théoriques et résultats, Information. Wissenschaft & Praxis 64(4), 175–184.

Rémillard, Gil/ Gall, Gerald/ Makin, Kirk (2017): Supreme Court of Canada. In: Wilson-Smith, Anthony: The Canadian Encyclopedia, abrufbar unter: https://www.thecanadianencyclopedia.ca/en/article/supreme-court-of-canada, letzter Zugriff: 05.08.2022.

Richter, Julia (2015): Die Konstruktion von Reputation. Verweise auf Ferdinand de Saussure in der romanischen Sprachwissenschaft. Bielefeld: Transcript-Verlag.

Rolek, Boguslawa (2019): Hedging in wissenschaftlichen Artikeln polnischer und deutscher Studierender. In: Cirko, L./ Pittner, K. (Hrsg.): Wissenschaftliches Schreiben interkulturell: Kontrastive Perspektiven. Bern/ Schweiz: Peter Lang, 225–247.

Roncador, Manfred von (1988): Zwischen direkter und indirekter Rede. Nichtwörtliche direkte Rede, erlebte Rede, logophorische Konstruktionen und Verwandtes. Reihe Linguistische Arbeiten 192. Tübingen: Max Niemeyer Verlag.

Rozumko, Agata (2017): Adverbial Markers of Epistemic Modality Across Disciplinary Discourses: A Contrastive Study of Research Articles in Six Academic Disciplines. Studia Anglica Posnaniensia 52(1), 73–101.

Röhl, Klaus Friedrich/ Röhl, Hans Christian (2001): Allgemeine Rechtslehre. Ein Lehrbuch. Köln: Carl Heymanns Verlag.

Sabban, Annette (1978): Verben der Redeeinleitung im Französischen und Deutschen. Ein Beitrag zum Problem der Redeerwähnung. Zeitschrift für französische Sprache und Literatur 88 (1), 28–63.

Salager-Meyer, Francoise (1994): Hedges and Textual Communicative Function in Medical English Written Discourse. English for Special Purposes 13/2, 149–170.

Schack, Haimo (2013): Wissenschaftsplagiat und Urheberrecht. In: Dreier, Thomas/ Ohly, Ansgar (Hrsg.): Plagiate. Wissenschaftsethik und Recht. Tübingen: Mohr Siebeck, 81–98.

Schecker, Michael (2002): Über den Konjunktiv in der indirekten Rede. In: Baudot, Daniel (Hrsg.): Redewiedergabe, Redeerwähnung. Formen und Funktionen des Zitierens und Reformulierens im Text. Tübingen, 1–14.

Scherr, Elisabeth (2019): Die Opazität epistemischer Modalverben im Deutschen. Funktion, Form und empirische Fassbarkeit. Reihe Sprache und Wissen 39. Berlin/Boston: De Gruyter.

Schlaich, Klaus/ Korioth, Stefan (2018): Das Bundesverfassungsgericht. Stellung, Verfahren, Entscheidungen. München: C.H. Beck.

Schmid, Wolfgang/ Stempel, Wolf-Dieter (1983) (Hrsg.): Dialog der Texte. Wien: Wiener Slawistischer Almanach.

Schröder, Hartmut (1998): „Ich sage das einmal ganz ungeschützt"—Hedging und wissenschaftlicher Diskurs. In: Danneberg, Lutz/ Niederhauser, Jürg (Hrsg.): Darstellungsformen der Wissenschaft im Kontrast. Aspekte der Methodik, Theorie und Empirie. Tübingen: Narr, 263–276.

Schubert, Charlotte (2013): Zitate und Fragmente. Die kulturelle Praxis des Zitierens im Zeitalter der Digitalisierung. In: Schubert, Charlotte/ Klank, Markus: Das Portal eAQUA—Neue Methoden in der geisteswissenschaftlichen Forschung III. Leipzig: Universität Leipzig, 3–30, https://doi.org/10.11588/ea.2012.2.11409.

Schulte-Middelich, Bernd (1985): Funktionen intertextueller Textkonstitution. In: Broich, Ulrich/ Pfister, Manfred: Intertextualität. Formen, Funktionen, anglistische Fallstudien. Niemeyer: Tübingen, 197–242.

Schulz, Lorenz (2018): Zur Funktion des obiter dictum. Zeitschrift für Internationale Strafrechtsdogmatik 10, 403–407.

Schulz von Thun, Friedemann (2010): Miteinander Reden, Bd. 1: Störungen und Klärungen. Allgemeine Psychologie der Kommunikation. Hamburg: Rowohlt Verlag.

Segal, Jeffrey/ Spaeth, Harold (2002): The Supreme Court and the Attitudinal Model Revisited. Cambridge: University Press.

Seibert, Thomas (1992): Vom Verfassungsrecht auf richtiges Zitieren. Zeitschrift für Semiotik 14(3), 263–270.

Shan, Chung-chieh (2010): The Character of Quotation. Linguist and Philos (33), 417–433.

Shapiro, Fred (1992): Origins of Bibliometrics, Citation Indexing, and Citation Analysis. The Neglected Legal Literature, Journal of the Association for Information Science and Technology 43(5), 337–339.

Slaughter, Anne-Marie (1994): A Typology of Transjudical Communication. 29 U. Rich. L. Rev. 99, 98–137.

Sobota, Katharina (1996): Argumente und stilistische Überzeugungsmittel in Entscheidungen des Bundesverfassungsgerichts. Eine Rhetorik-Analyse auf empirischer Grundlage. In: Dyck, Joachim/ Jens, Walter/ Ueding, Gert (Hrsg.): Rhetorik. Ein internationales Jahrbuch 15 (Juristische Rhetorik). Tübingen: Niemeyer, 115–136.

Songer, Donald (2008): The Transformation of the Supreme Court of Canada. An Empirical Examination. Toronto/ London: University of Toronto Press.

Spoerhase, Carlos/ van den Berg, Christopher (2013): Zweck, Zweckmäßigkeit. In: Ueding, Gert (Hrsg.): Historisches Wörterbuch der Rhetorik Online: St–Z. Berlin, Boston: De Gruyter, https://www.degruyter.com/database/HWRO/entry/hwro.9.zweck_zweckmaessigkeit/html, letzter Zugriff: 31.12.2021.

Stei, Erik (2007): Über Gebrauch und „Bedeutung" von Anführungszeichen. In: Brendel, Elke/ Meibauer, Jörg/ Steinbach, Markus (Hrsg.): Zitat und Bedeutung. Hamburg: Helmut Buske Verlag, 201–214.

Steigler-Herms, Joy/ Wittmann, Laura (2022): Zitat. In: Gutmann, Thomas/ Ortland, Eberhard/ Stierstorfer, Klaus (Hrsg.): Enzyklopädie Recht und Literatur, https://lawandliterature.eu/index.php/de/inhalt?view=article&id=32&catid=11, letzter Zugriff: 06.07.2023.

Steinbrink, Bernd/ Ueding, Gert (2011): Grundriss der Rhetorik. Geschichte, Technik, Methode. Stuttgart/ Weimar: J.B. Metzler.

Steinseifer, Martin (2019): Funktionen, Konstellation und Mittel der Wiedergabe—Ein dreidimensionales textpragmatisches Modell. Zeitschrift für germanistische Linguistik, 47(1), 147–215.

Steinseifer, Martin/ Feilke, Helmuth/ Lehnen, Katrin (2019): Eristische Literalität. Wissenschaftlich streiten—wissenschaftlich schreiben. Heidelberg: Synchron (=Wissenschaftskommunikation).

Stubbs, Michael (1996): Text and Corpus Analysis. Computer-assisted Studies of Language and Culture. Oxford: Cambridge.

Swales, John (1986): Citation Analysis and Discourse Analysis. Applied Linguistics 7, 39–56.

Swales, John (1990): Genre Analysis. English in Academic and Research Settings. Cambridge: Cambridge.

Szczyrbak, Magdalena (2014): Stancetaking Strategies in Judicial Discourse. Evidence from US Supreme Court Opinions. Studia Linguistica Universitatis Iagellonicae Cracoviensis 131, 91–120.

Tesnière, Lucien (1988): Élements de Syntax Structurale. Paris: Klincksieck.

Thompson, Geoff/ Ye, Yiyun (1991). Evaluation in the Reporting Verbs Used in Academic Papers. Applied Linguistics 4, 365–382.

Toska, Bledar (2012): Epistemic Hedges and Boosters as Stance Markers in Legal Argumentative Discourse. Topics in Linguistics: Approaches to Text and Discourse Analysis 10, 57–62.

Ulrich, Anna (2015): Gebaute Zitate. Formen und Funktionen des Zitierens in Musik, Bild und Architektur. Bielefeld: Transcript-Verlag.

Van den Berg, Willem (2000): Autorität und Schmuck: Über die Funktion des Zitates von der Antike bis zur Romantik, in: Beekman, Klaus/ Grüttemeier, Ralf (Hrsg.): Instrument Zitat: Über den literarhistorischen und institutionellen Nutzen von Zitaten und Zitieren. Amsterdam: Rodopi, 11–35.

Vass, Holly (2015 a): A Comparative Analysis of Hedging in a Corpus of Two Written Legal Discourse Genres. Dissertation Madrid, abrufbar unter: # https://core.ac.uk/download/pdf/148678663.pdf, letzter Zugriff: 08.09.2022.

Vass, Holly (2015 b): Analysing Hedging in Legal Discourse Using Small-Scale and Large-Scale Corpora. Research in Corpus Linguistics 3, 27–35.

Vázquez, Ignacio/ Giner, Diana (2008): Beyond Mood and Modality. Epistemic Modality Markers as Hedges in Research Articles. A Cross-Disciplinary Study. Revista Alicante de Estudios Ingleses 21, 171–190.

Vogenauer, Stefam (2009): Rule of Precedents. In: Basedow, Jürgen/ Hopt, Klaus/ Zimmermann, Reinhard (Hrsg.): Handwörterbuch des Europäischen Privatrechts. Tübingen: Mohr Siebeck, 1304–1306.

Voigt, Manfred (1981): Das Zitat vors Gericht!, Akzente 28, 357–366.

Volosinov, Valentin (1930): Marksizm i filosofija jazyka. Marxism and the Philosophy of Language. Aus dem Russ., übersetzt von: Ladislav Mateijka/ I.R. Titunik. New York: Seminar.

Washington, Corey (1998): Use/Mention Distinction and Quotation. In: Craig, Edward (Hrsg.): The Routledge Encyclopedia of Philosophy. London/ New York: Routledge, abrufbar unter: https://www.rep.routledge.com/articles/thematic/use-mention-distinction-and-quotation/v-1/bibliography/use-mention-distinction-and-quotation-bib, letzter Zugriff: 03.01.2022.

Weinstock, Melvin (1971): Citation Indexes. Encyclopaedia of Library & Information Science 5, 16–40.

White, Howard (2004): Citation Analysis and Discourse Analysis Revisited. Applied Linguistics 25(1), 89–116.

Wirth, Dieter (1996): Paraphrase und Übersetzung in einem Inhalt-Text-Modell. Tübingen: Niemeyer.

Wuttke, Eveline/ Seifried, Jürgen (2016): Formen, Funktionen und Effekte sprachlicher Instruktion und Interaktion am Beispiel von Fragen und Feedback. In: Kilian, Jörg/ Brouer, Birgit/ Lüttenberg, Dina (Hrsg.): Handbuch Sprache in der Bildung. Berlin/ Boston: De Gruyter, 346–361.

Xu, Zhongyi (2015): Modality and Evidentiality in Political Discourse: A Cognitive-Functional Account. Lancaster University, abrufbar unter https://eprints.lancs.ac.uk/id/eprint/74785

Yang, Linxiu (2013): Evaluative Functions of Reporting Evidentials in English Research Articles of Applied Linguistics. Open Journal of Modern Linguistics 3(2), 119–126.

Yu, Wei (2021): Reporting Verbs in Court Judgments of the Common Law. A Corpus-Based Study. International Journal for the Semiotics of Law 34, 525–560.

Zima, Peter (2000): Zitat—Intertextualität—Subjektivität. Zum Funktionswandel des literarischen Zitats zwischen Moderne und Postmoderne. In: Beekmann, Klaus/ Grüttmeier, Ralf (Hrsg.): Instrument Zitat. Über den literaturhistorischen und institutionellen Nutzen von Zitaten und Zitieren. Amsterdam: Avantgarde, 297–322.

Zweigert, Konrad (1961): Zur Lehre von den Rechtskreisen. In: Nadelmann, Kurt/ von Mehren, Arthur/ Hazard, John (Hrsg.): Twentieth Century Comparative and Conflicts Law. Legal Essays in Honor of Hessel E. Yntema, Leiden: A.W. Sijthoff, 42–55.

Legal Sources

Bundesverfassungsgerichtsgesetz (Gesetz über das Bundesverfassungsgericht, BVerfGG) In der Fassung der Bekanntmachung vom 11.08.1993 (BGBl. I S. 1473), zuletzt geändert durch Gesetz vom 20.11.2019 (BGBl. I S. 1724) m.W.v. 26.11.2019

Grundgesetz für die Bundesrepublik Deutschland (GG) vom 23. Mai 1949, zuletzt geändert durch Gesetz vom 29. September 2020

Strafgesetzbuch (StGB) in der Fassung der Bekanntmachung vom 13. November 1998 (BGBl. I S. 3322), das zuletzt durch Artikel 4 des Gesetzes vom 4. Dezember 2022 (BGBl. I S. 2146) geändert worden ist

Supreme Court Act, R.S.C. 1985, c.S-26/ Loi sur la Cour supreme L.R.C. 1985, ch. S-26 current to May 17 2023, last amended on December 18 2019

Urheberrechtsgesetz (UrhG) vom 9. September 1965 (BGBl. I S. 1273), das zuletzt durch Artikel 25 des Gesetzes vom 23. Juni 2021 (BGBl. I S. 1858) geändert worden ist

Tools

DATAtab Team (2023): DATAtab. Online Statistics Calculator. DATAtab e.U. Graz, Austria. https://www.datatab.de

Duden-Online: https://www.duden.de/sprachwissen/sprachratgeber/konjunktiv-1-oder-2, letzter Zugriff: 29.11.2020

R Core Team (2022): R. A language and environment for statistical computing. R Foundation for Statistical Computing, Vienna, Austria. https://www.R-project.org

Verbi Software (2022): MAXQDA, Software für qualitative Datenanalyse, 1989—2021, VERBI Software. Consult. Sozialforschung GmbH, Berlin, Deutschland.

FSC
www.fsc.org
MIX
Papier | Fördert
gute Waldnutzung
FSC® C083411

Kolibri 360 GmbH
Ferdinand-Jühlke-Straße 7
99095 Erfurt, Deutschland
produktsicherheit@kolibri360.de